Soldiers of Misfortune
The Somervell and Mier Expeditions

Soldiers of Misfortune

THE SOMERVELL AND MIER EXPEDITIONS

By Sam W. Haynes

University of Texas Press, Austin

First paperback printing, 1997

Requests for permission to reproduce material from this work should be
sent to Permissions, University of Texas Press, Box 7819, Austin, TX
78713-7819.

∞ The paper used in this publication meets the minimum requirements
of American National Standard for Information Sciences—Permanence
of Paper for Printed Library Materials, ANSI Z39.48-1984.

Library of Congress Cataloging-in-Publication Data

Haynes, Sam W. (Sam Walter), 1956–
    Soldiers of misfortune : the Somervell and Mier expeditions / by
Sam W. Haynes. — 1st ed.
        p. cm.
    Includes bibliographical references.
    ISBN 0-292-75118-4 (alk. paper)
    ISBN 0-292-73115-9 (pbk.)
    1. Texas—History—Republic, 1836–1846. 2. Mier Expedition,
1842. 3. Texas—Boundaries—Mexico. 4. Mexico—Boundaries—
Texas. 5. Texas—Foreign relations—Mexico. 6. Mexico—Foreign
relations—Texas. I. Title.
F390.H34 1990
976.4'04—dc20   90-33976

For
María Guadalupe

Contents

Preface

FEW EPISODES IN the history of the early Texas frontier are as well documented as the Somervell and Mier expeditions. The existence of such a large body of primary source material is hardly surprising; from the moment William Fisher's men decided to invade Mexico in defiance of their commander, Alexander Somervell, they became embroiled in one of the Republic's bitterest controversies. Censured by their government as freebooters and mutineers, many sought vindication and from prisons in Mexico wrote angry letters to newspapers and relatives blaming Sam Houston for their misfortunes. Many continued to defend their actions in the years that followed. Thomas Jefferson Green, Thomas W. Bell, and William Preston Stapp, eager to set the record straight and perhaps hoping to turn a profit from their misadventures, authored books on the affair when they returned to Texas. William A. A. "Big Foot" Wallace and John C. C. Hill related their experiences many years later to biographers (Wallace, who had an unusual talent for self-promotion, told slightly different stories to two of them). Others, like Joseph McCutchan, Samuel H. Walker, Israel Canfield, and James A. Glasscock, to name only a few, wrote not for posterity but to pass the time during their lengthy confinement in Mexico. Never intending their diaries and letters to be published, they are among the more reliable chroniclers of the expedition, although all served, to varying degrees, to propagate the view that the men who crossed the Río Grande contrary to orders did so with the noblest of intentions.

If the Mier men did not receive the attention they had hoped for upon their return from Mexico, they have not been ignored by Texas historians. Of these, certainly the most assiduous has been Joseph Milton Nance. In the final chapters of his exhaustive and meticulously researched study, *Attack and Counterattack* (1964), Nance examined the travails of General Alexander Somervell and the Southwestern Army of Operations' ill-fated invasion of the lower Río Grande Valley, concluding this work with the mutiny of Fisher's men in December 1842. Amateur historian Houston Wade's interest in the history of Fayette County, the home of many of the Mier participants, led him to compile a series of articles on the expedition which appeared in the *LaGrange Journal* and were subsequently published in two short volumes as *Notes and Fragments of the Mier Expedition* (1936). In *Black Beans and Goose Quills* (1970), James M. Day chose to examine the expedition from a literary rather than a historical perspective, evaluating the many diaries and journals written by the Mier combatants on the basis of each author's style and viewpoint. Both Nance and Day, as well as Marilyn McAdams Sibley, have made further contributions to the scholarship of this particular chapter of Texas history as editors of some of the most important published diaries of the expedition.

This study seeks to examine the Somervell and Mier expeditions in a political context, in order to assess their broader implications as determinants of Sam Houston's foreign and domestic policies during the years 1842–1844. The following narrative makes no claim to be the definitive military history of the campaign. Its purpose, rather, is considerably more modest: to show how these events helped create a climate of public opinion favorable to annexation, and to determine the extent to which political and diplomatic considerations played a role in efforts to gain the prisoners' release. Although both the Republic's border hostilities with Mexico and its annexation to the United States are topics with which students of Texas history are familiar, they have generally been regarded as two parallel developments, neither having much impact upon the other. Thus, it is hoped that this narrative will shed some light on the consequences of frontier adventurism, as well as help to bring the policies of the Republic's enigmatic president into sharper focus. The Mier Expedition has traditionally been viewed as a footnote in the history of the Republic, as an example of Texas vainglory which had little bearing on larger events. But the clamor for an invasion of Mexico in 1842, the defeat at Mier, and the lengthy incarceration of Texas prisoners in Mexico all created political crises which Houston's diplomatic initiatives were designed to remedy. Seen in this light, the misadventures of the men who participated in the Mier Expedition had far-reaching implications. Much more than a tragic sideshow, the expedition played a crucial role in the series of events which ultimately brought Texas into the Union.

Like so many episodes in early Texas history, the Mier Expedition remains steeped in lore and insulated by myth. In this study I have tried to steer clear of both, hoping to provide the reader with a concise narrative which does not glorify or romanticize these events. The pathos and tragic drama of the Mier Expedition must not obscure the fact that, for the most part, the Mexican government responded to this unauthorized invasion of its territory in a manner that was not unreasonable. By and large, the treatment of the Mier prisoners could hardly be considered inhumane, and indeed may have been better than the Texans had reason to expect under the circumstances. Such a view does not, of course, square with the testimony of the Mier prisoners themselves, who chafed at their confinement and whose own accounts offer a litany of indignities and humiliations suffered at the hands of their Mexican captors. But today even the most casual reader is struck by the unabashedly Anglocentric and self-serving tone of these accounts. This is not to say that excesses were not committed, or that the Mier prisoners were treated with the kind of clemency that might satisfy late-twentieth-century sensibilities. As with any conflict between Anglos and Mexicans during this period, the Mier Expedition reveals enough ignorance and cruelty on both sides to go around.

I have received so much help from so many quarters that at times this study has seemed like a collaborative effort. My special thanks go to Stanley Siegel, John Mason Hart, and James Kirby Martin of the University of Houston for their generous advice (to which I add the standard caveat that they bear no responsibility for any errors, the blame for which is mine alone). I am very grateful to my editors at the University of Texas Press, both for their professional expertise and for their patience in dealing with a first-time author. My brother, Charles Haynes, was both an accommodating host during my long sojourns in Austin and an enthusiastic advocate of this project. I would also like to thank Juan Pozas, with whom I retraced the steps of the Mier men in northern Mexico; Dorothy MacInerney and Teresa Franklin, for much-needed word-processing instruction and assistance; Marilyn Hartley, who helped with the translations of a number of Mexican sources; John Hartley, for his help with the maps; Jim McCaffrey for sharing with me his research on the Mexican War; and Laura Paschetag, for the peace and quiet of her family's hill country farmhouse, which enabled me to get some writing done. I would also like to thank the librarians and archivists—too numerous to mention individually—at the following institutions: the Barker Texas History Center; the Benson Latin American Collection; the Texas State Library;

the Texas and Local History Department, Houston Public Library; the University of Houston Rare Books Collection; and the San Jacinto Memorial Library. Finally, I would like to thank my wife, María Guadalupe Pozas, to whom this book is dedicated, for her perennial optimism and ceaseless encouragement. She has contributed to this book in more ways than I can list here, and in more ways than she can possibly know.

Sam W. Haynes
Houston, 1990

"Carthage Must Be Destroyed"

THE 1841 PRESIDENTIAL inauguration of Sam Houston was an event requiring all the pomp and pageantry the little town of Austin could muster. Behind the Hall of Congress—a rather grand name for a flimsy wood frame building not much bigger than a large dogtrot—a dais had been erected underneath an enormous purple canopy. A crowd of one thousand people spilled out from underneath the tent as they waited for the ceremony to begin.[1] They had come from all parts of the country to see Sam Houston sworn in on this crisp, clear day in mid-December, but most lived in Austin or its environs on the western fringes of the Republic. The inauguration represented a high-water mark for Austin society, and there were but few residents willing to miss the swearing-in ceremony, or the banquet and fancy-dress ball to follow.

At 11 A.M., Sam Houston and his Vice-President-elect, General Edward Burleson, emerged from the building and mounted the platform, escorted by a platoon of Travis Guards. They were followed by the leaders of the outgoing administration, Mirabeau B. Lamar and David G. Burnet, and a host of notables that included the U.S. chargé d'affaires and selected members of the Texas House and Senate.[2] All eyes, however, were on Sam Houston. His appearance drew an immediate murmur of astonishment from many in the crowd, as he must have known it would. In striking contrast to the somber attire of the other dignitaries on the stage, both Houston and his running mate were outfitted in frontier dress. Houston, who had a reputation as something of a dandy, on this important occasion looked downright shabby in a linsey woolsey hunting shirt, pantaloons, and an old white, wide-brimmed fur hat. It was clear that the President-elect, with his politician's flair for the theatrical, had cast himself as a man of the people and was determined to look the part. The irony of the situation did not escape notice. Here was the new chief executive of the Republic, dressed like a rube before his rural constituents, who had turned out for the event in their very best finery.[3]

If Houston saw any humor in this breach of protocol, there were probably not many who did. In spite of his victory at the polls the President-elect had few friends in the audience. Lamar was still a favorite with these western voters, while Houston was the preferred candidate in the more populated east. Among the many issues which divided the Houston and Lamar factions, certainly none was more contentious nor of more concern to the citizens who had gathered for the inaugural than the location of the seat of government. Austin had served as the capital for eighteen months, but in 1841 Lamar's prediction that the town would some day become "the seat of future Empire" must have seemed a remote possibility to all but the most credulous residents.[4] Situated on the edge of the frontier, it was dangerously isolated and subject to frequent Indian attack. The cabins west of Austin had been burned out by Comanches or abandoned, while in the capital itself few residents were bold enough to venture onto the streets after the sun went down.[5] The mass migration of settlers envisioned by Lamar had not occurred; indeed, many were leaving the frontier for the relative safety of towns farther east. At the time of Houston's inaugural the capital city of the Republic of Texas was little more than a string of crude shacks and barns nestled along Congress Avenue, a dirt track thirty yards wide leading down to the Colorado River. The President-elect, it was reported, "did not want to risk his scalp, up in that d——d hole," and favored moving the capital back to his namesake city, which had hosted the government during his first term.[6] But Austin residents were determined to keep the government right where it was, knowing full well that without it and the income it generated, their town would disappear, to be reclaimed by the wilderness, like so many other ambitious but unsuccessful urban projects on the Texas frontier.

Houston was prepared for a cool reception. Since his arrival in Austin earlier in the week he had kept quiet on the subject of a possible change of venue for the government. There was no need to raise the ire of these voters any more than he had done already. But in "dressing down" for his inaugural audience Houston seems to have won few converts. These men and women were not so easily fooled by his humble dress. Rustic garb could not conceal the fact that the flamboyant Houston was no friend of the western settlers.

After an invocation by the Reverend R. E. B. Baylor, the Speaker of the House and the President-elect rose from their seats for the oath of office. On the inaugural stand Mirabeau Lamar watched the proceedings in silence (he had refused to give a valedictory). As Houston kissed the Bible to seal his oath, a salvo of cannon erupted from the arsenal nearby, and the crowd, taken by surprise, joined in with polite applause.[7]

By all accounts, the new President's inaugural address was not a speech of hope and promise.[8] Many listeners were annoyed that Houston used this opportunity to remind the crowd of the dismal record of the outgoing administration and to recite at great length the successes of his first presidential term. But the new chief executive had good reason to lament the affairs of the nation which he now undertook to lead for the second time. After three years of Lamar, the young Texas Republic seemed to have made no headway in its efforts to carve a place for itself in the sprawling American southwest. The nation's currency was virtually worthless, and the public debt—owed in specie—had swollen from less than two million to more than seven million dollars during Lamar's term, although by some accounts the figure was even higher.[9] The foreign loans which Lamar hoped would inject new life into the country's flagging economy had fallen through. And yet the visionary Lamar was completely oblivious to the need for belt-tightening. He continued to create the illusion of empire, burdening the government with an unwieldy and expensive bureaucracy, outfitting a navy, and building a splendid executive mansion on a hill above Congress Avenue. The past three years had seen a succession of schemes come and go. Plans for a national bank, a national road, and a public school system were all abandoned due to lack of funds or as Lamar lost interest in them. Nor was the financial crisis the only obstacle Houston faced. In spite of Lamar's ruthless and costly policy of Indian extermination, angry tribes continued to threaten the lives and property of settlers on the frontier. In northeast Texas, a bitter feud between two rival bandit gangs had recently erupted into nothing less than a bloody civil war. The litany of problems seemed endless.

But Houston did not know the worst. The most distressing news of all had not yet reached Texas. Several hundred miles away, a ragged band of Texans was marching along a dusty road in northern Mexico—the miserable survivors of the Santa Fe Expedition. Three months earlier, in a last-ditch effort to rescue the failing fortunes of the Republic, Lamar had dispatched a force of 320 men across the desert to Santa Fe to establish a trade route with New Mexico. This lucrative market brought yearly revenues of five million dollars to merchants in the United States, revenues which could be diverted into the empty coffers of Texas. The Santa Fe region, he believed, was eager to gain its independence from Mexico and would welcome his offer of annexation and trade.

Lamar could not have been more wrong. From the start it was a quixotic mission with no hope of success. Ill-equipped and poorly led, the expedition soon ran into difficulty. After a tortuous march through uncharted territory, harassed by Comanches and weak from thirst and hunger, the exhausted Texans reached their destination only to find that the citizens of Santa Fe did not share Lamar's enthusiasm for his proposal. They surrendered to the Mexican garrison there without firing a shot.

What followed was a nightmare. The Santa Fe prisoners were marched south under the custody of a Mexican officer with a distinct penchant for sadism, who drove them mercilessly into such a state of exhaustion that escape was unthinkable. At night they shivered without blankets on the frozen ground, or were locked up in rooms so cramped they could not sit down and gasped for air, nearly dying of suffocation. Along the way men died of exposure or were summarily shot for lagging behind. Their bodies were stripped of clothing and left by the roadside. Their ears were hacked off with a machete; the Mexican officer pierced them and strung them on a strip of rawhide to wear as a grisly necklace. Upon reaching the Río Grande he was relieved of his duties and court-martialed for his excessive zeal. Thereafter the treatment of the prisoners improved, but the Mexican government, still smarting after its humiliation at San Jacinto and incensed that its former province now had the temerity to try and snatch away additional northern lands, was in no mood for clemency. The Santa Fe prisoners were marched one thousand miles into Mexico and thrown into prison.[10]

THERE WOULD BE no honeymoon for the incoming administration, for partisan sentiments ran high in the Sixth Congress, and its members were a contentious lot under any circumstances. Many seemed to have little in common with the voters who had elected them into office. Hardscrabble farmers could not neglect their fields nor afford the time and the expense to represent their districts. A considerable number of these officeholders were young, single men, often lacking prior political experience or a stable profession, the gadabouts and adventurers and those anxious to make a name for themselves in a new land. Most could claim some distinction on the field of battle, either at San Jacinto or in some Indian skirmish. Ned Burleson was barely literate, but such were his credentials as an Indian fighter that voters had seen fit to elect him to the nation's second-highest post by an overwhelming majority. One man who had known him some years earlier remarked that "no one could even have dreamed of predicting that he would ever have been 'thought of' as the vice president of a republic nation."[11] Evidence of valor was more than an asset for the would-be politician; it was virtually a prerequisite for office (and, for some, their only qualification). Not surprisingly, a spirit of calm deliberation was noticeably absent among such legislators. Debates were often boisterous affairs, and on occasion verbal attacks gave way to violence. Three weeks after the inaugural, David Kaufman, the former Speaker of the House, was shot and seriously wounded outside the Hall of Congress by Nacogdoches congressman James Mayfield.[12] The new President might have preferred a Congress with more statesmen than sharpshooters.

All seemed to agree, however, on the need for budget-cutting in view of the fiscal crisis. Houston set the example by having Lamar's grand presidential mansion boarded up, taking lodgings instead at the Eberly House. The legislators followed suit by cutting their own salaries from $5 to $3 per day, and Houston's annual salary in half, from $10,000 to $5,000. The swollen public debt was suspended until the Republic could meet its obligations. Government offices were abolished, and the responsibilities of remaining ones curtailed for lack of funds, while Houston's request for a modest $300,000 public loan was voted down.[13]

No sooner had Houston taken the oath of office than reports of the capture of the Santa Fe campaigners began to reach the capital, although it would be some time before these rumors were actually confirmed.[14] Outraged at the harsh treatment of the prisoners, the nation demanded that Houston take suitably aggressive action. Tensions between Texas and Mexico, largely quiescent since 1836, erupted with a new and disturbing intensity. One broadside entitled *A Voice from the West!!!* was indicative of the belligerent attitude:

> *Fellow Citizens—The piteous cries, and dying groans of our imprisoned and slaughtered countrymen, come to our ears in every breeze that sweeps over the Western prairies; and call upon us, in the language of incarcerated and murdered fellow beings, who are of our own country, of our own acquaintance, and of our own kindred, to rise up and march to their rescue, or to avenge their blood! Fellow Citizens, shall those cries be wafted to our ears in vain?*[15]

The Texas Congress insisted that the new President issue a direct challenge to Mexico for its treatment of the Santa Fe prisoners. Opposed to any move that might provoke further hostilities, Houston urged caution. His allies in Congress ignored his warnings and added their names to a sweeping bill passed by both houses authorizing the annexation of all Mexican territory north of the Río Grande and portions of the states of Coahuila, Tamaulipas, Durango, and Sinaloa as well. Thus Texas in effect laid claim to two-thirds of Mexico.[16]

Houston could only scoff at such a proposal, and vetoed the bill without hesitation. With Texas staring bankruptcy full in the face, Congress had ordered him to wrest from Mexico's control an area of land larger than the United States (excluding the territories), and yet it could not find the money to fund an adequate mail service within its own borders. His veto message was a plea for sanity. "Texas only requires peace to make her truly prosperous," he stated. "I am inclined to believe other nations would regard it as a legislative jest inasmuch as it would assume a right which it is utterly impossible to exercise."[17]

It was no jest. Congress, reflecting the public furor, passed the bill over Houston's veto. But if it could defy the President, it could not defy the simple truth: there was no revenue to proceed with a war against Mexico. When Congress adjourned as scheduled in early February, there were no plans for an invasion. The legislators had given vent to their rage with empty threats, but they had accomplished nothing. With his country tottering on the verge of collapse and its people bellowing for war, the President packed his bags and made the four-day trip by mule to Houston City, no doubt hoping that the crisis would soon blow over.

The controversy did not die with the close of Congress. Houston was assailed from all quarters for his refusal to be swept up by the martial fervor. Even some of his political allies and closest associates counseled aggressive action. "In the name of outraged humanity, can we not—shall we not mete out to the authors of so much barbarism and cruelty the full measure of a nation's vengeance?" Washington D. Miller, the President's young secretary, asked his chief. In a distinctly rabid tone Miller continued:

"Let the avenging sword be drawn! . . . Westward the star of empire makes its way," and like the wise men of old, the Anglo-american race will be true to its course. . . . Fully do I believe, that as sure as the morrow's sun will rise, the irrevocable destiny of that people points to an absolute dominion as extended as the continent itself. Heaven has decreed it; and will employ agents equal, by benign favor, to the splendid accomplishment. "Delenda est Carthago." [Carthage must be destroyed.][18]

Sam Houston could not share his young colleague's flight of fancy. Realistically, Texas could not hope to wage an offensive war against Mexico. Houston estimated that an invasion would require no less than five thousand men at a cost of $2,500,000.[19] And yet Texas had no standing army. Prior attempts to raise one had been disastrous, for Texas soldiers—from commanding officers to the lowliest privates—had little taste for discipline. There was only one arsenal, and this was so depleted by the Santa Fe Expedition and Indian raids that the government could lay its hands on no more than 395 rifles and 581 barrels of powder.[20]

In the minds of most Texans, these were trifling matters. Few shared the President's fear that another invasion of Mexico might end in tragedy. The Santa Fe Expedition had not tarnished the Republic's self-image of invincibility (although Andrew Jackson believed that Lamar's "wild goose campaign" had done the reputation of Texas such damage that it would take three San Jacintos to restore it).[21] An unswerving faith in their own fighting abilities and the supremacy of the Anglo-Saxon race stilled all doubts. The Mexicans, they were convinced, were simply no match for them; it was cowardice even to contemplate defeat against so unworthy an adversary. Cultural chauvinism ran rampant in North America in this age of Manifest Destiny, and nowhere were such views more in evidence than in Texas, where the Revolution appeared to portend the inexorable advance of the white race across the continent. The miscegenation of the Indian and Hispanic peoples had created a lower breed, Anglo-Americans believed, rendered all the more inferior by a hot, tropical climate which left them listless and phlegmatic.[22] Joseph Eve, the U.S. chargé d'affaires in Texas, offered his own "impartial comparison of the character of the two races of men" in a report to President Tyler which, it hardly needs to be said, reflected a point of view shared by most Anglo-Saxons living west of the Sabine:

> . . . the Texans [are] bould and fearless to a fault, chivalrous, intelligent enterprising and patriotic, who fight in defence of their all, their wives and children, their homes and property, and their civil and religious liberty; whilst the Mexicans are a feeble mongrel Priest riden race, composed of Spanish Indian and negro; nine tenth's of them ignorant and servile, bound in chains of superstition, which hangs upon them like an incubus, and holds all the faculties of the mind in a hopeless state of stupidity and bondage extinguishes every inducement to noble valorous and patriotic deeds and leaves them in the lowest depth of poverty misery and woe almost beyound the reach of remedy. . . .[23]

But if the Texas experience was any indication, the Anglo-Saxon destiny to rule the continent was, in 1842, anything but manifest. Despite the imperial ambitions of Houston's predecessor and the grasping aggrandizement of the Sixth Congress, Texas could do no more than hold its own, occupying a belt of land from the Sabine to the Colorado rivers. The Republic existed in a curious state of limbo, still claimed by a nation whose culture and customs it abhorred and denied a union with the country to which it felt a natural allegiance. Although the problems which beset the infant Republic were many and complex, Texans attributed their woes to a single source—Mexico, which periodically threatened to reconquer its former province. Although it had as yet made virtually no effort to do so, American and international banks were unwilling under the circumstances to provide the capital Texas so desperately needed. "[Mexico] is the cause of all our difficulties," the Austin *City Gazette* editorialized, "the source of a heavy national debt—crippled commerce—neglected if not paralyzed husbandry; and an emigration, less by four-fifths, than it would have been under other circumstances." [24]

Many Texans believed that the looming specter of Mexican invasion was the sole source of the Republic's problems; remove that specter with a profitable invasion of its own, so the reasoning went, and Texas would find the prosperity that had thus far eluded it. Indolent and idle though the Mexicans were believed to be, the towns in the lower Río Grande Valley were reputed to be rich and would yield valuable plunder to a conquering horde of Texans. Silver and other valuables were there for the taking, livestock could be captured and driven north across the river, indemnities could be paid by Mexican towns to be spared from the torch. Francis Moore, the editor of the *Telegraph and Texas Register,* suggested that no less than $100,000 could be extorted in this manner from Monterrey and Saltillo alone, as well as "a proportional sum from other towns." The newspaperman declared: "Our citizens could not engage in a more lucrative business than in carrying on offensive war with Mexico." [25] A policy of government-sponsored pillage seemed a convenient and acceptable way to sustain the Republic during its current economic crisis.

The furor that followed the news of the Santa Fe Expedition had its origins in six years of frustration. Underlying the outrage which Texans expressed at the mistreatment of the Santa Fe prisoners was the conviction that an inferior people had managed to deny them their rightful place on the continent. At a public rally at Houston in March, citizens cheered as one speaker promised that "the insults of that weak, imbecile, and *nigger* republic of Mexico would be avenged in the most signal manner."[26] In the prevailing climate of economic uncertainty, Texans were particularly anxious to seek redress for their martyred and imprisoned countrymen. Despite the Republic's misfortunes, its reputation for Spartan heroics remained a wellspring of national pride; indeed, the martial symbols of its brief but violent past would ultimately prove more enduring than the nation itself. Francis Moore called upon "the unemployed young men who are not yet engaged in permanent business" to equal the heroic accomplishments of 1836.[27] With a talent for hyperbole unmatched among the gazetteers of Texas, Moore predicted that "the footsteps of their enslaved countrymen traced in blood . . . shall guide them in the path of glory."[28] In the aftermath of the Santa Fe episode, the desire for retribution had become nothing less than a quest for national vindication. The Republic had suffered too many setbacks to ignore this most recent affront to its legitimacy. "Vengeance," Washington D. Miller conceded, "is all that is left us."[29]

In 1842, few believed that San Jacinto had been the final, decisive conflict. The Anglo and Latin American cultures seemed destined to clash again. Not since the Revolution had Texans been so determined to wage war against their southern neighbor. Many Texans had come to the conclusion that the time had come to settle the matter once and for all. Recklessly, impulsively, they howled for war.

The Vásquez and Woll Incursions

FOR THE PAST six years, ever since Santa Anna's humiliating capture and the utter rout of his army in the tall grass of Buffalo Bayou, the reconquest of Texas had been for Mexicans a rallying point, a national goal. But while Mexican leaders vowed that this stain on the country's honor would be erased, they had been unable to muster the resources necessary to mount an effective campaign. Beset by chronic political instability and economic decay, Mexico was in no position to make good its threats. Its standing army, while larger than that of the United States, had long been corrupted by factionalism and political intrigue. Mexican leaders, whose power was limited in the best of times, were also unwilling to hazard a second invasion of Texas while they faced more pressing problems of internal unrest. Since 1836 the country seemed to be crumbling away at the edges as outlying provinces rose up in revolt, demanding greater autonomy and in some cases complete independence. In part, the absence of national cohesiveness was inevitable; Mexico's very size was a handicap which would have posed nightmarish administrative problems for even the most efficient and benevolent government. Upon the great central plain the bureaucracy functioned well enough, but as the roads disappeared into dense jungles to the south, miles of empty desert to the north, and high mountain ranges to the east and west, the government's grip became noticeably weaker.

In 1840 federalist rebels in the northern states of Coahuila, Nuevo León, and Tamaulipas declared their independence from Mexico and established the Republic of the Río Grande. No sooner had this uprising been put down than a similar revolt flared in another far-off corner of the country, the Yucatán. Stamping out these insurrections had become an all-consuming task for a government saddled by mounting debt. But it was the Texas Revolution, the most successful separatist movement, which underscored the government's inability to control the land it claimed. Mexico had inherited from Spain an empire in decay, but an empire nonetheless, and with it came an understandable if obsessive desire to maintain its territorial integrity. It was a point of honor that could not be compromised.

Perhaps no one wanted to bring Texas to heel more than Antonio López de Santa Anna, whose political exile after San Jacinto had been remarkably brief. Two months before Houston took office, Santa Anna had once again seized power, proving if nothing else that the self-styled "Napoleon of the West" was a man with an uncanny ability to sense and seize the moment, a political acrobat who could stumble and still land squarely on his feet. Like his predecessors, the new President of Mexico was painfully aware that a full-fledged invasion of Texas was out of the question. With government expenditures often four and five times greater than revenues, Mexico—like Texas—simply could not afford to wage war. The rebellion in the Yucatán peninsula demanded immediate attention, and the army could not manage two campaigns at once. At least for the foreseeable future, Santa Anna's plans for revenge would have to wait. He could not, of course, place these facts before the Mexican people. The promise of reconquest had been made too often and too loudly; the government could not keep face and allow Texas to go unpunished.

There was, however, an alternative to a financially ruinous invasion. A swift, retaliatory strike north of the Río Grande would spark national pride and divert attention from the chaotic affairs of state, giving the new President the political capital he needed to shore up his public support. Moreover, the appearance of Mexican troops on the west Texas frontier would also serve to discourage Anglo-American settlement, which could not be allowed to continue if Mexico was ever to entertain hopes of regaining its errant province. Since the Texas frontier was thinly populated and completely undefended, the risks involved in such a show of force were negligible. If Mexico was at present unable to win a lasting victory, it could at least send a clear message that it was not yet prepared to concede defeat.

Three days after making his triumphant entrance into Mexico City, Santa Anna instructed General Mariano Arista, his commander of the Army of the North, to reopen hostilities against Texas.[1] With the objective of harassing the Texas frontier, Arista was to send a portion of his army against San Antonio, "to surprise its garrison and take it captive, or to put it to the knife should it offer obstinate resistance."[2] It was a simple raid, nothing more, but it was important to keep up appearances, and Santa Anna grandly declared that Mexico would soon plant "her Eagle Standards on the banks of the Sabine."[3]

In the spring of 1842 a Mexican army marched into Texas. Under General Rafael Vásquez a force of seven hundred men crossed the south Texas plain, arriving in San Antonio on March 5. Most Anglo-American residents had already hastened toward the interior, but a small force made preparations to defend the town. Heavily outnumbered, they were allowed to withdraw, leaving San Antonio open to Vásquez and his men.[4]

The news of the invasion threw Texas into a panic. Hundreds of settlers fled to the more populated and safer towns in the east, taking only the belongings they could load into their wagons, in an evacuation reminiscent of the Runaway Scrape of 1836. Rumors were wild and abundant; Vásquez was reported to have as many as fourteen thousand troops, and the seizure of the capital in Austin, it was said, would surely be his next objective.[5]

While many settlers abandoned their homes, many others rallied to the defense of the Republic. Without waiting for their government's call to arms, volunteer companies were formed and rushed to the frontier. Within a few days as many as three thousand men were on their way to San Antonio.[6] Those who could not join the jubilant crusade contributed generously to the cause. Merchants donated goods to outfit the new recruits, and in Galveston men sold property and even slaves to raise money for the war effort. Women sold their jewelry to purchase ammunition.[7] The entire country seemed to have caught the war fever.

But President Houston remained immune. He was worried that if farmers abandoned their plows during planting season, the country might well face a serious food shortage the following winter. He ordered them to return to the cultivation of their fields. By this time news had reached Houston City that Vásquez had occupied San Antonio only two days and was now retreating back across the south Texas chaparral. It appeared that this was only a hit-and-run attack, not a full-scale invasion. Unwilling to allow the martial spirit to carry the nation headlong into a war it did not need, Houston dispatched General Alexander Somervell to command the volunteers who were now assembling at San Antonio. Houston's greatest fear was that the volunteers would rush toward Mexico "without orders and in a tumultuous mass."[8] Thus, Somervell was instructed to attack the Mexican army if practical, but the President remained firm in the belief that an invasion of Mexico was out of the question for want of ammunition and supplies.

Houston chose Somervell, the senior-ranking officer on the frontier, to lead the defense of the west knowing full well that the general did not enjoy the support of those men who were most anxious to proceed with an invasion. There were others, notably his own Vice-President, Edward Burleson, who were eager to place themselves at the head of an army and sweep down across the Río Grande. Houston seemed well pleased with the appointment, if only because of the frustration he knew it would cause among those who hungered for martial glory. "You would be amused and miserably provoked at some of our 'Heroes,'" the President wrote to William Henry Daingerfield, his secretary of the treasury. Burleson and others were "all burning with revenge to cross the Rio Grande and 'damning the President' that he would not let them go on. Oh, they were snorting! . . . Somebody will be taken down a button hole or two." [9]

In the meantime, Houston added to the excitement on the frontier by ordering the transfer of the government archives from Austin to Houston, where they would be safe in the event that Vásquez decided to make another assault on the western settlements. Ever suspicious of Houston's motives, the frontier settlers regarded this action as the first step in an attempt to rob Austin of its place as the seat of government. Determined to resist the President's order, they seized the arms and ammunition of the government arsenal there and prepared to defend the town. The obstinate westerners, it was clear, were ready to fight both Santa Anna *and* Sam Houston. For the time being, Houston thought it best not to press the issue, and the archives remained where they were.

When Somervell arrived in San Antonio, he found that Edward Burleson had dashed to the frontier ahead of him with three companies of volunteers. Claiming the right to choose their own officers, the men gathered at San Antonio had already elected Burleson to command the new army. The Vice-President was usually a loyal soldier, but a few of the anti-Houston firebrands had gained his ear in San Antonio, and he was now so excited by the troops' vote of confidence that he refused to give up his post. Somervell, bearing orders from the President of the Republic, might have stood firm, but as later events were to demonstrate, he utterly lacked the kind of resolute character necessary for frontier leadership. Without so much as a word of protest Somervell withdrew, complaining afterward that "political intrigue has been at work" by men who sought to usurp his command and gain "immortal glory for themselves." [10]

Burleson eventually realized that this kind of discord and disobedience were detrimental to the war effort. He resigned from the post to which the rank and file had elected him. [11] Now the army had no commander. Meanwhile, Vásquez and his army had safely crossed the Río Grande.

This kind of confusion and insubordination were unfortunate characteristics of the Texas army. The self-willed frontiersman was a splendid fighter but a poor soldier; submissive obedience was foreign to his very nature. Unruly, undisciplined, and untrained, this was a people's fighting force, which scorned military pomp and exemplified the egalitarianism of the frontier. Officers were elected, not appointed, and they could just as easily be removed if they failed to lead by example. In a nation that glorified combat and heaped accolades upon its heroes, it was no wonder that so many were eager to distinguish themselves by acts of courage and daring. It was an army of paladins, in which every man sought to win the laurels of battle, in which every man considered himself best suited to generalship. Cooler heads could rarely prevail among men who equated caution with cowardice. And the result was chaos.

Houston had nothing but contempt for those who sought to undermine the government's authority with talk of war. They were the same kind of reckless men whose utter lack of restraint had very nearly robbed Texas of victory in the Revolution. In 1836 insubordinate commanders routinely disobeyed their orders, while Houston himself was nearly overthrown by mutinous troops on the eve of San Jacinto. Even after the war was over the rebellions in the ranks continued. It soon became clear that a standing army was a greater danger to the Republic than the lack of one, for in the hands of hot-headed generals it could never be left standing for long. With the wealth of Mexico within reach, they were eager for plunder and ready to march on Matamoros. Houston had skillfully managed to thwart all attempts to cross the Río Grande during his first term, but keeping these firebrands at bay remained his most formidable and exasperating problem. "Texas," he grumbled, "will 'whip herself' without the assistance of Mexico." [12]

In 1842, the clamor for war had never been louder, nor the Republic's citizen-soldiers more unmanageable. They had had enough of Houston's temporizing. While the danger of a Mexican invasion had clearly passed, the President still faced mounting pressure to wage war on Mexican soil and avenge the recent insults to national pride. The American chargé d'affaires was only one of many visitors who did not know what to make of this impetuous frontier breed that seemed bent on self-annihilation. Texas, he wrote incredulously, was "a young nation just emerging from its cradle with a population of less than 100,000 souls without a dollar in its Treasury, nor a single soldier belonging to it, without credit sufficient to borrow a dollar at home or abroad, constantly at war with numerous tribes of canibal [sic] Indians, and at the same time making offensive war upon a nation of eight millions; strange as it may seem such is the fact." [13]

To the exasperation of his critics and many of his friends, Houston continued to urge a policy of retrenchment. He was convinced that Mexico lacked the wherewithal to mount an invasion with the objective of regaining its former province. If Texas stayed on the defensive, he believed it could never be conquered. He was unwilling to tempt fate and order a second quixotic mission into Mexican territory, and certainly not one of hot-headed adventurers whom he could not control. Shortly before the Vásquez raid he had expressed his thoughts on the military situation as follows: "To defend a country requires comparatively but little means—to invade a nation requires everything. To conquer Mexicans in Texas is one thing—to battle with Mexicans in Mexico is a different kind of warfare. The true interest of Texas is to maintain peace with all nations and to cultivate her soil." [14]

But Houston was nothing if not unpredictable. He would soon abandon his reservations—or at least appear to do so—and startle his critics by sounding the tocsin with as much enthusiasm as the most zealous war hawk. Houston ordered county militia units to be ready to march at a moment's notice and invited volunteers from the United States to join the campaign. He went further and announced a blockade of Mexican harbors. [15] To appropriate funds and empower him to wage war against Mexico, the President called for a special session of Congress to convene in June. "We invoke the God of Armies," he declared to a Galveston editor. "War shall now be waged against Mexico, nor will we lay our arms aside until we have secured recognition of our independence." [16]

What made him change his mind? Houston was no doubt aware of several factors that weighed in favor of an abrupt political about-face. Most important, he could not run the risk of sending signals of weakness to Santa Anna. If Texas was incapable of raising an army against Mexico, Houston could not afford to publicize the point. It was essential that Texas give every impression that it could respond to the recent invasion with one of its own. Houston also knew that Great Britain and the United States were anxious to negotiate a peaceful settlement between Texas and Mexico. By appearing to push his country to the brink of war, Houston may have hoped to pressure the two major powers to step up their efforts at bringing about Mexico's recognition of Texas independence.

Nor could Houston much longer continue to ignore the public outcry in favor of an invasion. If he could match the bluster of the firebrands it would defuse much of the criticism against him. This would be particularly helpful in appeasing western voters, whose relations with the President were strained to the breaking point. The demand for war was strongest in the west, and the possible transfer of the government from Austin and the loss of income threatened by the move had the frontier settlers literally up in arms.

Thus Houston found himself in the contradictory but necessary position of advocating a war he neither wanted nor planned to carry out. Rather than be swept aside by the current of public opinion that rushed toward war, Houston rode the wave. Even as the army in San Antonio began to disperse for want of leadership, Houston was proclaiming a bold new policy. Not to be outdone by Santa Anna's bombast, he taunted the Mexican President with some fiery rhetoric of his own: "ere the banner of Mexico shall triumphantly float upon the banks of the Sabine, the Texian standard of the single star, borne by the Anglo-Saxon race, shall display its bright folds in Liberty's triumph on the isthmus of Darien."[17]

IF TEXANS IN the west were heartened by Houston's new-found belligerence, their elation was offset by one infuriating bit of news. Empowered by the constitution to relocate the government in case of an emergency, the President insisted that the special session of Congress meet in Houston City. He argued, with some justification, that the Vásquez raid was proof of the danger of maintaining the capital on the frontier. "We should be the laughing stock of the world," he said, if Santa Anna—who knew the indignity of falling into enemy hands—could capture the legislature in session.[18]

Throughout the spring and early summer Houston continued to act warlike. He could afford to; it was easy enough to call for the blockade of Mexican ports when the Texas Navy—three vessels—was sitting in dry dock in New Orleans. The last session of Congress, in spite of its ambitious plans for territorial expansion, had released no funds for a campaign, and Houston well knew they would not be forthcoming at the next session, for such funds simply did not exist. Nonetheless, the volunteers were now gathering on the frontier near Corpus Christi, in anticipation of a campaign into Mexico. The enlistees were generally adventure-seekers and soldiers of fortune who came to Texas with the intention of winning spoils and rich prizes from Mexico. Lacking food and provisions that the government could not supply, they quickly turned hostile and mutinous. Their commander dispatched a string of plaintive notes to his President, admitting that he was unable to control them. Houston was unsympathetic. "How can men with naked feet talk of Matamoros, Monterrey, and other places?" he asked, when informed that his soldiers were restless and itching for their marching orders.[19] He had called for volunteers to intimidate Mexico, but he had never intended to use them. His only concern was that the men not march on the Río Grande.

In late June, Congress met in Houston City to enact war legislation. The western legislators had threatened to boycott the session, but now that the President seemed ready to prosecute the war they wanted, they had little choice but to obey. In 1842 Houston was a town of some two thousand inhabitants, many of them gamblers and young men in search of business opportunities. Although touted by its enterprising founders as "handsome and beautifully elevated,"[20] the town was built on lowland marshes, making it ripe for outbreaks of yellow fever and cholera. It may not have been the "greatest sink of dissipation and vice that modern times has ever known," as one visitor chose to describe it, but its reputation as the wildest of the Texas boom towns was well-deserved.[21]

Houston opened the session with an address to the Congress in Government House. No doubt to the amazement of many legislators, the tone of his speech was not anything like the bold talk of recent months. As if he had never said a word about an invasion of Mexico, Houston implored Congress to weigh the consequences of waging war. He was not, he told them, "an advocate of offensive measures."[22] The War Party, as the President's enemies were collectively known, had come to Houston City with the purpose of punishing Mexico, and they quickly set about drafting legislation that would force Houston's hand. Both houses passed by a wide margin a bill authorizing the President to call up one-third of the country's young men and sell off ten million acres of land to finance the invasion. The President himself was to lead the campaign.

Houston received the bill and took no immediate action. Anticipating a veto, the war hawks were enraged. Nacogdoches congressman James Mayfield, a former secretary of state under Lamar, accused the President of having "lulled and deceived the people by open promises of war, while his secret machinations were at work to dismay the public hope and chill the general enthusiasm to avert war if he could, and leave the people to submission and despair."[23] "The Bill presented for your consideration and signature opens to yourself a field for glory which has had no parallel since Napoleon crossed the Alps," pleaded Memucan Hunt, the former Texas minister to the United States.[24] The mood in the capital was tense as all waited for Houston's decision. The insufferable heat made for hot tempers. Small knots of armed men, many of them deserters from the army, gathered on the streets; some talked openly of Houston's assassination. Fearing reprisals, some cabinet members considered resigning their posts. The President shunned the advice of friends to station guards at his house, preferring instead to court danger by keeping his lamps burning late into the night. Through open windows and blinds he could be seen passing from room to room, an easy target, as his wife Margaret sang and played the piano or harp.[25] Still Houston held onto the war bill and waited.

On July 2, one day before the session was due to adjourn, Houston surprised no one by sending Congress his veto message. Among other reasons, he argued that the war bill did not provide him with the financial means necessary to prosecute the war. The sale of public lands could not be expected to raise sufficient revenue in a nation with more land than it could possibly use, in which squatters' rights were often the rule. Land scrip was already selling at a fraction of its original value. Moreover, as Congress intended to pay its soldiers in land under the headright system, the government would have great difficulty disposing of the allotted ten million acres before hostilities began. Unable to resist a final jab at his opponents, the President who had so often been accused of megalomania observed that the war bill conferred upon the chief executive virtually dictatorial powers in time of war, and would therefore be unconstitutional.[26]

Once again Houston faced the fury of his enemies. Even Secretary of War George Hockley, a friend of the President's since his Tennessee days, could no longer tolerate a policy of inaction and resigned in disgust. But after the tension of recent weeks the excitement quickly subsided. The panic caused by the Vásquez raid had been largely forgotten; it was now evident that it had never been intended to be the first wave of a full-scale invasion. Although there had been some skirmishing on the frontier between Mexican *defensores* and Texas militia units in July, the country did not appear to be in any immediate danger. The American volunteers encamped near Corpus Christi, tired of waiting, were packing up and going home. Commodore Edwin W. Moore of the Texas Navy declared he had been "humbugged" by the President when it became clear that he would not be receiving any money to blockade Mexican ports.[27] In the western districts, critics heaped scorn upon the administration's "ludicrous military farce" and decried the President's "ingenuity for new excuses and pretexts" in avoiding war with Mexico.[28]

The President, on the other hand, could afford to be well pleased with his adroit handling of the situation. The firebrands, for all their bluster and loud talk, would not be marching down into the Río Grande Valley after all. The nation's financial woes and the hostility of the western voters were problems that would have to be dealt with, but Houston could look back at the first nine months of his administration with considerable satisfaction. Twice Texans had demanded an invasion of Mexico and twice Houston had managed to deny them the opportunity. The furor over the veto quickly died down, and one Houston critic believed that the President was now more popular than ever.[29]

But Houston's respite was to be short-lived. In Mexico City, Santa Anna's government greeted the news of the Vásquez raid with parades and the firing of cannons and rockets. The purpose of the raid, the government explained, had been to test the Texan defenses in preparation for a full-scale invasion. The conquest of Texas still remained a dream, but the enthusiasm with which the Mexican people had received this small victory seems to have convinced Santa Anna that such half-measures were enough to satisfy public opinion.[30] Arista resigned that summer, and it fell upon Isidro Reyes, his successor as commander of the Army of the North, to further implement Santa Anna's policy of border harassment. Reyes chose Adrian Woll, a Frenchman who had risen to the rank of brigadier general, to lead another expedition across the Río Grande.

With elections to the new Texas Congress to be held in early September, Houston was now urged to consider relocating the capital yet again, if not back to Austin then to some other frontier town, as a peace offering to his opponents in the west. Houston City was proving to be an unpopular choice for the seat of government, its residents having found there was more inconvenience than prestige in playing host to a penurious body of legislators. Washington-on-the-Brazos, on the other hand, promised to be more accommodating, and preparations were made once again for a change of venue for the wandering government. As the government property was being packed, Houston received the news that, for the second time in six months, a Mexican force had captured San Antonio.

AT DAWN ON September 11, under the canopy of a heavy fog, General Adrian Woll marched into San Antonio at the head of an army of fourteen hundred men. Unlike the earlier Vásquez raid there was little advance warning, Woll having followed an old smuggling trail through the hills west of San Antonio. The Anglo-American residents nonetheless managed to put up a spirited, if brief, defense of the town. From Samuel Maverick's house in one corner of the plaza, no more than sixty Texans battled Woll's force for half an hour, until the fog lifted and they saw that they were completely surrounded. District court had been in session that week in San Antonio, and the captives included the judge and two members of Congress, as well as several attorneys and clerks.

For a week General Woll held the town, as Texans once again rushed to the frontier. Since the Vásquez raid the west had been virtually de-

fenseless. The only regular force (but irregularly paid) was a company of
rangers under Major John C. Hays. An aggressive, self-confident leader,
the boyish-looking, twenty-five-year-old Hays had already established a
reputation on the frontier as a daring fighter of Indians. According to one
historian, Hays "possessed those qualities that made him an excellent
officer: he mixed kindness with strictness in such a way as to command
respect and obedience, [and] he knew the potential of his men both collectively and individually." [31]

Among those in Hays' company were men who were also to figure
prominently in the early history of the Texas Rangers. They included Ben
McCulloch, a native of Tennessee who had ventured to Texas on the eve
of the Revolution. He planned to rendezvous with one of his neighbors,
David Crockett, in Nacogdoches but was taken ill along the way, and
Crockett went on to the Alamo without him. Another was twenty-seven-
year-old Samuel Walker, who had run off from his job as a carpenter's
apprentice to fight Indians while still in his teens. After a failed business
venture in Florida, he drifted to Texas, arriving on the frontier in January
1842. [32] Taciturn and unassuming, he kept mostly to himself, but in the
face of danger exhibited a recklessness and wanton disregard for his own
safety that quickly won him the admiration of the others in Hays' outfit.
"There was nothing in the personal appearance of Capt. Walker that de-
noted the hero," one acquaintance recalled. "His intellect was mediocre,
and not much cultivated, but he was modest, moral, high-minded, and
the bravest of the brave." [33] A soldier who knew him well wrote, "War
was his element, the bivouac his delight, and the battlefield his play-
ground." [34] In Texas, Samuel Walker seemed to have found his niche. Destined to become the most famous of them all was William A. A. "Big
Foot" Wallace, a colorful character whose anecdotes about life on the
frontier would in later years make him something of a Bunyanesque character in Texas lore. The twenty-five-year-old Virginian had come to Texas
in 1837 upon learning that his brother and cousin had died in the Goliad
Massacre. Lacking a trade and intent upon avenging their deaths, he soon
signed up with Jack Hays' company on the frontier. [35]

Hays and his men now joined forces with volunteers from the surrounding countryside. The volunteers elected as their commander Math-
ew Caldwell, a well-known Indian fighter and signer of the Texas Declaration of Independence who was known as "Old Paint" for the gray
streaks in his dark red hair. As a member of the Santa Fe Expedition, he
had only recently been released from a Mexican jail. Broken in health but
hungering for revenge, Caldwell saddled up again for what would prove
to be the last time.

On the morning of September 17 Jack Hays and a contingent of mounted rangers rode across the chaparral to the outskirts of San Antonio, within shouting distance of Woll's men, hoping to lure them out for a fight. They were spotted immediately by the sentries, and within minutes a cavalry regiment was in hot pursuit. The rangers took off for the Salado, a stream five miles east of town, where Caldwell's men, now some two hundred volunteers, were waiting in a dense thicket in the creek bottom, a position which afforded ample protection and a clear view of several hundred yards of open prairie.

Seeing that the Texans would not be easily dislodged, the Mexican cavalry halted at a safe distance and sent back word to San Antonio that reinforcements would be necessary. Woll had actually planned to abandon the town and move his troops south that day, the limited objectives of his mission having been accomplished. Although he was under orders from the high command of the Army of the North not to attack the Texans, Woll decided to meet their challenge, reasoning that the enemy was gaining strength hourly as more volunteers arrived on the frontier. With a quick victory against Caldwell's inferior force, Woll hoped to prevent the Texans from mounting an effective attack, allowing him to make good his retreat across the Río Grande.[36]

Woll left a small part of his force to hold the town and marched his men out to the Salado. It was almost midday before the Mexicans were ready to launch their assault. As lines of infantry started across the prairie, Caldwell addressed his men: "keep cool and recollect for what we are fighting—it is for liberty and our insulted country." He then called for a few words from a Baptist preacher in his ranks, who responded with the following invocation: "Let us shoot low, and my impression before God is that we shall win the fight."[37] The Mexicans made repeated attempts to dislodge the Texans with cavalry and infantry, but on each assault the lines broke and fell back before they reached the thicket. One Texan died, but as many as sixty of Woll's troops were killed in the fighting.[38]

Late that afternoon Woll received news that another group of Texans was on its way to the battlefield. Frustrated and determined to end the day with a victory of some kind, Woll dispatched two squadrons of cavalry to crush the Texan reinforcements. Captain Nicholas Mosby Dawson and fifty-two of his neighbors from Fayette County had made a forced march from LaGrange in forty-eight hours, having heard of Caldwell's plan to attack Woll's army. Among Dawson's men were seventy-nine-year-old Zadock Woods and his two sons, Norman and Henry. One mile and a half from the Salado they saw the approaching cavalry units sent to intercept them. Caught in the middle of a wide-open prairie,

Dawson and his men headed for a mesquite grove, the only cover available.[39]

As the Mexicans rolled a light artillery piece into position, Dawson was offered terms of surrender. He unwisely rejected them. At first the Texans repulsed the Mexican cavalry assaults, but their numbers were quickly reduced as the cannon found its range and grapeshot ripped through the trees. The gray-haired Zadock Woods was shot down by musket fire, and his son Norman fell to the ground with a bullet in his hip. Severely wounded, Dawson emerged from the thicket with a blanket on his rifle, the only thing he could find that might signify a white flag. In the confusion some of his men continued firing, and Dawson fell under the renewed Mexican barrage. Dismounting, the cavalrymen entered the grove with their sabers drawn, cutting down the Texans in fierce hand-to-hand combat. Only two of Dawson's men managed to escape, one of whom was Norman's brother Henry. Fifteen of Dawson's men were spared; the rest shared their captain's fate.[40] Later that afternoon Woll's soldiers came back to strip the corpses of their clothing and valuables. Among the mangled bodies they found Norman Woods, with five gaping saber wounds and a shattered hip, but still alive. He was brought into San Antonio with the Mexican wounded that evening.[41]

Two days after the battle the Mexican troops made their exit from San Antonio, taking with them their Texan prisoners, including Norman Woods, who made the trip by oxcart, and as many as two hundred Mexicans who had welcomed the invaders and feared reprisals if they remained. Hays and Caldwell followed the retreating Mexican army, and near the Hondo River attacked Woll's rearguard. But once again, the Texan efforts were foiled by a total lack of discipline. The inability of the two commanders to coordinate their movements forced them to break off the pursuit. Caldwell was unfairly blamed for the mix-up, and he returned home in disgrace, scorned by his own men.[42] Like so many leaders of the Republic, Caldwell found that the Texas volunteer owed his allegiance to no man. He died in bed three months later.

News of the invasion quickly spread across the country, sparking a new wave of patriotism. Houston could only watch helplessly as ablebodied men girded themselves once again for war. One Galveston judge, who was trying a woman for the murder of her husband, dismissed the court and put the woman on bail when he heard the news. The judge, attorneys, and other court officers immediately joined the army.[43]

In a letter to President John Tyler, the U.S. chargé d'affaires summed up the situation in Texas in the fall of 1842. The Republic, he explained, might "be well compared to a ship upon a stormy sea without sail or ballast where every mariner claims to be the pilot, and where it requires great firmness prudence and tallents [*sic*] to save it from being capsized by the waves of popular dissension, or strand[ed] upon the beach by the Mexican bayonet."[44] For the past ten months the Texas President had labored to prevent the storm-lashed Republic from running aground. But since the Santa Fe Expedition, war sentiment had grown as one crisis followed another. Not even Sam Houston could keep his nation at peace. With telling prophecy he had written earlier in the year: "I foresee the evils which must befall us before we can learn wisdom. At least two massacres must take place, and fierce adversity will then make us rational."[45] Now the very scenario that Houston feared—that of an unruly band of adventurers descending on Mexico under the Texas flag—was about to be enacted.

The Southwestern Army of Operations

IF THE PEOPLE of Texas were hell-bent on launching a campaign against Mexico, Houston was obliged to give them one. But although circumstances beyond his control had forced his hand, the President was no more enthusiastic about an invasion than he had been ten months earlier. Publicly, he called for Texans to wreak a terrible vengeance on Mexico for the recent incursions; privately, he appears to have still been searching for ways to avert a course that he was convinced would lead to disaster. Clearly, Houston could no longer deny the War Party the opportunity to mount a campaign. But it was now mid-September; if the invasion took two months to get organized, it would have to be postponed until spring, for even the war hawks could not expect to invade Mexico in the winter. By that time, Great Britain and the United States, which were both anxious to maintain peace in the region, might be able to prevail upon Santa Anna to cease his border harassment. Texas tempers would have cooled and a campaign could be put off indefinitely.

Time, therefore, was the President's most valuable ally. Like the rest of the country, he had been very much concerned by the early reports of the second attack on San Antonio, and he took immediate steps to secure the defense of the western frontier by calling up the county militias for active service the day he received word of the invasion.[1] But once it became clear that Woll intended merely to harass the frontier rather than overrun it, Houston proceeded with plans for offensive operations with considerably less dispatch, waiting until he reached Washington-on-the-Brazos before organizing the campaign and appointing a commander. By all appearances, Houston was now ready to prosecute the war on Mexican soil, having been reluctantly forced into such a posture by the ever-mounting pressure of the War Party which could no longer be ignored. But the evidence suggests that the President was not yet ready to allow his enemies their moment of glory.

It was not until October 2 that the government wagon train rumbled into the little village of Washington-on-the-Brazos. Conditions in Washington were undeniably primitive; Houston was a city of sophisticated elegance by comparison. The House of Representatives assembled in rooms above Hatfield's saloon, while the Senate debated on the upper floor of the general store. In shanties scattered throughout town could be found the various departments of government. Secretary of State Anson Jones conducted the affairs of Texas diplomacy from a carpenter's shop, while the President went to work in a newly built one-room shack just off Ferry Street, which led down to the Brazos River. Lodgings for the Houstons proved to be something of a problem. The rent on the house they had planned to live in was exorbitant and demanded in advance. Judge John Lockhart, one of the town's prominent citizens, was anxious that the Houstons' stay in Washington be a pleasant one and kindly offered the first family the use of his main bedroom.[2]

Once the Houstons were settled in, the President turned his attention to the war against Mexico. For a commander to lead the campaign, he chose Alexander Somervell, again snubbing Vice-President Burleson, who still burned with military ambition. Weak-willed and unpopular with the men, Somervell seemed the perfect choice to head up the campaign; the last person the President wanted was a general like Burleson whom the Texans could rally behind. A scapegoat was needed, someone loyal enough to follow orders, naïve enough to think Houston wanted such a mission to succeed, and inept enough to make sure that it did not. If the expedition failed, the blame would lie with Somervell, not Houston. The President could claim he had done all in his power to satisfy the public appetite for war.

Many Texans correctly guessed, however, that Houston's enthusiasm for a campaign into Mexico was still less than lukewarm. His choice of a general who had been rejected by the army six months earlier was hardly reassuring. The *Telegraph and Texas Register* likened the Somervell appointment to "the casting of a firebrand among inflammable materials." Editor Francis Moore added that the appointment "is but an indication that he still secretly wishes to break up the present army, and thus defeat the contemplated campaign."[3] Nelson Lee, who served as a scout under John Hays, agreed; "President Houston," he would later write, "though apparently yielding to the popular demand was, nevertheless, at heart, opposed to the project."[4] After arriving in Washington-on-the-Brazos with dispatches from Hays informing the President of the pro-war feelings in the west, Lee was dispatched to Galveston with instructions to prevent volunteers from joining the expedition, ordering them instead to defend the city from possible attack by sea. So slight was the fear of a possible naval attack by Mexico, however, that Lee returned to San Antonio with twenty citizens of Galveston, including Colonel John H. Walton, the city's mayor.[5]

In the western counties, mistrust of the President was now so great that any move on his part would be questioned by those who had called in vain for war in the past. Houston seemed to take a malicious delight in rankling his critics, and they responded with an equally stubborn determination to wreck administration policy. Given this atmosphere of suspicion and hostility, Alexander Somervell's job was an unenviable one. As a Houston man, the commander of the Southwestern Army of Operations would have a hard time winning the loyalty of the men he would now attempt to lead.

The President authorized Somervell to proceed to the frontier and place himself at the head of the forces gathering there. If the general believed a campaign into enemy territory could be undertaken "with a prospect of success," he was to advance on Mexico as soon as possible. In these and other orders to Somervell, Houston stressed one all-important theme: "Insubordination and a disregard of command will bring ruin and disgrace upon our arms."[6]

Houston suggested that Somervell organize his troops at a point along Cibolo Creek, a few miles above San Antonio.[7] The town itself was a much more suitable location, but Houston did not want the army mustered there, he claimed, for security reasons (the Mexican inhabitants were not believed to be loyal to the government, and might relay valuable information to the enemy below the river).[8] But the Texans riding to the frontier for the anticipated campaign were unaware of these orders, and they headed straight for San Antonio anyway. The President had waited so long to issue Somervell his instructions that the army was ready and waiting by the time the general arrived. Somervell was therefore unable to muster his army at a spot on the frontier more to Houston's liking; his men had made the decision for him.

Singly, in small groups, or in full-fledged companies, the Texans converged on San Antonio. Jack Hays and his ranger company were the first to appear, after their recent skirmish with Woll's army, and made camp outside the town. En route to the frontier Colonel Joseph L. Bennett's militia company from Montgomery County passed through Washington-on-the-Brazos. Houston and his staff visited the men where they were encamped for the evening. The President called upon all his considerable powers of oratory and gave the men a rousing speech, never betraying his true feelings about the mission. He predicted that they would invade Mexico, release all Texas prisoners, and administer to the enemy a stern rebuke for the raids on the frontier.[9] Earlier in the day, however, he had written to a friend confessing his misgivings. "What the men of Texas will do no one can tell, for we must look at them as men, but not as an organized body. To do any good we must unite and act in harmony, or we cannot exist as a nation."[10]

SAN ANTONIO WAS situated in a basin surrounded by rolling hills dotted with mesquite and prickly pear. Looking down upon the town from the hills, one could see imposing white stone buildings built around the plaza and long rows of adobe homes fanning out toward the river: evidence that at one time this was the capital of Spanish Texas and the cornerstone of Spain's vast domain north of the Río Grande. In contrast to the makeshift character of Austin, Houston City, or Washington-on-the-Brazos, San Antonio gave the very definite appearance of prosperity and permanence.

But a closer inspection revealed a much different picture. The town lay nearly in ruins. In recent years it had been a most convenient battleground, a place where the Anglo-American, Hispanic, and Indian cultures met and crossed swords. At one time it had boasted a population of five thousand, but that figure had dwindled steadily with each new outbreak of violence. Weakened and unprotected after the Revolution, it had been the frequent target of Comanches, who were in the habit of making off with horses, supplies, and the occasional scalp until they were massacred on the streets of the town in the vicious Council House Fight in 1840. Now, with renewed hostilities between Texas and Mexico, San Antonio was once again the center of conflict.

There was hardly a building that had not been scarred by violence. Grapeshot had ripped enormous chunks of plaster from the low-slung, white-washed adobe homes. The belfry of the San Fernando Church was honeycombed with musket balls. The missions, too, were in pitiful disrepair, abandoned even by the local clergy who were supposed to maintain them. Blanketed by moss and weeds, the walls were crumbling or had already collapsed. A few of the poorer Mexican families lived in huts of mud and wattles inside the enclosures.[11]

The small Anglo population of San Antonio had evacuated the town after the Woll invasion, leaving some fifteen hundred war-weary Mexicans, who observed the arrival of the volunteer and militia companies with stoic detachment. Quickly and quietly, they herded their livestock away from town and hid their valuables. Armies of any stripe were unwelcome visitors.

As the soldiers arrived in the early weeks of October, they made camp in the general vicinity of the San Juan and Concepción missions, about four or five miles south of town. Expecting a brief campaign, the volunteers brought with them few supplies or warm clothes. Almost immediately their war spirit was dampened by bad weather. Heavy rains and fierce winds buffeted the open prairie where they were encamped. The missions were in such a filthy state that many soldiers refused to take refuge inside them, preferring instead to remain outdoors with only the thinnest of blankets to shield them from the fury of the storm. It was so severely cold that no guards were posted, and the men were scattered throughout the nearby thickets, taking shelter wherever they could find it.[12]

Somervell had not yet arrived in San Antonio, and in the absence of an army quartermaster to procure supplies, the volunteers made do with whatever they could find. Anything of use to the army was confiscated. Lumber was hauled away for firewood, and the residents' corn supply was quickly exhausted. The Concepción copper baptismal font was used to make soup for one company.[13] As the men waited on the outskirts of town for their commander, they had plenty of spare time and little to do. They hunted and fished, and some of the more enterprising ones gathered pecans along the river bottoms and sold them in town for a dollar a bushel, using the money to buy coffee, tobacco, and other provisions. They wandered among the missions, particularly the Alamo, where behind the chapel could still be seen ashes, charcoal, and remnants of bones where Santa Anna's troops had built a bonfire to burn the bodies of the Texans killed seven years earlier. A good many wood and stone figures, the work of Spanish craftsmen, were pried from the walls with Bowie knives and carted off as souvenirs.[14]

In the middle of October "General" Thomas Jefferson Green—like so many Texans he preferred to be known by his Revolutionary rank—rode into camp. With his medium height, prominent nose, and brown hair that curled around unusually large ears, Green's physical appearance was not particularly impressive. Still, he managed to cut a flamboyant figure and quickly became one of the most visible men in camp. But the soldier-adventurer was not all he seemed. Those who did not know Green might not have guessed that he had never seen combat in his life. In this army the general was unattached to any militia or volunteer company, and he held the rank of a common private. The arrival in camp of this strutting, swaggering prima donna suggested that the expedition might well be headed for the kind of calamities President Houston feared. Brash, impetuous, and utterly lacking respect for authority of any kind, Green was a compulsive agitator. Whether seeking the spotlight or plotting behind the scenes, he had been a thorn in the side of the Texas government since the early days of the Republic. One soldier gave this description of him:

> *He was possessed with that degree of vanity that prompted him rather to rashness than cool, determined valour. He might be termed, by some, a man of tallent [sic], which he did to some degree possess, but they were of an order that I would believe quite ordinary. Vain, bombastic, fond of praise, and withall, ambitious of military glory, he could well be called darring [sic], even fearless; but he was unfit to command an army . . .*[15]

Sam Houston's estimate of Green was even less charitable. The two men had long been bitter enemies, developing a loathing for one another that had grown rather than diminished over the years. A master of insult when riled, Houston saved some of his choicest barbs for Green, whom he once described as a man with "all the characteristics of a dog except fidelity."[16] On another occasion he declared: "I would not advise any decent and respectable person to touch him with a fifteen-foot pole, unless he had gloves upon his hands of double thickness, and then he should cast away the pole to avoid the influence of the contaminating shock."[17]

While not a product of the frontier like some volunteers, Green nonetheless had in abundance the wanderlust and keen sense of adventure that drew many men to Texas. Born into a prosperous North Carolina planting family in 1802, Green was apparently ill-fitted to the elegant life of the Southern tidewater aristocracy. He enrolled at the University of North Carolina and later West Point, lasting but a short time at either institution. In 1836, upon hearing the news of the rebellion in Texas, Green made his way to east Texas. He signed on as a volunteer, but soon parlayed his rather limited military education into a brigadier general's commission.[18] Green's orders were to return to the United States to recruit volunteers for the cause. He was successful in enlisting more than two hundred men, "some of the roughest specimens of humanity the *purlieus* of New Orleans could furnish."[19] But, alas for Green, the Revolution was already over.

Green and his men sailed to Velasco, where the Texas government had established temporary headquarters after the Battle of San Jacinto. When they arrived they found another ship, the *Invincible*, docked offshore with Santa Anna and his staff aboard. The Mexican President, having signed a peace treaty with the Texas rebels, was being allowed to return to Mexico. When Green learned of Santa Anna's imminent departure he demanded that Acting President David Burnet stop the ship from sailing, for only the Texas Congress, which had not yet been elected, could decide what to do with this enemy of the people. Sam Houston, the only figure with any real authority, had already sailed for New Orleans for treatment of an ankle badly shattered at San Jacinto. The army had marched south in pursuit of the remnants of Santa Anna's forces. Most of the Texans at Velasco also believed that the Mexican President should not be allowed to escape so easily, although no opposition to the government's decision to release him had developed before Green arrived. Heavily outnumbered and fearing for his own life if he refused, Burnet gave in and handed Santa Anna over to Green's custody.

Green found the Mexican general in a state of extreme agitation at the thought of being delivered into the hands of a lynch mob on Velasco Beach. To allay his captive's fear, Green transferred Santa Anna to his own vessel, and that evening the two men shared a pot of stew on a bench in Green's cabin. Green remarked that if he ever visited Mexico, he expected Santa Anna to give him coffee in brighter metal than the smoked tinware in which they were being served. "Ah! Yes, my dear General, I do long for this unfortunate episode to be over," Santa Anna is reported to have replied, "and then I want to see you in Mexico where I can reciprocate your kindness." [20]

The next day Santa Anna was thrown into chains. He was held under lock and key for several weeks until Houston returned to countermand the order, although he would not return to Mexico for another year. Santa Anna later repudiated the peace treaty he had signed on the grounds that its terms had been violated by Green and his men. Seemingly ignorant of all the trouble he had caused, Green would boast of his role in this episode for several years, until he found himself a prisoner in Mexico. He could not have been surprised when Santa Anna's promised hospitality was not forthcoming.

Within a few months after his arrival in Texas, Green quarrelled with most of the men who were to shape the new Republic. Following the Velasco incident he schemed to gain command of the Texas Army, although he had not participated in a single battle. He refused to serve under two different commanders, Mirabeau Lamar and Thomas Rusk, but was later rebuffed when the Senate refused to confirm him as senior brigadier general. As a member of the First Congress, Green devoted most of his time to promoting his own business interests as one of the major stockholders of the Texas Railroad, Navigation and Banking Company. The backers of this scheme planned to build a series of canals and railroads linking the Río Grande to the Sabine, and ultimately a network of transportation facilities as far as the Pacific Coast. A bill of incorporation was passed, but the plan fell through amid allegations that the backers had grossly underestimated the cost and sheer size of the undertaking. Houston spoke out against the company, and this marked the beginning of a feud that was to span nearly two decades.[21] In recent years Green had speculated in lands and operated a racetrack, keeping a stable of horses that competed in Texas and the United States.[22] A strident critic of the new Houston administration, Green had not lost his taste for political intrigue, and frequently denounced the President for his timidity in prosecuting the war.

Sowing seeds of dissension wherever he went, Green continued to stir up trouble as the Southwestern Army of Operations gathered at San Antonio in the fall of 1842. In the days ahead he would rarely miss an opportunity to thwart the official objectives of the expedition. With such men in the ranks whose disloyalty was well known, the success of the expedition was jeopardized from the very outset.

Somervell did not appear in San Antonio until November 4, by which time many soldiers had been waiting at the frontier for nearly a month. During this critical period his absence allowed troublemakers like Green to foment unrest. Somervell found his army unruly, disorganized, and, as the rains continued, increasingly demoralized; in short, totally unprepared to take up the line of march.

Somervell's task could not have been more difficult. Many of his men, like Green, had refused to serve under him in March. This time they accepted his leadership grudgingly, for they knew that it was only with Somervell in command that the government would permit the expedition to get underway. A short, plump man, Alexander Somervell did not give the appearance of a man born to lead, at least not to the frontiersmen who comprised his army. "[H]is very looks and deportment combined to prove him no General," said one soldier.[23] Good-natured and jovial, he was popular among the soldiers he knew personally. And yet even among these men Somervell seems to have inspired little loyalty, for he lacked that ineffable quality that lifts a leader above the rank and file. He was "a very nice kind Gentleman," observed a private in Captain Samuel A. Bogart's company, "But no more fit to Command an Army of men in those times, than a ten year old Boy."[24]

Many problems were entirely of Somervell's own making. Had he approached his task with energy and a sense of purpose, he might have won the respect of his men, but Somervell was well aware that there were many in camp who resented his leadership, and he chose to avoid them rather than win them over to his side. Somervell established his headquarters in town, thus exposing himself to charges that he was unwilling to share the privations of the common soldier. Men grumbled that their commanding officer was enjoying the comforts and pleasures of San Antonio while they shivered in the cold. To make a bad situation even worse, Somervell chose to remain aloof, visiting only occasionally the campsites scattered outside town, and even then communicating to his soldiers through his officers. Rumors quickly spread—no doubt started by the Houston critics in camp—that General Somervell was spending his time in the arms of Mexican women at the fandangoes held nightly in San Antonio and was too busy to call on his troops.[25]

Ignoring the problem of morale, Somervell addressed himself to other matters, equally serious. The army still needed to be outfitted and supplied for a campaign into Mexico. He could expect no help from President Houston. When Colonel William G. Cooke, his quartermaster general, tried to obtain provisions from Washington-on-the-Brazos, he was bluntly informed that "the Government has not the means to purchase a single ration."[26] Houston's orders were explicit: all purchases the quartermaster required were to be made on credit, although the administration could not guarantee that citizens who furnished the army with supplies would ever be repaid. Receipts were to be sent to the capital, and compensation, if any, would be determined at a later date. Under no circumstances, Houston informed his commander, could the army confiscate supplies without permission; all donations to the war effort must be voluntary. The President knew this was an impossible demand. The citizens of Bexar were under no illusions about the government's ability to repay them and were hardly likely to contribute livestock and supplies for patriotic reasons.

As for ammunition, the War Department had dispatched some ordnance to the army, but no one seemed to know where it was. The powder and lead, the secretary of war and marine explained lamely, had been handed over to "irresponsible individuals" and were "scattered all over the Western Country," making it extremely doubtful that they would ever reach San Antonio.[27] Somervell put in a request for heavy artillery, although Houston advised against it. Somervell insisted; so a cannon was sent up from Gonzales, but it too was taking several days to arrive. The message to the general of the Southwestern Army was clear. An expedition had been authorized by the government, but it was entirely up to Somervell to get it underway.

HOUSTON HAD ASKED Congress to convene in the middle of November, but the western legislators were slow to arrive, and a quorum could not be reached until December. The Seventh Congress was no better than the last as far as Houston was concerned. What little western support the administration had enjoyed in the past had been due to the popularity of Vice-President Edward Burleson. This goodwill had vanished since Burleson's open break with his chief over the leadership of the Mexican campaign. Houston's opponents found they could override his veto almost at will, and they took no small amount of satisfaction in thwarting the President on every issue.[28] Houston continued to lecture the legislators on the problems facing the nation, pointedly addressing those who pined for a return to the grand old days of Mirabeau Lamar: "The chimera of a splendid government administered upon a magnificent scale has passed off and left us the realities of depression, national calamity and destitution."[29]

Congress chose to ignore these admonitions, and showed a conspicuous lack of interest in the pressing matters that generally occupy the time of a responsible government. More often than not they chose to do no work at all. The editor of the Houston *Morning Star* rode out to the new capital to report on the legislative session, and he was not favorably impressed by the political inactivity which he observed. "The Senate, I learned, was waiting for the House to progress with business, and the House, I suppose, often waits for the Senate, and in the mean time certain members steal away occasionally, and *'consult the book of prophecies'* alias a pack of cards. Thus do our legislators *labor* for their country."[30] Another visitor found the honorable members of Congress seated on candle-boxes and sugar casks or anything else they could find, "whittling away without intermission."[31]

In the western counties, what few settlers remained were still upset over the removal of the legislature from Austin, and they were in no way pacified by the choice of Washington-on-the-Brazos as the new seat of government. Even as Somervell's Southwestern Army of Operations was preparing to take the war onto Mexican soil, many western settlers were giving up and moving east. San Augustine and other East Texas towns were said to be bustling as a result of the depopulation of the western settlements, while the Brazos River, it was predicted, would soon be the new frontier.[32] Visitors to Austin reported that the former capital, if not quite a ghost town, had steadily declined since March. The President's mansion, the Hall of Congress, and other official buildings lay deserted.[33] No government property remained except the archives, and these Houston now ordered brought to Washington-on-the-Brazos. But the angry townsfolk had no intention of surrendering the documents to that "dam blackguard indian drunk," as one of them called Sam Houston.[34] When a government agent arrived to collect the archives, a mob shaved the mane and tail of his horse and rudely escorted him from town. The citizens established a vigilance committee to protect the archives and held a kangaroo court, charging the President in absentia with "moral treason."[35] Everywhere respect for the law and the government seemed to have reached its lowest ebb.

But if the Houston administration seemed to be regarded as little more than a pariah in many quarters of the Republic, it could at least take comfort from the fact that it enjoyed considerable support abroad. Weak as it was, Houston's one-horse government was viewed with much more than passing interest in the corridors of power in Whitehall and Washington. The major powers had formally recognized Texas as a separate and independent state and were urging Mexico to do the same. Houston's roving minister-at-large in Europe, Ashbel Smith, had for the past several months been trying to arrange a tripartite agreement between Great Britain, France, and the United States, by which the three nations would jointly bring pressure to bear upon Mexico to abandon its efforts at reconquest. Houston did not yet know that the plan had fallen through; owing to increasingly tense relations between the United States and Great Britain, Lord Aberdeen, the British foreign minister, had refused to participate.[36] Nonetheless, both powers had very strong reasons of their own to keep the Republic from self-destructing and could be relied upon to continue to work separately to bring about a peace between Texas and Mexico. Whether these efforts would be sufficient to bring about any change in Mexican policy, however, was another matter. The major powers had important commercial and financial interests in Mexico, and recognized the need to tread lightly. All were anxious to appear as neutral bystanders, ready to lend their good offices if called upon to do so to work for the best interests of both parties.

In the United States, where the issue of expansionism was the principal source of sectional discord pitting North against South, both sides desired a quick solution to the border war along the Río Grande, albeit for entirely different reasons. U.S. President John Tyler and his secretary of state, Daniel Webster, best personified this awkward marriage of convenience between the two regions. For Tyler, a southern planter and slave-owner, the annexation of Texas meant the acquisition of new cotton lands and a stronger voice for the slave-holding states in Congress. Daniel Webster, on the other hand, was unalterably opposed to annexation; like many New Englanders, he believed that California, with its fine port of San Francisco, was the richer prize. Notwithstanding these conflicting foreign policy objectives, both men recognized the need for peace between their two southern neighbors. If Mexico managed to resubjugate Texas, this prime piece of real estate and valuable addition to the slave empire would be lost to the South forever. Northern politicians were equally anxious to keep the Texas issue in the background to eliminate any possible sources of tension between the United States and Mexico, hoping to purchase California at some later date.[37]

Houston's clear preference was for annexation. One of his first acts as President had been to order the Texas chargé d'affaires in Washington, James Reily, to quietly alert American foreign policy makers that Texas would be receptive to a proposal of annexation if one was offered.[38] These overtures had gone nowhere; President Tyler, though enthusiastic to re-opening the annexation issue, was involved in a bitter struggle with members of the Whig Party which had left him with little clout in Congress. Whig leaders had nominated Tyler as William Henry Harrison's running mate in 1840 knowing full well that he had little in common with the mainstream of the party, but reasoning that his presence on the ticket would attract much-needed southern votes. No sooner had the "Tippecanoe and Tyler Too" bandwagon rolled to victory, however, than Harrison was dead, the victim of pneumonia after a needlessly long inaugural address in bitingly cold weather. To the Whigs' horror, they found they had won the election but lost the presidency. A man of strong states' rights principles, Tyler had much more in common with the Democratic Party than his own, and proceeded to use his veto pen to block the nationalist Whig program.

A consequence of these difficulties was that Tyler could not command the two-thirds majority required to ratify a treaty of annexation in the Whig-controlled Senate. The U.S. President advised Reily to wait for a more favorable opportunity to pursue annexation, preferring that Texas in the meantime devote its diplomatic efforts to obtaining Mexican recognition of Texas sovereignty.[39] This would remove one of the major stumbling blocks to annexation, for many senators feared war with Mexico would result if the United States attempted to take land claimed by Mexico. Although Webster had no interest in his chief's long-term plans, the secretary of state agreed with the President that the resolution of the question of Texas sovereignty would be best for all concerned. Accordingly, Webster proposed that the United States mediate between Texas and Mexico, but added that his government would take no action unless both parties accepted the offer. Webster asked the Houston administration to suspend hostilities until these options could be explored further.[40]

For its part, Great Britain was adamantly opposed to annexation, having watched with growing displeasure the emergence of the United States as a new rival power in the western hemisphere. The British government was committed to a free and independent Texas, which would put the brakes on any future American westward territorial ambitions. Moreover, Texas would provide a valuable source of cotton for Britain's bustling textile mills. To that end, Her Majesty's government had appointed Charles Elliot, a clever and energetic captain in the Royal Navy, to serve as British chargé d'affaires in Texas. As a diplomatic troubleshooter, the forty-one-year-old Elliot had already displayed a talent for provoking controversy. Until recently he had served in China, where he had played a conspicuous role in the Opium War and the British annexation of Hong Kong. The government of Lord Aberdeen at first showed little interest in the sprawling infant Republic, but this attitude quickly changed as the commercial possibilities and strategic advantages of a pro-British state in North America became apparent.[41]

Although Elliot had only arrived in Galveston in late August, he was already on unusually close terms with Sam Houston. It was to be expected that Houston would develop a good working relationship with the representative of a powerful government that had evinced a willingness to come to the aid of the Republic. But the President seems to have genuinely liked Elliot, and the two men developed an intimacy that went beyond mere diplomatic protocol. No doubt Houston enjoyed the company of the urbane and sophisticated Elliot simply for its own sake. He may also have seen that Elliot was a man after his own heart: a diplomat who disdained formal channels and orthodox procedures when they did not suit him, and who understood that great things were accomplished not by governments conducting public policy, but by individuals who lived by their wits and made their own opportunities.

At the same time, however, it was not out of character for Houston to gain the maximum political advantage he could from all his personal relationships. After only two meetings, Houston was expressing a confidence in the diplomat's abilities that seems suspiciously premature, intimating to the British chargé that he wished him to play a key role in the affairs of Texas. In early November Houston had written to him: "You are aware of my intense anxiety for peace with Mexico. To obtain it I do not care to pursue formal means. I know of no Gentleman, whose agency in my estimation would go farther in the attainment of the object than your own were it possible to obtain your services."[42] Such flattery, it should be noted, was repaid with interest in Elliot's dispatches to London. "He is the fittest man in this Country for his present station," Elliot wrote a friend in the Foreign Office. "His education has been imperfect, but he possesses great sagacity and penetration, surprising tact in his management of men trained as men are in these parts, is perfectly pure handed and moved in the main by the inspiring motive of desiring to connect his name with a Nation's rise."[43]

Exactly what role Houston had in mind for Elliot he did not say, and perhaps at this time he did not know. Nonetheless Elliot was certainly under the impression that he had won the President's trust and confidence, and this may well have been Houston's sole intention. Houston must have known that Elliot's influence in Texas would not sit well with American politicians who, whether they decided to annex Texas or not, regarded the North American continent as their own special preserve and resented any interference in the region from their archrivals, the British. It should be added that at no time did Houston fail to treat the American representative with the proper courtesy and respect, but in the months ahead it would become increasingly obvious and worrisome to Washington policy makers that it was Elliot who seemed to enjoy the closest access to the President of the Republic.

Thus, in the winter of 1842 Houston hoped to obtain through the mediation of the major powers a recognition of Texas independence by Mexico, or at least a cessation of hostilities which would bring an end to the turmoil along the border. Annexation to the United States, it seems clear, was never far from Houston's mind, but he seems to have reconciled himself to the fact that there could be little reason for optimism on that front so long as stiff opposition to the measure existed in the Senate. In spite of the failure of Ashbel Smith's tripartite agreement, international mediation remained a possibility worth pursuing—indeed, at the present time it was the only way that Texas might achieve through diplomatic means the peace it so sorely needed. But Houston cannot have had any illusions about the ability of Great Britain and the United States to influence Mexican policy. Both powers were determined to remain strictly neutral, and could do no more than issue mild protests when Mexican troops showed themselves along the Texas frontier. It remained to be seen whether the kindly solicitations of Great Britain and the United States would translate into tangible and meaningful guarantees of security for the Republic.

In November, Charles Elliot and Joseph Eve paid a brief visit to Washington-on-the-Brazos. The two diplomats were received with "every mark of politeness and kindness by the President officers of government and members of Congress," Eve observed, but the animosity between the chief executive and a sizable portion of the legislature did not escape the American chargé's notice.[44] Many western delegates complained bitterly to Eve that Houston was responsible for the defenseless position of the western frontier and cursed his decision to abandon Austin as the seat of government. Ironically, although it was these same delegates who had clamored so loudly for war against Mexico, many were coming to the conclusion that peace was far preferable to a constant state of turmoil. These frontier representatives were anxious to know what progress Eve's government had made in securing Mexico's recognition of Texas independence. The visiting dignitary could offer them little solace, advising them only "to breast the storm awhile longer."[45]

No doubt Eve and Elliot discussed the matter of mediation in their private meetings with the President, but at this point neither had received any news from home, and they could only reiterate their governments' earlier positions on the subject. Neither government was anxious for Texas to carry the war onto Mexican soil. Secretary of State Webster had repeatedly instructed Eve to prevail upon Houston to refrain from reprisals until the mediation efforts of Waddy Thompson, the U.S. minister to Mexico, could be allowed to run their course. Captain Elliot heartily disapproved of the impending campaign, and in his dispatches to the Foreign Office predicted, "they are without discipline and I am afraid there can be little doubt that the result will be signally disastrous."[46] Still, both diplomats were of the opinion that the President had no choice in the matter. Having watched at first hand Houston's vain attempts to keep the War Party at bay, they understood better than their superiors why the President had bowed to the cries for an invasion of Mexico.

The two distinguished guests did not stay at Washington-on-the-Brazos for long. The hamlet's two taverns were already filled to capacity with members of Congress, and lodgings for Elliot and Eve were not easy to find. In the end they were put in a room Eve described as "not ceiled or plastered, without a fire place or stove, and without windows, with four other persons."[47] Houston confided to Elliot that conditions in Washington-on-the-Brazos were indeed "rather raw."[48] Not particularly impressed by the new seat of government, the two diplomats hastened back to Galveston at the first opportunity.

AS SOMERVELL WAITED for the cannon and tried to procure the necessary supplies, his little army lived from hand to mouth, foraging for food when not trying to keep warm and dry. Shortly after arriving in San Antonio the general ordered the army to camp farther west along the Leon and Medina rivers, where game was plentiful in the heavily wooded area nearby. Large numbers of deer were killed, and the men who needed warmer clothes made trousers of the skins.[49]

One afternoon a shot rang out from the woods, and sometime later a few of the men in Captain Bogart's company marched into camp carrying a fat, three-hundred-pound bear. This touched off a wild melee as scores of men took off for the thicket to try their luck. Soon more shots were heard. One soldier, creeping stealthily through the underbrush, had been mistaken for a bear and shot in the arm. In spite of this mishap, the entire company looked forward to a meal of roast bear, until it was learned that the men who had shot the animal had no intention of sharing it with anyone. They erected a barbecue spit and proceeded to eat their dinner alone, while the heady aroma of roast bear pervaded the camp, tempting those who munched on acorns or gnawed on strips of jerky or salt pork.

Late that night one of the sentries in Bogart's company, claiming to see an Indian skulking about at the edge of camp, gave the alarm by firing his rifle. The soldiers were ordered to fall in and search the area, but they would find no one; the alarm was simply an attempt to steal some of the bear meat. The ruse failed when those who had killed the bear stayed behind to guard their prize, suspecting some sort of trickery (or perhaps because anxious sentries had given so many false alarms that their warnings were now often ignored). A few days later another bear was killed, and this time it was divided among all the men in the company except, of course, those who had been so stingy with their own.[50]

The conduct of the officers was little better than that of their men. They squabbled constantly, with self-interest and jealousy outweighing any common sense of purpose. When Somervell ordered Captain Bogart's company to fall in with the Second Regiment, Bogart refused. His men had been among the first volunteers to arrive in San Antonio, and they wanted the privilege of serving as spies, as the scouts were called, not regular soldiers. Somervell agreed to let Bogart and his sixty men join the Hays ranger company. But Bogart did not want to play second fiddle to

Jack Hays. He insisted on equal and separate status for his company, and proposed an arrangement: he would serve under Hays, provided that any reconnaissance parties would be drawn equally from both units. The responsibility of leading the scouting parties would be shared by the two commanders. When one was out with the spies, the other would be in charge of the soldiers left behind. Somervell balked at this demand, but since he needed the men, he had little choice; Bogart was threatening to pack up and leave with his company if he did not get his way.[51]

As the weeks passed Somervell's men grew bored and restless. It was time that might have been spent training the troops, organizing them into a well-disciplined army. A few captains took it upon themselves to put their men through rudimentary drills, but Somervell himself seems to have taken little interest. Discipline in the army quickly broke down, if indeed it had ever existed. Some of the men got drunk and ventured into town, where they plundered homes, including that of the widow of Revolutionary hero Deaf Smith, and raped several women. Wrote one volunteer in disgust, "to gratify their beastly lusts," they have "compelled the women and girls to yield to their hellish desires, which their victims did under fear of punishment and death."[52]

Reports of these activities were not well-received at Washington-on-the-Brazos. On November 9, Secretary of War M. C. Hamilton found it necessary to warn Somervell: "You will under no circumstances permit liquor to be brought within the limits of your encampment, nor within the reach of the troops."[53] Ten days later Hamilton dashed off a stinging message that left no doubt as to the President's displeasure, deploring the conduct of the volunteers and Somervell's inability to control them. This would never have happened, Hamilton wrote, presumably at Houston's direction, if Somervell had organized the army on the Cibolo Creek as per his instructions.[54] But there may have been another reason for the President's irritation, one that had little to do with the outrages committed in San Antonio. Houston could not call off the campaign without risking an insurrection in the west, but the evidence suggests that he wanted Somervell to do it for him. If he could not dissuade the war hawks of the folly of an invasion, he could probably convince his timorous commander. Thus, every dispatch was worded to impress upon Somervell that the chaos and disorder in San Antonio were but a prelude to the disaster that would surely follow if he took up the line of march. Hamilton wrote:

> It was not the design of the Government to keep an undisciplined and disorganized army stationed on the frontier merely for the

*purpose of consuming the little substance remaining of a popula-
tion already nearly reduced to starvation . . . Your communication
of the seventh of November has just been received, but it affords
no information as to the probable number of men at your encampment, how they are supplied, when you can probably take
up the line of march, or whether it will be practicable . . . to carry
out, at this advanced season of the year, the objects contemplated.
If it is, you will see the necessity of prompt and energetic movement. If it is not, why it is hoped you will see the propriety of
disbanding the troops at once—they have now been on the frontier six weeks, and are seemingly as little prepared for the march
as when they first arrived.*[55]

The President was actually reprimanding Somervell for failing to sur-
mount the obstacles he had personally thrown in his path. But the
subtleties of Texas politics were lost on Somervell. Silently he bore his
chief's merciless criticism and continued to prepare for the campaign as if
this were indeed what the administration wanted.

Somervell might soon have to disband his forces whether he wanted to
or not. Winter had come early to west Texas, and there were no signs of
relief from the unseasonably cold, wet weather. Already much of the surrounding area was under water, and the swollen rivers would soon be im-
passable. More important, the weather was having a disastrous effect on
morale. The middle of November brought more torrential rains. Small
tents of blankets and stretched beef hides were erected to keep the ammunition and baggage dry, but as only a few men could get under them at
one time, most were compelled to withstand the fury of the storm. Men
crouched underneath trees and brush with only a blanket to shield them
from the pelting rain. At night they spread their blankets on beds of mesquite branches to avoid sleeping on the rain-soaked earth. Few of the men
could sleep under these conditions; instead they tried to keep a fire going
by which they could warm themselves until daybreak. "I stood up by the
fire all night & got as wet as a drowned rat," one soldier lamented.[56] Unable to keep their blankets dry, they stole extra ones from the hapless citizens of Bexar. Some, rather than return to the miserable conditions in
camp, simply turned the Mexicans out of their houses and waited out the
storm.[57]

It all proved to be too much for many of them. Those who had arrived
in the early days of October were ready to go home. Having rushed to the
frontier soon after the Woll invasion, they had not anticipated a pro-
longed campaign. "This morning it is very cold," one soldier wrote on

November 12, "and most of the men suffer very much, being very thinly clad, & having come out with the intention of having a fight with the enemy at or near San Antonio & then returning home."[58] Cold, hungry, and fed up with the apparent inactivity of the high command, small bands of men began to slip out of camp at night. "[Their] example caught like wild-fire," wrote another, "infusing itself more or less throughout camp, and every one who wished to leave felt at liberty to do so."[59] Desertions soon became so widespread that soldiers made little effort to conceal their withdrawal. Somervell ordered some of the first deserters arrested, but this did not deter others from leaving. So nasty had the mood of his troops become that Somervell actually feared an uprising in the ranks, and was obliged to let them go unmolested.[60]

Within ten days, the Southwestern Army had dwindled to a mere 750 men; close to 500 had deserted and gone home. The militia regiments had the highest attrition rate. The Washington and Montgomery County outfits disappeared almost entirely. These men had been drafted into service and were anxious to get back to their farms and families. Poorly equipped for even the briefest campaign, the East Texas troops were not directly threatened by the recent Mexican incursions and did not share the frontier settlers' eagerness for reprisal. They had been called up for a ninety-day period, and fully half that time had been spent in inactive service.[61] A large number of volunteers also deserted. Some said they were going home for warmer clothes or a better horse, but never returned. The problem of desertion became so serious that whole companies had to be dissolved, new ones created, and old ones reorganized.

And yet there were still some 750 men waiting anxiously to move south. The danger from Woll's invading force had passed, but for seven weeks they remained in camp, cursing the mud, the rain, and their commander who, they believed, was exhibiting such extreme reluctance to pursue the enemy. Why had these men stayed on?

Their motives were as personal as they were patriotic. Revenge was foremost in the minds of many. Some, like Big Foot Wallace, had lost relatives in the Revolution. The Fayette County volunteers also stayed, looking to avenge the deaths of their neighbors who had so recently perished with Captain Dawson. The commander of the Fayette company, William M. Eastland, was Dawson's cousin. One soldier serving under him was Benjamin Boone, the grandson of Daniel Boone and brother-in-law of a man who had died in the Dawson Massacre.[62] More than a dozen members of the army had gone along on the disastrous journey to Santa Fe the year before.[63] The terms of their parole were clear: they would be shot if they took up arms against Mexico again. But no sooner had they made their way back to Texas than they jumped at the chance for revenge. To all these men, there was nothing abstract about their desire for retribution. Personal injuries had been suffered, and the ethos of the frontier dictated that they be repaid in kind.

Many western farmers simply wanted to put an end to the chaos and disruption which the recent Mexican incursions had caused, and believed that peace along the frontier could be obtained only by a policy of retaliation. "Our homes are endangered; our property has been pillaged," one volunteer had written to his sister three months earlier. "Our people have been murdered, and there is no peace, no security left for us, unless we carry the war into the enemies' land." [64]

But not all were farmers with property and families to protect. Many, quite simply, had little else to do, there being scant opportunities for young men in the prevailing climate of economic uncertainty. Thomas W. Bell, a volunteer in Captain William Eastland's company, had written to his father some months earlier: "I am again out of employment and as times are so dull I do not know that I can be better employed than by serving my adopted country." [65] This footloose group also included an unsavory element, common to all armies, who waited for Somervell's orders to march south because warfare had its own rewards, who "went in for making the thing pay." [66] Houston had authorized the army to live off the land, and this could mean nothing else but that they were entitled to all the loot they could carry home with them. This was not, of course, what the President had intended, but it was a sad fact that Somervell's army contained more than a few freebooters, who could not have been pleased with the slim pickings in San Antonio. They looked forward to the pillage of towns in the Río Grande Valley when the campaign at last got underway.

There were young, adventurous spirits, too, who had come to Texas seeking the raw excitement of the frontier. Gideon Lewis quit his job as a cub reporter on the New Orleans *Daily Picayune* when he learned of the trouble on the Texas border. George Crittenden, a recent West Point graduate and the prodigal son of a Kentucky senator, also made tracks for Texas, neglecting to notify his father until he was well on his way. [67] William Preston Stapp was another volunteer who could not resist an expedition which "wore at its outset the most attractive hues of daring chivalry and high adventure." [68] Theirs was a highly idealized view of warfare which owed much to the romantic novels of Sir Walter Scott. Like the knights-errant of Arthurian legend, they hoped to distinguish themselves and win renown on the field of battle. Samuel Walker spoke for many when, shortly before his arrival in Texas, he wrote of "that unextinguishable love of chivalric immortal fame. . . . The love of fame still urges me on." [69]

Many were seasoned veterans of the Texas frontier. Among them was Ewen Cameron, a Scotsman who had come to Texas to fight in the Revolution. Like Jack Hays, he had become something of a celebrity through his activities on the frontier; one newspaper which reported his adventures gave him the sobriquet "Bruce of the West." [70] A man of enormous strength and little education, Cameron was a stonemason, although he had not plied his trade in Texas. After San Jacinto, cattle-rustling was more profitable. Below the Nueces River, in the area claimed by both Texas and Mexico, Cameron and his cowboys raided Mexican ranches, stealing cattle which they would then drive to Goliad for sale. Officially, the government condemned these attacks, but as Cameron's men seemed to distinguish between Texan and Mexican property—there were many bandits in the area who clearly did not—they were given the status of "permanent volunteers" and called upon from time to time to aid in the defense of the frontier.[71]

For several years Cameron and his men were the scourge of the lower Río Grande Valley. In 1839 they crossed the river to join federalist rebels who were trying to establish an independent state in northern Mexico. For twenty-five dollars a month and a share of the spoils, they temporarily put aside their hatred of Mexicans. They fought savagely against the centralist forces, helping the federalists establish the Republic of the Río Grande. But the uneasy alliance did not last. Once unleashed, the Texans could not be controlled, pillaging the very towns the rebels hoped to win over to their cause. The Texans never understood their federalist comrades, nor could they conceive of a struggle for independence that was anything but total war. After a series of setbacks the federalists resolved their differences in a secret treaty with the centralist government. Both sides agreed that the "adventurous strangers" would have to be left to their own fate.[72] Unaware of this subterfuge, the Texans accompanied the rebels into battle at Ojo del Agua, near Saltillo. At a given signal the federalists galloped toward the enemy lines. Not a little bewildered by this abrupt turn of events, Cameron and the others fell back to a nearby hacienda, where they successfully staved off an attack of the centralist forces and their former allies. At nightfall they beat a hasty retreat, pursued by the Mexicans all the way to the Río Grande.[73]

Captain William S. Fisher also led a contingent of Texans in the Federalist War. Gentlemanly, well-learned, and "one of the tallest men in the country," [74] Fisher had seen as much combat in the Revolution as any Texan, taking part in the battles of Gonzales, San Antonio, and San Jacinto. A former secretary of war in the Houston cabinet, he fought Cherokees and Comanches before throwing in his lot with the federalists. Penniless and discouraged after the war, Fisher made his way to New Orleans. Here the soldier of fortune penned a letter to a former comrade in which he laid out his plans for the future. Mexico, he concluded, was a land of opportunity for the "discontented spirits who are in the same threadbare condition as myself." Fisher predicted that Texas would soon be invaded by Mexico. The result would be that the helpless and ungovernable Republic would turn not to its inept volunteer army, but to the leaders of mercenary bands who would rush to Texas and join the cause. It was a struggle that Fisher believed Texas would ultimately win, but the real victors in a war between two such weak and fragile regimes would in fact be the mercenaries themselves. "I have determined to go immediately to Texas," Fisher wrote, "and among my old associates and the disbanded soldiery to raise a force from 5 to 600 men. . . . I will receive no Commission or authority from the Government of Texas and will be governed alone by the fixed principle of . . . rewarding those who serve under me with the riches of the land and the fatness Thereof. . . ."[75]

While Fisher correctly predicted that Mexico would attack Texas, his independent army of adventurers never materialized; Houston had made sure that there would be a government-sanctioned expedition or no expedition at all. But the official status of the Somervell Expedition meant so very little to Fisher and to others like him that, for all intents and purposes, the forthcoming campaign was not unlike the one he had planned.

Revenge, security, plunder, adventure—or a combination of the four— kept these men huddled by campfires along the Leon River. Not the weather, nor a commander they regarded as incompetent, nor a President they regarded as pusillanimous was going to deprive them of this opportunity. The faint-hearted sunshine patriot with no stomach for fighting had already drifted away. Certainly the men who waited this long to descend on the Río Grande were eager for a fight. They were, as Big Foot Wallace described them:

A motley, mixed-up crowd, you may be certain—broken down politicians from the "old States" that somehow had got on the wrong side of the fence, and had been left out in the cold; renegades and refugees from justice, that had "left their country for their country's good," and adventurers of all sorts, ready for anything or any enterprise that afforded a reasonable prospect of excitement and plunder. Dare-devils they were all, and afraid of nothing under the sun (except perhaps a due-bill or a bailiff).[76]

Quite a few of these "renegades" were some of the Republic's most prominent young men. A sizable number had dabbled in politics, and some would make a career of public service, such as John Hemphill, chief justice of the Supreme Court. Many had served at one time or another as senators or representatives. William Fisher and Alexander Somervell had both served in Congress, and Thomas Jefferson Green would ultimately hold the distinction of having served in the legislatures of four states. There were several erstwhile cabinet members, such as Memucan Hunt, who had served as Texas minister in Washington and secretary of the navy, and James Mayfield, a former secretary of state, as well as a postmaster general and a commissioner for Indian affairs. Somervell's aide-de-camp, Peter H. Bell, would be elected governor of Texas seven years later.

By the middle of November Houston was doing all he could to discourage Somervell, with each dispatch reminding him of the dangers of undertaking the campaign with winter fast approaching. "[It] is worse than useless to remain on the frontier inactive," came the advice from the capital. "By this time the fact must be apparent whether you can prosecute the campaign with success or not."[77] Nor was Somervell alone in hearing of the government's displeasure with the campaign. William Cooke, who was still unable to procure the supplies he needed, received stern rebukes from Secretary Hamilton, who blamed the quartermaster for failing to make arrangements for the transportation of ordnance to the frontier, although by his own admission he did not know where any could be had. If the expedition should fail for any reason, Hamilton took pains to point out on two separate occasions, whatever provisions the quartermaster had managed to acquire were to be properly stored before the army disbanded.[78] Thus, while Houston continued to send Somervell instructions regarding the campaign, the signals from Washington-on-the-Brazos were anything but encouraging.

But Somervell had his orders to move the army south, and he felt duty bound to carry them out. After three weeks of inactivity in San Antonio, the general came to the conclusion that the situation called for extreme measures. On November 23, Somervell directed his quartermaster to confiscate from local residents whatever items the army needed.[79] This was, of course, a serious violation of Houston's instructions, but the general decided to risk his President's displeasure in order to fulfill the primary task of getting the campaign underway. Once the order went out, the supplies were quick in coming. Cooke's men scoured the area, snatching up everything they could find. Quantities of salt, corn and lead were stolen from the French consul at gunpoint.[80] About three hundred head of cattle were driven from nearby ranches to feed the men on the march south. At last the cannon, a brass six-pounder, arrived from Gonzales, and the Southwestern Army of Operations was ready to proceed.

On the morning of November 25, the army struck camp. Behind the main contingent of men were driven the three hundred cattle and two hundred pack mules. The cannon, however, would not accompany the army. After traveling some six muddy miles, Somervell realized that it would be too cumbersome on the march. Incredibly, the artillery piece for which the army had waited three weeks was returned to San Antonio, much to the amusement of the general's antagonists.[81]

In spite of the dissension and chaos that had accompanied the preparations for the campaign, the mood of the army was one of exuberance and optimism as it finally got underway. Each man set out with high hopes of making his mark, of winning the laurels of battle, of returning covered in glory. The rains that had been the cause of so much discomfort had ceased for the time being, and the army moved forward under a bright, clear sky "in high spirits and bright anticipations," wrote one volunteer, "proudly looking forward to the time when, face to face we should meet our country's foe, and hurl his haughty insolence back, to his teeth!"[82]

The March to Laredo

THE EUPHORIA DID not last long. The trek across south Texas proved to be far more hazardous than anyone had expected. From the encampment along the Medina River Somervell marched west, not toward Laredo, his real destination, but Presidio, with the intention of confusing any Mexicans in the Bexar area who might be spying on the army's movements.[1] After covering a distance of several miles, the army pulled away from the Presidio road and marched south in the direction of the Laredo road, making camp at a waterhole for the night. Somervell was correct in thinking there were Mexican spies in San Antonio, who did indeed manage to relay their information to General Reyes' forces below the river.[2] But Somervell's luck would remain unchanged. The detour was to cost his army considerably more in lost time than it could ever have gained in the element of surprise.

The following day, the army was up at dawn and traveled some eight miles before coming to a sudden halt. Hays and his spy company had expected to find the Laredo road, but in fact they had already crossed it; with the entire region under water, one dirt track looked much like another. And now it began to rain again. As the thunderstorms returned, so did the grumbling among Somervell's men. "If this was not suffering for ones Country . . . then I do not know what to call it," one miserable, rain-soaked sentry wrote.[3] Unable to find the right road, they headed south in the general direction of Laredo. The little army would spend the next three grueling days in what became known as the Atascosa bogs, trying to get its bearings. Pack mules, horses, cattle, and men all sank in the loamy soil, which had turned into virtual quicksand after weeks of heavy rain. The animals became so deeply embedded in the mud that it took several men to get each one of them out. In the worst places it was necessary to roll a helpless mule or horse "over and over until a firm standing place was obtained."[4] The animal would then get to its feet, go one hundred yards, and the process had to be repeated again. Many animals, exhausted, refused to budge, or could not be pulled from the mud and had to be shot. A considerable number of those that did survive were so fatigued or injured during the ordeal that they were unfit for later use.[5]

All semblance of a military operation disappeared in the morass. "The coffee-pots and frying pans would go one way, and the *aparajos* [harnesses] and other camp appurtenances another." It was a scene one described as "ludicrous beyond all power of description."[6] The army stretched for miles, the men scattered in every direction, all trying desperately to extricate their animals, all furiously cursing their commanders who had led them here. Wrote one soldier: "Captain Hays . . . was the pilot and between him and General Somervell lies the blame!"[7] If there was any consolation in their misery it was the sight of these officers in the same predicament as themselves. "Never before in my life have I seen men on as equal a footing as they were in this instance," one volunteer recalled. "Genls, Majors, Colonels, Captains and other *tall* men were brought down to the humiliating Condition of being in mother earth as deep and as dependent as the lowliest private."[8]

At last Somervell's army found the Laredo road on November 29. Sickened by the hardships encountered thus far, about twenty men decided to return home.[9] Bogart and his men were also unhappy, for their rivalry with the Hays ranger company was still unresolved. When Hays went on ahead to reconnoiter that evening, Bogart ordered the rangers to pitch camp for the night at a certain spot. They refused—only Jack Hays was going to tell them where they could and could not camp. Bogart insisted he had authority over both companies in Hays' absence, as Somervell had promised him in San Antonio. Tempers flared, and insults and abusive language were hurled back and forth. The fracas might well have ended in bloodshed had not Hays arrived in time to restrain his men.[10] That evening Somervell made an appearance at the camp of the two spy companies to put an end to the bickering. Tired of Bogart's persistent griping, the general reversed his earlier decision and stripped the Bogart unit of its status as a spy company. He knew that as the ranks of the Southwestern Army dwindled, it was impractical to allow 120 men—a major part of his force—to march in advance of the main contingent. Only Hays and his rangers would be given the honor of scouting detail. Bogart would have to be satisfied with marching at the vanguard of the army with Somervell.[11]

But Bogart was not satisfied. At dawn he and his men mounted their horses and quickly rode off before the rest of the army broke camp. Some of the men in the Hays company spotted them and alerted the others. They were not going to surrender to Bogart the prestige of heading the expedition. Within minutes they had caught up, and Bogart's company quickened its pace. Hays' rangers also spurred their horses. The two groups were now galloping across the prairie, faster and faster, neither one allowing the other to take the lead, "trying to outstrip each other for the highest post of honor. . . . like two gloomy clouds . . . in opposing columns, frowning darkly at each other." [12]

This petulant parade continued for four miles until Somervell, "be-smeared with sweat and almost foaming with rage," managed to catch up with it. [13] He demanded that Bogart obey his order and fall in with the army. Bogart rode back to camp, but a short time later sent one of his officers to ask permission for the company to return home. Somervell refused, using, "as he thought, many reasons why our company should not be dissatisfied with the status assigned it." [14] That night Bogart held a meeting of his men. Although many now wanted to return home, they eventually decided to remain with the expedition, reasoning that if they turned back and the campaign was unsuccessful, they would be blamed for having weakened the strength of the army.

Somervell and his men moved out across the seemingly endless south Texas chaparral; terrain which one soldier described as that of "profound and cheerless desolation." [15] There was little to eat except panola (corn-meal) and small rations of beef (the cattle the army had herded from San Antonio were quite lean). Many soldiers dug up a plant resembling a turnip which tasted rather like a potato when roasted. By the time the army reached the Nueces these men were seriously ill. All recovered, but not before they were "punished by a few hours of torturing sickness, some even with thoughts of death." [16]

The army reached the Nueces River on December 2. Recognized by Mexico as the southern boundary of Texas, the Nueces was a thin stream most of the year, but had overflowed its east bank during the recent heavy rains and was now more than two miles wide. "Had it not been for the timber rising from it," one soldier remarked, "we might well have believed that we had struck an arm of the Gulf of Mexico." [17] The men dismounted and led their horses across the flooded prairie, where the water mostly stood one to three feet deep, though in some places much deeper, and a soldier would occasionally take a misstep and find himself up to his neck in mud and water.

The advance party cut down trees on both banks of the river and, using brush and reed cane, managed to build a crude bridge, allowing the army to cross the Nueces without swimming. Somervell permitted his men to rest here for two days while they slaughtered the last of the cattle and jerked the meat in preparation for the last leg of the march to Laredo. On the second night a fierce thunderstorm blew up. Horses and mules stampeded amid the thunder and lightning, racing through camp as soldiers rushed to avoid being trampled.[18]

Meanwhile, Hays and his spy company had left camp a day early and headed toward the Río Grande. Along the way they captured two Mexican *rancheros* who provided quite accurate information about the strength and position of the Mexican forces. The bulk of the Army of the North, under General Reyes and General Woll, continued to expect a Texan assault on Presidio del Río Grande and was concentrated on the opposite side of the river due west of Somervell's army. The defense of the towns above Matamoros had been left in the hands of some militia and presidial troops under the command of Colonel Antonio Canales. Hays sent two Lipan Indian scouts to tell Somervell and recommended that he march on Laredo immediately before it could be reinforced. One of the Mexicans escaped during the night when his guard, unwilling to stay awake keeping an eye on his prisoner, hit upon the idea of using him as a pillow and promptly fell asleep. The *ranchero* gently placed a saddle under the ranger's head and slipped out of camp, returning to Laredo to give the alarm.[19]

While the army rested back at the Nueces, a message for Somervell arrived from Washington-on-the-Brazos. George Lord, an Englishman in Captain Cameron's company, came forward many years later to tell of a conversation he overheard that night between General Somervell and Colonel James R. Cook. According to Lord, Somervell's new orders from Houston were to abandon the campaign and withdraw from the frontier. Cook reportedly replied: "Gen[eral] we cannot break up this expidition [*sic*], the men will mutinize, they are determined to cross the Rio Grande and fight the enemy, but my advice is to fling every impediment in its way and let it break itself up."[20] This communication, Lord maintained, was kept secret from all but a few of Somervell's senior officers. While no such dispatch from Houston has ever been found, a messenger from Washington-on-the-Brazos passed through LaGrange on or about December 2 with orders from the President to General Somervell. According to the *Telegraph and Texas Register,* these orders would delay the march of the Southwestern Army of Operations.[21] Years later, Houston would admit, rather vaguely, that Somervell returned "in conformity with his orders."[22] Judge John Lockhart, who knew the general well, wrote that Somervell "was recalled before crossing the [Río Grande]."[23]

It is improbable that Houston, whose meaning was often obscure even in the best of times, was so precise in his instructions. Houston had no wish to go on record recalling the expedition, nor did Somervell ever say that he did. It is more likely that the President simply used all his powers of logic and persuasion to convince his commander in the field that nothing could be gained from the campaign so late in the year. Somervell had failed to get the message in San Antonio; no doubt this time Houston was more explicit.

It must have been finally clear to Somervell that he lacked not only the support of his men but the support of the government as well. The lonely general was mulling over his misfortune and wondering what to do about it when Hays' Lipan scouts rode up with the report that Laredo could be taken with little effort. Here, at last, was some good news. A quick victory might be enough to satisfy his war-hungry men, after which he could march home with at least a small measure of success. He jumped at the opportunity.

Having decided that the Southwestern Army of Operations would get its first taste of battle in Laredo, a day's march away, Somervell issued an address to his men. If meant to inspire, the speech fell short. Still refusing to formally address his troops in person, Somervell had it read to them by a member of his staff. But it was probably intended to be not so much an appeal to their valor as a plea for their good conduct:

> We have lamented [the Vásquez and Woll raids]—let them now be avenged. Let us even turn them to profit, by teaching us to adopt that harmony in council, that unanimity in action and that subordination united with energy, the want of which has hitherto paralyzed all our efforts. They are as necessary to the safety of the soldier as they are to the honor of the country.[24]

Somervell ordered Colonel James Cook to cross the Río Grande and approach the town with half the army from the south, hoping to cut off the Mexican garrison's escape. But owing to the heavy rains Cook was unable to cross the river as planned and instead had his men take up positions on the outskirts of Laredo to wait in the darkness for the main army. That night the men busied themselves with their equipment, checking and oiling their firearms in preparation for the following day's battle.

At dawn on December 8, Ben McCulloch detained a young boy along the bank of the river, from whom he learned some disappointing news. The Mexican garrison, apprised of the Texan advance, had already withdrawn across the Río Grande. With Somervell and the rest of the army only a short distance behind them, Cook and his men entered the town and hoisted the Texan flag from the church tower.[25]

Far from meeting with resistance, the soldiers were embarrassed to find that they were received warmly by the townsfolk of Laredo. The Mexicans may not have been particularly happy to be visited by a horde of desperate-looking Texans, but had little choice but to put the best face on things. Greeting Cook and his men as liberating heroes with shouts of "¡Buenos hombres, buenos Americanos!" women and children came out of their homes to give them "cakes & many other things."[26] Some fifteen minutes later Somervell and the main force arrived, whereupon the alcalde, Florencio Villareal, formally surrendered and placed the town at the Texans' disposal. Levying a requisition for food, blankets, and clothing, Somervell then marched his army to a gorge outside town to camp and await the supplies. "[A]fter the brilliant capture of this place," one disgruntled soldier remarked, "whose only Inhabitants were women, children & dogs, we repaired to the ravine."[27] The Southwestern Army of Operations had captured its first town.

If there was to be no battle, Somervell's men were at least looking forward to being furnished with the provisions which they had done without on the march to the Río Grande, such as coffee, sugar, plentiful rations, and warm clothing. Exhausted by the needlessly long march—which had taken seventeen days instead of the usual seven[28]—they waited for the requisition order, but once again they were to be disappointed. Laredo could offer little in the way of supplies. Caught in the crossfire of the Federalist War and the object of frequent Indian attacks, the town had suffered considerable hardship in recent years. That spring, the Río Grande had overflowed its banks and done considerable damage to the town.[29] Now, having been forewarned of the Texan occupation, many residents, like those in San Antonio, had gathered what few valuables they owned and driven their livestock across the river or beyond the town, out of reach of the scavenging army.[30]

Consequently, the supplies that were sent into camp by Villareal in response to General Somervell's requisition were meager indeed. The Texans received fewer than a dozen cattle, barely enough for one day's rations of beef, and a few sacks of flour. There were no fresh horses, no clothing, and no blankets.[31] To men who had long heard of the riches of the Río Grande Valley, these meager provisions were an insult. Many had gone along on the expedition solely for plunder. Convinced that the Mexicans were hiding their goods, they were determined to find them.

Somervell knew what his men were capable of. He had seen their rowdy conduct in San Antonio and urged them not to give a repeat performance in Laredo. But that is exactly what happened. He took no steps to enforce discipline, and a number of men returned to the town that afternoon, got drunk, and looted houses and stores, making off with whatever they could find. Somervell's decision to move the army to another campsite for better protection against a possible surprise attack put a halt to the pillage, but only for the time being.[32]

At dusk, without orders from Somervell, Thomas Jefferson Green took five men and crossed the Río Grande. Riding into the plaza of the little town of Galveston, Green planted the Texian banner before a handful of bewildered Mexicans and demanded five mules. The alcalde was quick to hand them over, and the animals were brought back to camp.[33] This impromptu raid was allowed to go unpunished, but when Green returned, Somervell issued strict orders to the sentries to stop any men from leaving camp without orders from company commanders.

In spite of this directive, as many as two hundred men returned to Laredo the following morning. Some simply ignored their officers' request to remain in camp, others actually obtained leave "with no declared object beyond that of examining the place," no doubt from captains who were eager to defy their unpopular commander.[34]

The soldiers went immediately to the commissary stores. These were locked, but some cypress beams were found and put into use as battering rams, and with a few running charges the doors gave way. The stores were ransacked "from top to bottom" in the general rush to grab the most valuable items.[35] In the mad free-for-all, loaded rifles were left by the doors as the men ripped open boxes of cigarettes and stuffed them in their pockets. The fever of pillage spread among the others, who were afraid that all the best things would be taken if they did not join in. As more soldiers arrived, the looting became more indiscriminate, more frenzied. Soon the town was an orgy of pillage. Those items that the soldiers did not want were left scattered in the doorways and streets.

The pillage continued well into the afternoon. Small groups of men wandered through the streets with cypress beams, breaking down all doors that barred their way. Three men grabbed Alcalde Villareal and threatened to kill him unless he told them where he had hidden his silver. They had a gun at his head and a rope around his neck when Major Henry Davis arrived and demanded they release the frightened Mexican official. Davis, whose men had earlier robbed the French consular agent in San Antonio, was so disgusted with the conduct of his men that he resigned his commission and went home, saying that he would have no more to do "with men who would rob in their own country."[36] One group of soldiers made their way to the local jail, where they chased off the guards and ordered the twenty convicts inside to give three cheers for Texas. They did, and were promptly released.[37]

Not until two o'clock did Somervell take steps to put an end to the looting. Some soldiers would later claim that the general actually gave his tacit approval to the pillage, "but when it became too formidable then another face had to be put to it."[38] While this seems unlikely, it is hard to explain the fact that wholesale robbery was allowed to take place for several hours before Somervell intervened. As much as one-third of his entire force was in Laredo that day, and most of the men were there contrary to his explicit instructions.

Somervell ordered his officers to go to Laredo and have all the men return immediately, but not to reprimand the looters or attempt to take anything from them.[39] Guards were stationed in a V formation leading into camp, so as to catch the culprits as they came in. All the plunder except the blankets, clothing, and other army supplies Somervell had requisitioned the previous day were to be deposited near the camp guard fire. Most of the stolen articles were recovered in this way, but a few men who had done well for themselves in Laredo and "who smelt the rat in time" managed to get outside the lines to hide "their ill gotten gains" until things "blew over."[40]

As the men straggled back from town, they seemed to be carrying the sum total of the citizenry's belongings. Driving the livestock before them, the looters laughed and cheered, their horses dragging toward camp under the weight of immense loads of plunder. Wrapped about the bodies of men was clothing of every conceivable variety—coats, hats, trousers, blankets, even nightclothes; piled high upon the backs of mules they had stolen in town were saddles, bridles, and cooking utensils. They "looked more like a troop of equestrian harlequins, than brave and manly soldiers," remarked William Preston Stapp, who had remained in camp.[41]

Many of the looters were surprised and angry when ordered to come forward and deposit their vast array of spoils at the camp fire. Some insisted that they had paid for the items; others argued that they were enforcing Somervell's requisition of the previous day. Some of the items pitched into the pile at the camp guard fire were of little use or value. There were baby clothes, pillows, and embroidered cushions, even the "miscellaneous decorations in use amongst the gentler sex, that our blushing muse forbids us to catalogue," as one sensitive soldier recalled.[42] By the time the last of the looters deposited his plunder, the pile was enormous, as big as "a good large house," according to one soldier.[43] Said another: "It was a Mountain of no inconsiderable size."[44]

Many of the culprits defended their actions on the grounds that they had merely taken the customary spoils of war. Thomas Jefferson Green was quick to excuse the conduct of the men. "Did not the Texians have a clear right to lay every Mexican town upon the frontier ashes? Did not the burning of our towns in 1836 give them this right? It clearly did!" Green was equally quick to censure Somervell, who evinced a greater interest in "the *'poor Mexicans'*" than his own men.[45] (Years later, Sam Houston would accuse Green of having personally led the marauding soldiers on their rapine plunder, although Green denied it and no other source directly links him to the episode.) [46]

Among those who stayed behind at camp during the pillage, the general reaction appears to have been one of shame and indignation. "Here was a Town," one wrote, "on the soil claimed by Texas; its inhabitants, claiming to be Texians, had opened their doors to us, as to friends . . . and yet, those inhabitants were not safe in the possession of their private property. Suffice it to say, Texas must wear a stain for the conduct of a few disorderly volunteers." [47] An English traveler visiting Texas shortly after the sack of Laredo commented: "These men were *loafers*—the dangerous and unprincipled set of people of whom General Houston is so anxious to free the country. One of the few respectable individuals who took part in the expedition told us, that they were heartily ashamed of being there, and, for his own part, he felt 'dreadful small' on the occasion." [48]

With the exception of much-needed provisions such as clothing, coffee, sugar, flour, and saddles, the stolen property was returned to the citizens of Laredo. His little army having overstayed its welcome, Somervell gave the order to break camp. One of his junior officers was sent into town with the general's letter of apology to Alcalde Villareal:

> *I regret to learn that some bad men belonging to the army under my command have committed Acts of outrage in your town. The Army is composed of volunteers and is difficult to control. But I am proud to state to you that these Acts have excited the indignation of a large portion of the Army and are utterly reprobated by myself and officers under my command. We will make you all the reparation in our power, by returning all such articles as are not essential to the Army.*[49]

Late that afternoon the Mexicans came with carts to collect their belongings as the Texans resumed their march, heading east along the bank of the Río Grande. Peter Bell, the officer conveying his general's apology to the townspeople of Laredo, stayed behind to supervise the return of the plunder. No sooner was the army out of sight than the Mexicans who had been hiding their animals in the chaparral returned to find their homes ransacked. Bell made his exit only with some difficulty. Not wanting to give Somervell's men a reason to return to Laredo, Alcalde Villa-real arranged to have Bell escorted safely out of town.[50]

AFTER PROCEEDING ALONG the riverbank for several miles, the army abruptly turned left into a dense chaparral. Somervell believed that Mexican forces from Presidio and Matamoros were on their way to intercept his army, and he hoped to conceal it in this inhospitable countryside. For several hours the Texans wound their way through prickly pear and thorn bushes, sitting cross-legged on their mounts to avoid being lacerated by cactus spikes. At ten o'clock that night the army camped in a mesquite flat, having covered a distance of only seven miles. The wearisome march and the unpleasant events in Laredo earlier that day had put the troops in a bad temper. There was no water and only a little dried beef to eat. In spite of the cold weather only a few campfires were permitted, Somervell being fearful of Mexican spies in the vicinity, and this added to the dissatisfaction in the ranks. Tired of their general's cautious tactics, many soldiers grumbled that the object of the expedition was to stand and fight, not avoid the enemy.[51]

There were rumors in camp that Somervell had no intention of crossing the Río Grande, but instead was moving his troops, slowly and circuitously, toward the San Antonio Road, which would lead them home. Most of the men were now convinced that Somervell had indeed received instructions from Houston to break up the campaign. A private in Captain Bogart's company wrote in his diary: "It was said that [Somervell] had secret orders from Genl Houston to drag the men round till they would be glad to get home again, and if nothing else would do them, to cross the Rio Grand, but not disturb the [Mexican] people."[52]

Somervell's predicament at this critical juncture of the expedition was a difficult one. He had undoubtedly received some word from the government, either ordering him to return or, much more likely, discouraging him from continuing the campaign. In view of the misfortune which had characterized the expedition thus far, he surely needed no prodding. But if he marched north without facing the enemy he would return in disgrace, and the disposition of his troops was such that they might not accompany him anyway. The pillaging of a defenseless town had added the stain of dishonor to the campaign, and Somervell no doubt still hoped to achieve something that might redeem the expedition that would hereafter bear his name. At the same time, the general had little reason to be optimistic if he remained on the Río Grande. His troops lacked horses and provisions and could not be expected to continue much longer without them. He also knew that the Mexican army was mobilizing against him and would soon be in a position to overwhelm his fractious force. Somervell was unable to sleep that night as he pondered the quandary in which he now found himself.[53]

The following morning the army went in search of water, and after finding a muddy stream a few miles to the east, Somervell held a council of war with his officers. The majority wanted to keep going, though a few captains were strongly against the idea at this point and voted to return home. Somervell, fraught with indecision, unable to decide which counsel to take, opted to put the future of the campaign in the hands of his men.

The general seems to have realized that the low esteem in which he was held by his troops had contributed to the failure of the mission thus far. Now, for the first time since taking command of the army in early November, he tried to win their confidence. The men were mustered in an open prairie where Somervell personally addressed them. The general reproached those who had taken part in the plunder of Laredo and gave his permission for any soldiers who wished to withdraw from the expedition to do so. But Somervell was still willing to march into Mexico and meet the enemy, and he called upon his men to follow him. In a dramatic gesture, he offered to resign his commission and to cheerfully serve as a common private if the army wished to choose a new leader. Somervell's appeal was so impassioned, and his offer to serve in the ranks so unexpected, that even those who had been loudly critical of his conduct felt a sudden change of heart, and he was elected "volunteer leader" by acclamation.[54]

But this play for popularity was only partially effective. There were 187 men who had had enough.[55] Many were drafted militiamen who had been eager to quit the campaign for quite some time; only the stigma of desertion had prevented them from abandoning the cause in San Antonio. The rigors of the march had left many dispirited. Others believed nothing significant could be accomplished at this stage, and there were no doubt a few men who had managed to keep some of the property they had stolen in Laredo and were satisfied with their plunder. One looter was said to have stolen one hundred gold doubloons and a number of valuable blankets.[56] Under the command of Colonel Joseph Bennett, these men marched north the following morning, December 11.

His army now reduced to less than 550 men, Somervell was more convinced than ever that he lacked the strength to meet Reyes' forces. Once again he chose a serpentine path through difficult terrain to conceal his army's movements from the enemy, moving along the east bank of the Río Grande in order to cross at Guerrero, a town of two thousand inhabitants some fifty-four miles below Laredo. Almost immediately the vote of confidence given him by his troops, who wanted to cross the river at once, turned to furious condemnation. Guerrero could have been reached in a two-day forced march, but instead the little Southwestern Army of Operations meandered through the chaparral on the east bank for an entire week. "This tardy and zigzag march," exclaimed Thomas Jefferson Green, "completely bewildered the enemy, and they took for a cunning military manoeuvre what the tattered pantaloons and sore shins of our men too plainly told them was an unpardonable piece of stupidity and a cruel waste of time." [57]

Before crossing the river near Guerrero, some sheepherders informed the Texans that there was no Mexican force in the town. The commander of the militia units, Colonel Antonio Canales, had ordered all available troops to Laredo, expecting to find the invaders still there. The Texans found two canoes in the bushes along the bank, and these were used to carry men and baggage, while the horses swam across. The process was slow, and after three hours only seventy-five men from the Bogart and Hays companies had managed to make the crossing. [58]

Thomas Jefferson Green was one of the first to reach the west bank. Always restless and willing to take charge, he set off along the road with Captain Bogart to scout the area while the army was ferried across the river. Two miles away, they came upon the crest of a small hill to find a large force of Mexican mounted *defensores* (local militia) riding toward them. Wheeling their horses, Green and Bogart raced back to the river with the cavalrymen in pursuit. Green's horse stumbled and appeared to be losing ground to the fresher mounts of the Mexicans. Pulling a red silk handkerchief from his hat, Green held it between his teeth and let it flutter behind him. The *defensores,* fearing an ambush, promptly broke off the chase and fanned out on either side of the road about half a mile from the river. [59] After some initial confusion Bogart and Hays got their men into battle lines, in anticipation of an assault. The Mexicans, however, were content to parade in and out of the enemy's field of vision so as to create the impression of a larger force throughout the remainder of the afternoon. That evening the Mexican cavalry withdrew, leaving Somervell's army to cross the river safely, although it was not until the following morning that the entire force stood on the west bank. [60]

At daylight the alcalde and one or two other citizens of Guerrero approached the Texan camp under a white flag. Brought before General Somervell, they had heard of the pillage of Laredo and begged him to spare their town from a similar fate. Somervell assured them their lives and property would be safe, but levied an order for food and provisions, as he had done in Laredo. Among the list of supplies demanded were warm clothing, for the Texans' recent marches through the chaparral had left their trousers ripped and torn and of little use in the bitterly cold weather.

Toward evening the army moved closer to Guerrero and camped along a little stream, the Salado, where the requisitioned items were to be deposited by the villagers of Guerrero. A heavy rain began to fall and continued throughout the next day. The troops were drenched to the skin, and their mood did not improve when the supplies provided by the citizens of Guerrero arrived. The clothing so desperately needed consisted of no more than ten pairs of shoes, six or eight "well worn, *very aged*" hats, and a few old and now very soggy blankets.[61] The quantities of food were equally unsatisfactory: ten pounds each of coffee and sugar, a few cattle, and less than a quart of corn for each horse. The one hundred horses the alcalde had promised were not brought in. The requisition "should have been an insult to the general as [it was] to the men, and the very insufficient quantity of rations more calculated to make men mad than to allay their hunger."[62]

The soldiers were by this time so angry that many urged Somervell to strike the town and seize by force whatever the army required. But the general had learned his lesson in Laredo. Fearing another riot, he hastened to move his men as far as possible from the town. The companies were ordered to march back to the Río Grande and make camp on the *east* bank, which suggests that Somervell had at this point already decided to terminate the expedition. Jack Hays and a small detachment of men rode into Guerrero to demand $5,000 from the alcalde in lieu of the supplies, with the warning that the town would be sacked if the indemnity was not paid. No doubt the Mexicans took this threat very seriously, but it made no difference; they were still unable to raise the sum. For an hour and a half Hays and his men waited in Guerrero, while the alcalde managed to collect only $381, claiming that the wealthier townspeople had fled as the Texans approached. Placing the official under arrest, Hays and his rangers returned to the Río Grande.[63]

One soldier would later write that General Somervell flew into a rage when Hays informed him of the paltry sum raised by the Mexicans.[64] Another offered a very different account, maintaining that Somervell said "if that is all they can do, tell them to take it back with them."[65] In any case, the alcalde was soon released, for Somervell was now much more concerned with the disturbing reports he was receiving of the enemy's movements. Mexican troops were said to be moving from Presidio and Matamoros toward Guerrero to reinforce the auxiliary militia under the command of Colonel Canales, who had refrained from fighting the Texans on the west bank of the Río Grande two days before. This intelligence was not quite accurate. In fact, General Reyes had dispatched no troops from Presidio, and General Pedro de Ampudia, who commanded the garrison at Matamoros, had already conceded the loss of Guerrero to the Texans. Ampudia resolved to make his stand at Mier, which he believed to be the next target of the invading force. Bad weather delayed his march, and he would not reach Mier, some thirty miles south of Guerrero, until December 23.[66]

Whatever inclination Somervell may have had to pursue the campaign into Mexico now vanished. Believing he had tarried too long in enemy territory and that a Mexican attack was imminent, he decided to make tracks for Texas. Somervell had clearly lost both the confidence of his men and his nerve. "[H]e got awfully *scared*," said one soldier.[67]

Some of the men took refuge from the downpour in the huts of local Carrizo Indians. It was so cold that many of the horses froze to death where they were tied. That night, when Somervell ordered the boats used to ferry the troops across the river destroyed to hinder any pursuit by the Mexicans, his men hid them further downstream, convinced that he now intended to terminate the mission.

Their suspicions were well founded. The next morning, December 19, Somervell issued what would prove to be his last order to the Southwestern Army of Operations. The expedition was over; the army was to march north to Gonzales, where it would be disbanded. Later, in his report to the secretary of war, Somervell explained that it was the threat of attack from a force larger than his own which prompted him to turn back. "[H]aving been eleven days upon the river," Somervell wrote, "and knowing the various positions of bodies of the enemy's troops, I was satisfied that they were concentrating in such numbers as to render a longer stay an act of imprudence."[68]

If the order came as no surprise, this did not prevent the scene of mass confusion that followed. The entire camp was thrown into an uproar by the news, and the men "became perfectly wild" when they learned of Somervell's decision.[69] The hostility between Somervell and his renegade soldiers which had been smoldering for the past five weeks now erupted in mutiny.

Five of the eight company captains—Ewen Cameron, William Fisher, William Eastland, William M. Ryon, and John G. W. Pierson—were determined to continue the campaign. They held a vote among their men, most of whom were overjoyed at the prospect of an expedition without the hated Somervell at the helm. With this vote of confidence, the five volunteer officers went to Somervell and announced that they were separating from his command. His staff stood by him, arguing that the army was courting disaster if it remained on the river.

One of the reasons later given by the men who broke from the army was that insufficient supplies would have made the march back to the settlements of Texas hazardous, certainly an important consideration in view of the hardships they had faced thus far. Memucan Hunt of Fisher's company later wrote that his captain's objective was "to proceed . . . down the river far enough to procure horses for those of his company who were on foot, or whose horses were unable to carry them, and a necessary supply of food." [70] Fisher, he wrote, expected to be a day or two behind the army at the most. In a final attempt to avert the crisis, Hunt urged a compromise solution. Not too long ago he had compared the invasion of Mexico to Napoleon's crossing of the Alps; now he asked Somervell only to prolong the expedition one or two more days, at least until fresh horses and provisions could be found for what promised to be a dismal march home. But it was too late for any hope of reconciliation. Somervell, who expected to see the Mexican army on the horizon at any moment, had at last made up his mind: he was marching home that morning. As for Fisher, Cameron, and the rest, the general seems to have realized that he was powerless to stop them.

Fisher and the other filibustering men of the expedition would not have been satisfied with Hunt's suggestion in any case. They had been waiting for this opportunity to go off on their own since San Antonio. Having endured the hardships of a three-hundred-mile march, they had no intention of turning back without firing a shot at the enemy. "We crossed the river to stir up the whirlwind of war," one of the mutineers later explained; "we were more afraid of being branded on our return as recreants, than we were of the worst possible results to be apprehended from such disobedience." [71] Said another of the mutineers: "The Idea of encountering the fatigues of a five hundred miles march, to no purpose, did not set well with [our] belligerent spirits and dauntless hearts." [72]

Nor were they pleased with the thought of going home empty-handed. They fully expected to turn a nice profit for their time and trouble by rustling as many cattle and Spanish horses as they could manage before heading north. [73] Several years later, William Fisher would argue that the sack of Laredo was in large part responsible for the expedition that followed, for many who refused to join Somervell did so because they were "determined to blot out in our own blood, if necessary, the foul stain which had been cast upon us by the acts of others."[74] Many, however, were clearly swayed by more mercenary motives; Ewen Cameron reportedly gave the men a rousing speech, telling them "how easy it would be to make a fortune in a few days . . ."[75] Guy Bryan, whose brother Austin was a lieutenant on the expedition, later wrote that only three of the sixteen Brazoria County volunteers who joined with Fisher were residents of the area; the others he classified as "transients," who "would obey no one." "All of those who had an interest in the country returned with Somerville," Bryan wrote. "Brother says about three-fourths of those who went on were expressly for plunder . . . who had nothing and wished to make something by the expedition."[76] One Texan credited hard times in the Republic as a factor in the decision of many soldiers to press on into Mexico. "Their object was plunder. They had nothing at home, nor in fact *no homes* & many of them went forward as an alternative, having no fear of Houston."[77]

Nearly all the men under the command of the five captains chose to stay on the Río Grande; Memucan Hunt was the only member of Captain Fisher's company to fall in with General Somervell. Many soldiers from other companies also joined the mutineers. A few who abandoned Somervell secretly wanted to return with him, but were afraid of being labeled cowards by their more reckless comrades. One young soldier, who was suffering from a cactus needle lodged in his knee, admitted later that he "would have been rather glad to go back . . . but had not the courage to express myself."[78] More baffling was the case of Ezekiel Smith, sixty years old, who joined the mutiny while his two sons went home.[79]

On the afternoon of December 19 the army broke up, and Somervell headed north with the remnants of the Southwestern Army of Operations. He was accompanied by his staff and the last of the militiamen from the eastern counties. Jack Hays and Ben McCulloch did not return with Somervell, but they would not join Fisher's expedition either. They agreed to perform scouting duties for the unauthorized campaign for a few days before making their way back home. Some of Hays' rangers, among them Samuel Walker and Big Foot Wallace, chose to join the mutineers. In all, 189 men now turned their backs on the Río Grande and marched north with General Somervell.[80]

The bulk of his army, more than three hundred men, most of them volunteers from the west, stayed behind. They had been the most vociferous in their denunciations of Houston and were now ready to show their timid President what an army of Texans could do. There was loud talk of an easy victory.[81] But only a few were seasoned veterans; many had never seen combat. They elected as their new commander William Fisher, who knew the terrain well from his days in the service of the federalists. Thomas W. Murray was chosen as adjutant-general. Up to this point Fisher had enjoyed the highest respect of the soldiers dissatisfied with Somervell. But their disobedience did not spring entirely from Somervell's poor leadership, and Fisher would soon find it a thankless task to lead an army of self-willed adventurers.

THE MARCH TO the Río Grande had been a difficult one, but the return journey, without food or fresh horses, with many of the men on foot, was to prove doubly exhausting. Along the way the army disintegrated, spread out for miles across the vast chaparral, each man fending for himself and trusting his own instincts of survival to get home. "The provisions of many gave out, and to add to our perplexity, no one knew where we were or to what point we were moving,—all were lost, and our march was somewhat like that of the Children of Israel through the wilderness of old." [82] But Somervell was no Moses, and many refused to be led by him, attaching themselves to other commanders, including Flacco, one of Hays' Lipan Indian scouts. Reduced to near-starvation, they ate their horses and fed on roots and herbs. When they struck the San Antonio Road on January 1, their ordeal was nearly over. "The exultation was boisterous, and the shout proceeded from one end of our line to the other,—those in the rear catching it up, until, like one vast halleluha, it seemed to shake both earth and sky." [83]

The citizens of Texas were blissfully unaware of the fiasco in which their country's forces were engaged. Newspaper reports, in fact, had painted a rather glowing picture of the exploits of the army, whose sudden and unexpected appearance on the Río Grande had "spread terror and consternation throughout the whole country." [84] Once the facts were in and the true, tragicomic story of the campaign became known, condemnation of Somervell (and, of course, President Houston) was severe. On January 18 a lengthy article written by Memucan Hunt summarizing the expedition appeared in the Houston *Telegraph and Texas Register.* Hunt was sharply critical of his commander, who, he maintained, could have swept through the Río Grande Valley from Laredo to Matamoros had he acted with decision and energy.[85]

Francis Moore, the newspaper's editor and a staunch Houston enemy, remarked in that same issue that Houston's policy of vacillation was indeed suspicious, suggesting that the President by his own actions had actually served to sabotage the campaign. "We have no disposition to censure Gen. Somervell for his conduct during this disgraceful campaign. He was doubtless acting under the orders of the President," the newspaperman wrote. He added:

> We confess, when we examine carefully the conduct of General Somervell, we cannot discern what object he had in marching to the Rio Grande. If, as it appears, his object was merely to march to Laredo or Guerrero, and then return without even exchanging a single shot with the enemy; so far as the honor and credit of the Republic is concerned, he might better have merely marched his army up the first hill west of Bexar, and then marched down again, and then disbanded his troops and gone home. . . . [H]e certainly would have done less injury to the country, and have gained more glory, than he has acquired by the marching all the way to Guerrero and back again without capturing a single prisoner of note, or fighting one battle.[86]

The Somervell Expedition had come to an end. The Mier Expedition, as this new chapter in the history of the Republic would be called, was to suffer a fate even more inglorious than that of its predecessor.

The Battle of Mier

FOR THE FIRST time since breaking camp at the Leon River nearly one month before, Fisher and his men were in high spirits, and they moved forward, said one, with "a confidence and intrepidity that flung over the future the happiest auguries."[1] On the morning of December 20, the little army marched east along the bank of the Río Grande. Thomas Jefferson Green's furious opposition to Somervell the day before was rewarded by Fisher, who now told him to take the boats Somervell had ordered destroyed and follow the current of the river, keeping pace with the army during its march. While these instructions did not confer upon Green any particular status or higher rank, he interpreted them as such, and henceforth he emerged as second-in-command of the expedition. Warming to his task, Green pinned his red-silk handkerchief to the mast of his "flagship" and floated downstream, burning any boats that might be of use to the Mexicans. Green's swaggering bombast did not sit well with some of the men, who soon took to calling the makeshift flotilla "the Texian Fleet" and their self-proclaimed leader "the Commodore."[2]

Their destination was Ciudad Mier, a small village situated in a bend of the Río Alamo (also known as the Río Alcantro), which flows into the Río Grande four miles farther east. Both the land and the river parties encamped seven miles above the town on the evening of December 22. The next day Fisher and a group of men rode into the plaza and demanded adequate provisions for the renegade army.

The Texans remained unconvinced of the destitute nature of these Río Grande Valley towns. Mier, they had been led to believe, was the largest and richest upon the river save Matamoros.[3] The church possessed some valuables, for the local padre had been instructed by the archdiocese to send the "jewels and silver" of his parish to Monterrey or, if that could not be done, to conceal them where they could not be found when the Texans arrived.[4] But the people of Mier, like those of Laredo and Guerrero, were poor subsistence farmers. Once again Mexican villagers were ordered by the invading army to meet a requisition which they simply could not supply: five days' rations for 1,200 men, including 1,200 pounds of sugar and 600 pounds of coffee.[5] To ensure the fulfillment of the order, Alcalde Francisco Pérez was taken hostage and brought back to camp.

On the way back an unfortunate incident occurred involving Jesse Yocum, fourteen, and John Christopher Columbus Hill, fifteen, the two youngest members of Fisher's army. Hill had gone along on the expedition with his father and older brother as members of the Fayette County volunteers. Yocum had joined up with the Montgomery County militia regiment before it set out for San Antonio, and decided to stick with Fisher after the others went home. Only a short distance from camp, the two boys were climbing a brush fence that blocked the trail when Hill's gun discharged accidentally. The bullet hit Yocum in the back, killing him instantly. He was carried into camp and buried in a shallow grave.[6]

The movements of Fisher's army had not gone unnoticed. As Alexander Somervell had feared, the Mexican army had been apprised of the Southwestern Army of Operation's campaign to the lower Río Grande Valley from the outset. Even so, General Isidro Reyes had taken surprisingly few steps to check the Texan advance. The commander-in-chief of the Army of the North still feared the Texans intended to strike the towns along the upper river, and had collected the bulk of his forces, one of two divisions and a reserve brigade, at San Fernando de Rosas. With the other division garrisoned at Matamoros, this left Laredo, Guerrero, and Mier protected only by the *defensores* under the command of Colonel Antonio Canales. Since the first week in December, Canales had dispatched a string of urgent messages to his superiors begging for reinforcements, considering it prudent, in the meantime, to merely observe the enemy's movements.[7]

While Reyes temporized, General Pedro de Ampudia, commander of the Matamoros garrison, moved promptly when he learned of Canales' predicament. Dividing his division in half, Ampudia led one brigade in support of Canales, leaving the other in Matamoros to defend the city. On December 16, Ampudia's force of four hundred men left Matamoros, while the general went on ahead to organize militia companies in towns along the river. Morale among the Mexican regular troops must have been low. Ampudia's soldiers had not been paid in four months, subsisting on meager army rations alone. They now embarked on an exhausting forced march in heavy rains, and although rain-swollen rivers slowed their progress, they reached Mier on December 23, joining forces with Canales and his three hundred *defensores* a few miles below the town.[8]

On December 24 Fisher's men moved several miles downriver to the spot designated by Pérez where they would receive the provisions. The army waited all day, but the supplies did not arrive. It was not until Christmas morning that the Texans learned from a Mexican sheepherder that General Ampudia had joined forces with Colonel Canales and had arrived in Mier, countermanding the requisition order. Their combined force, the Mexican reported, totalled 700 men.[9] The Texans would later claim that the true size of Ampudia's army was much larger, numbering between 2,000 and 3,000.[10] The Mexican's estimate was closer to the mark; however, in addition to his own troops and the *defensores* under Colonel Canales, Ampudia's forces also included 100 sappers and 105 additional auxiliary troops from Nuevo León, bringing his combined troop strength to slightly more than 900 men.[11] To this figure must also be added the *presidiale* companies from the small towns along the river, which had been hastily organized as the Texans approached.

The two Mexican commanders were not unknown to William Fisher. It was Canales, in fact, who, as a leader of the Federalist War in northern Mexico two years earlier, had recruited Fisher and other Texas mercenaries for the rebel cause. Since his abortive attempt to establish a republic, Canales had served the government loyally, commanding the auxiliary forces which protected the border towns along the river. In the federalist revolt Pedro de Ampudia had been on the other side, establishing a reputation as a tough, ruthless adversary. On one occasion he had ordered the body of an executed federalist leader decapitated, and had placed the severed head on a pike in front of the man's home, in full view of his family, as a warning to the insurrectionists.[12]

William Fisher called a council of war and proposed to attack the town. His officers agreed without a single dissenting voice; it did not seem to matter that they were outnumbered three to one. With a vaunted regard for their own fighting abilities and nothing but contempt for their enemy, they appear to have harbored no doubt as to the outcome. The little army broke camp and began crossing the river, leaving forty men behind to guard the baggage. Alcalde Pérez asked to be left behind; he had a wife and children and had done all he could to comply with the Texans' orders. These protests were ignored, and with a "dolorous" countenance the alcalde accompanied Green and his men on their march to Mier.[13] Meanwhile, Fisher had sent the spy company on ahead to reconnoiter. On the outskirts of the town it stumbled into a party of Mexican cavalry, and the Texans quickly dispersed in all directions. Samuel Walker and two men spurred their horses, making a wrong turn down a side street that came to an end at a high bullrush fence. They dismounted, and Walker's two companions clambered over the top. Walker paused to fire one shot before following them, but during the chase he had lost the percussion cap of his rifle, and when he squeezed the trigger, the hammer clicked harmlessly. Walker turned to the fence and started over, but before he could make his escape, the Mexican cavalrymen grabbed his legs and wrestled him to the ground. The battle would have to go on without him.[14]

Ampudia had not planned to fight the Texans in the town of Mier. He had initially decided to make his stand at the confluence of the Río Grande and the Alamo, and had waited in ambush for them there on the evening of December 24. Upon learning that Fisher's men had already made camp at a ranch farther upriver, Ampudia returned to Mier that night. The following morning he set out again for the Río Grande, but was informed that the Texans were already crossing it, whereupon he doubled back and began preparations to defend the town. Leaving a contingent of cavalry along the banks of the Alamo, Ampudia set up his headquarters in the town square. Two brass six-pound cannon which he had brought up from Matamoros guarded the entrances to the plaza, while scores of infantrymen took positions on the rooftops.[15]

By nightfall on Christmas the Texans occupied a steep hill on the east side of the Río Alamo. The town appeared deserted, its lamps extinguished, its streets empty. In total darkness and a drizzling rain, Green and a number of men, including the unfortunate alcalde, felt their way down the bluff toward the water. The Mexican cavalry detachment on the opposite side of the river could be heard by the rattling of gear when the horses shook themselves. Leaving Captain John R. Baker's company to open fire on the enemy to give the impression that the Texans intended to cross the Alamo at this point, Green moved farther upstream in search of a more suitable crossing. Meanwhile, Captain Charles Keller Reese and Joseph Berry created an additional diversion by firing on a picket guard which had been spotted across the river. As they scrambled over the rocks to make their way back to Fisher's main force, Berry fell from a ledge into a deep ravine and broke his leg. Dr. John J. Sinnickson and a guard of seven men stayed behind, used rope to lift him to safety, and carried him to a little hut nearby.[16]

In single file the main group of Texans moved down the bluff to the water's edge, sliding down in places where it was too steep to walk. Green, leading the vanguard, forded the icy waters of the Alamo at a place where the sound of the swift current allowed the men to reach the opposite bank undetected. A cavalry picket spotted them as they reached the other side and opened fire. In the confusion the alcalde bolted from his captors and "bounded with the strides of a chamois" into the darkness toward town.[17]

The Mexican cavalry wheeled their horses and fell back into Mier, where the bulk of Ampudia's force had taken up positions. The Texans followed, but soon encountered stiff resistance in their push toward the square. With the artillery company firing two rounds of grape and canister per minute down the street, Ampudia's infantry opened fire from the rooftops. Forced to abandon the assault, Fisher's men took cover in one house at the corner of a street leading into the plaza. With the aid of a crowbar, breaches were made in the dividing walls of the house next door, and then the next, enabling the Texans to move from house to house, closer to the cannon emplacement in the square. All were vacant, but the Texans did find a plentiful supply of warm bread, jerked meat, and freshly filled water jars, left there by residents who had evidently evacuated the town in some haste.[18] Two companies gained entrance to buildings on the opposite side, and soon the entire army had found refuge from the hail of musket balls that raked the street.

Some of Fisher's men tried to sleep, while others busied themselves by knocking holes in the walls from which to fire upon the Mexicans in the square some fifty yards away. Ampudia's soldiers kept up an incessant fire throughout the night, as barricades were erected in the streets. Nineteen-year-old Joseph McCutchan described his first battle:

> *There is no sight more grand or sublime than the flash of opposing firearms at the hour of midnight . . . no sound [can] produce such an idea of grandure, and engender such intense excitement as the ringing report of rifles, the hoarse roar of musquetry, the awful thunder of artillery, and encouraging shouts of man, opposed to man, all mingled in dinn an[d] confusion.*
>
> *This night was by far the most exciting Christmas scene that ever I had witnessed!*[19]

The battle began in earnest before dawn. At five o'clock one of the six-pounders in the square opened fire on the houses occupied by Fisher's men, but with little effect. The grapeshot and cannonballs glanced off the walls and hurtled down the street, sending broken bits of cobblestones and chunks of adobe brick flying in all directions, allowing the Texans to make wider openings in the walls to give them a better shot at the enemy.

All morning they jostled for space at the window gratings and loopholes, and by nine o'clock the cannon at the end of the street had fallen silent, two companies of artillerists lying dead beside it. Ampudia's men used a rope to pull the cannon back to the plaza, out of the Texans' line of fire, where it continued to pound away at their position. Deciding that it was time to go on the offensive, Fisher ordered an immediate attack on the square, hoping to drive the Mexicans from the town. Not all the company commanders agreed with the idea, however, and the plan had to be abandoned.[20]

The Mexican infantrymen crowded on the rooftops fared little better than the gunners in the street. Although a three-foot-high parapet that extended along the roof provided some cover, the Texas marksmen unerringly found their targets. This sniper fire continued for several hours, until "there were but few soldiers bold enough to raise their heads above their ramparts," and by mid-afternoon the drainspouts that jutted from the walls spilled blood onto the cobblestones below.[21]

Up to this time Joseph Berry and the men detailed to tend to him had watched the action from the hut on the opposite side of the Río Alamo. Unwilling to remain bystanders as the battle raged, they took the opportunity to fire upon a cavalry unit as it passed by, making their presence known to the Mexican army. Reinforcements and the second artillery piece were immediately called up, forcing the Texans to make a dash for the river in an effort to rejoin Fisher's men on the other side of the Alamo. Leaving the wounded Berry with Dr. Sinnickson, they ran from the hut, but the Mexican cavalrymen ran them down, killing three with their sabers before the Texans reached the river. The Mexican soldiers burst into the hut and bayoneted Berry in his bed. Three were captured, and two men, one of whom was Berry's brother, managed to reach the houses occupied by their comrades in Mier.[22]

It was now General Ampudia who decided to dislodge the enemy with a frontal assault. The cannon was silenced, and the infantry were withdrawn from the rooftops and mustered in the plaza. In closed ranks the Mexican soldiers advanced upon the Texans' position. Fisher stepped out onto the avenue and ordered some of his men, perhaps fifty in number, to line up to meet the assault. At a distance of eighty yards the infantry halted and fired. When the smoke cleared, a number of Texans had fallen out of line, wounded, but only two lay motionless in the street. It seems likely that many of the flintlock firearms used by the Mexicans, which had a reputation for being unreliable, had misfired in the light rain. His right thumb shattered by a musket ball, William Fisher may not have given the order to return fire. Nonetheless, the Texans, most of whom used percussion-cap rifles which would have been largely unaffected by the weather conditions, replied with a volley that inflicted numerous Mexican casualties. Ampudia immediately ordered a second assault. Ranks were closed; muskets were reloaded. Fisher's men hurriedly regrouped and fired again. A third time the Mexican infantrymen pushed forward, and a third time they were sent reeling back to the square.[23]

Although Ampudia's losses were heavy, the lack of discipline among the Texas soldiers was beginning to take its toll. Fisher's wound, which had left him dazed and nauseous, may have impaired his ability to command in this critical stage of the battle. Both Cameron and Green tried desperately to rally their men. At one point Green jumped up on a table in one of the houses to shout above the din, but to no avail. Confusion reigned in the Texan ranks. No one was in command; everyone was shouting orders.[24]

Ampudia now pressed his advantage, sending one hundred militiamen to attack the Texan position from the rear. Behind the buildings were small courtyards where the villagers kept their livestock. Cameron and his Nueces cowboys rushed to the back to find the Mexicans massing behind a stone wall. Seven of his men were killed in this exchange. Unable to reload, Cameron grabbed two loose cobblestones from the courtyard and heaved them at his attackers. His men followed suit, and the Mexicans were forced to withdraw under a heavy barrage of rocks.[25]

After this assault, Ampudia made no more attempts to dislodge the Texans. The streets of Mier were quiet once again, and Fisher's men used this opportunity to pull the wounded back into the houses. The silence was suddenly broken when a loud cheer went up from the men at the windows. A man waving a white flag was walking from the plaza down the street. Thinking they had won the contest, the Texans now waited to hear General Ampudia's terms of surrender. The bearer of the white flag was Dr. Sinnickson, who had been captured in the hut across the river. But the doctor brought bad news; it was General Ampudia, he told them, who called upon the Texans to surrender. While Fisher and his captains considered the situation, several Mexican officers, some of whom had fought alongside the Texan leader in the Federalist War, approached to discuss with him the terms of capitulation. Colonel Rómulo Díaz de la Vega, Ampudia's second-in-command, granted the Texans a one-hour cease-fire, at the end of which time no quarter would be given if they had not laid down their arms.[26] Infuriated by this breach of security, Green, who believed the Mexicans had penetrated the Texan lines to gauge the strength and morale of their enemy, demanded that they be summarily executed, or at least taken hostage. Fisher, who in spite of his wound could still think clearly, was becoming increasingly frustrated by the contrariness of his officers, and rejected both of Green's requests.[27]

Green and Cameron wanted to fight their way out of the town rather than give in, and spent the hour drumming up support among the men for such an escape. But not all the Texans were so sanguine about their chances. There were many who doubted that a retreat could be made without tremendous casualties, and who talked of accepting the Mexican terms. Their supplies of ammunition were almost exhausted, and few were ready to abandon the wounded to Mexican captivity.

Notwithstanding the discord among his men about what should be done, Fisher was still hopeful that the day might yet be saved if the Texans stood their ground. At the end of an hour he walked up to the square. General Ampudia greeted Fisher courteously, although their discussion was brief. When told that Fisher had decided to reject the Mexican terms, Ampudia replied that hostilities would resume in ten minutes.[28]

Fisher did not know it, but he was no longer in a position to speak for his men. Back in the houses at the other end of the street, the scene was one of indescribable chaos. Some had already left their posts and were prepared to lay down their arms. Others agreed with Green and Cameron and were ready to make a dash to the Río Alamo, loudly proclaiming that they preferred annihilation to the ignominy of surrender. A large number did not know what to do, but showed little inclination to follow the leader whom they had chosen only a few days before. Like his predecessor, Fisher had become a commander without a command.

When he returned, Fisher was met on the street by several of his men who were walking toward the plaza. He ordered them to stop, but "no command or entreaty could induce them to return to their duty."[29] When others began to follow their example, Fisher realized that these defections in the ranks made further resistance futile. Refusing to be swayed "by the clamor of a few harebrained men and silly boys" who, in spite of the confusion, continued to argue in favor of fighting their way out of Mier, Fisher immediately returned to Ampudia's headquarters and notified the Mexican general that he had changed his mind. "I decided to avail myself of the terms proposed before it was too late, and entered into terms of capitulation after at least one half of the force had already surrendered upon the verbal promise of Ampudia to spare their lives."[30] Still there were those who refused to budge from their positions and from the windows cursed their comrades who trooped off down the street. But slowly even Green's group of die-hards conceded defeat, and one by one they came out of the stone houses and followed the others into the square to stack their arms.

Many survivors of the Mier Expedition unfairly blamed Fisher for the fiasco. Green would later argue that Fisher's wound rendered him incapable of command, although the injury was clearly not so serious as Green suggested in his account of the battle.[31] Others offered a harsher assessment of their commander, alleging that Fisher was guilty of timidity, if not outright cowardice. One Texan condemned his leader's conduct as "perfectly stupid . . . had Co'l Fisher exibited [*sic*] the least bravery or decision the victory would have been ours in a short time."[32] Entirely ignoring the confusion and panic which had seized the men during Fisher's absence, many Texans were convinced they had won the battle, and claimed that General Ampudia was preparing to withdraw from the town in the event that his terms were rejected. There is no evidence to suggest that the Mexican general was planning such an evacuation, although his offer was no doubt intended to prevent further loss of life in his already depleted ranks. While Ampudia's casualties were far heavier than Fisher's, it was the Texans—on foot and far from home, outnumbered and with no chance of receiving aid—who were in the weaker position. It had not escaped Fisher's notice that General Ampudia, anticipating a possible attempt by the Texans to head for the Río Grande, had deployed his forces to cover the only routes out of town.[33] Surrender, then, seemed to Fisher the only answer. As commander of the expedition, he was primarily concerned with the safety of his men, and he believed that Ampudia and Colonel Canales could be trusted to treat their prisoners honorably. He later gave his own account of his actions:

> *I capitulated at Mier because under the circumstances . . . I considered it the only means of saving the lives of even a portion of the command. Had I fortunately been placed in the same irresponsible situation as General Green, I also might have "blustered, vapored [and] tore my hair" . . . ; but alas, as the lives of two hundred and forty one men and the issue of happiness or misery of their families depended on my decision, I acted as I did.*[34]

The charge that poor leadership had contributed to the defeat at Mier wounded Fisher deeply. Any blame for the failure of Texas arms against Mexico rested instead with the rank and file, whose "overweening self-esteem, and arrogant assumption of unlimited superiority," he wrote not long after the surrender, "has already filled 'Texas' with widows and orphans, and will I fear produce yet greater disasters. All admit that the Mexicans are far inferior to us in the use of arms. As to the extreme cowardice so generally ascribed to them, it is altogether a popular fallacy, for

... they stand killing as well as the bravest, and are moreover comparatively perfect in that system of military subordination which enables enemies to gain victories and improve advantages—that system in which we are so miserably deficient, or to speak more properly, which we possess not at all." [35]

For many Texans the surrender was nothing less than traumatic. When it came time to stack their arms, Thomas Jefferson Green angrily smashed his rifle on the pavement rather than turn it over to his Mexican captors. [36] "Never shall I forget the humiliation of my feelings," Big Foot Wallace later remarked, "when we were stripped of all our arms and equipments, and led off ignominiously by a guard of swarthy, bandy-legged, contemptible 'greasers.' ... [D]elivered over to the tender mercies of these pumpkin-colored Philistines. ... I could have cried ... if I hadn't been so mad." [37]

At least two men at the battle of Mier managed to elude capture. [38] Whitfield Chalk, an ordained Methodist minister, was one of the Texans in favor of the plan to fight their way out of the city. He convinced a friend, Caleb St. Clair, to hide with him in a bake oven in the courtyard of one of the houses held by the Texans. Unknown to the others, they hid there until nightfall and then slipped out of town. St. Clair sprained an ankle jumping over a wall, but the two men managed to reach the Texans left behind on the Río Grande with the horses and baggage early the next day. [39]

Meanwhile, there had been much dissension among the camp guard that waited at the river. Some men hoped that the sounds of battle they had heard a few miles distant the previous day signaled victory for the Texans, while others, fearing the worst, had already headed north. With the bad news brought by Chalk and St. Clair, the small force decided to remain in the vicinity no longer. They withdrew just as a cavalry unit dispatched by General Ampudia to round up the remaining Texans appeared on the river. Two men who lagged behind were captured; one managed to escape, and the other, George Bonnell, at one time Houston's commissioner for Indian affairs, was shot. [40] The rest returned safely to the settlements of Texas.

They reached the frontier by the middle of January, just before Congress adjourned. Houston already had his hands full; two weeks earlier, a detail of twenty men had been dispatched to seize the government archives in Austin in a predawn raid. The vigilance of boarding house proprietor Angelina Eberly had prevented Houston's men from escaping unobserved, and three days later a posse of angry residents caught up with them and forced them to hand over the papers, bringing to an end the long-simmering feud between Houston and the townsfolk of Austin known as the Archives War.[41] The remnants of Fisher's army left behind at the Río Grande brought more bad news for the administration. Francis Moore, the choleric editor of the *Telegraph and Texas Register*, simply refused to accept the story he heard from the escaped men. "It seems incredible," he wrote, "that nearly three hundred Texans, all well-armed, and having at least fifty rounds of ammunition each, while strongly posted in stone houses, should have tamely surrendered to fifteen hundred or two thousand Mexicans." Such circumstances "exhibit a picture of imbecility and cowardice so totally at variance with the former achievements of the gallant Fisher [and] Cameron . . . that we still view these statements with suspicion." [42]

The Texans lost a total of sixteen men in the battle of Mier, including those who later died of their wounds, and another seventeen severely wounded.[43] According to Colonel Canales, forty Mexican soldiers were killed in the battle, and more than sixty wounded.[44] Fisher's men believed they had killed as many as five to seven hundred soldiers; some estimates ranged as high as one thousand. These were wild claims, even though it is quite possible that the death toll was higher than Colonel Canales' estimate, for Ampudia would later admit that the blood of his soldiers "flowed in the gutters of Mier," [45] and his report contained no mention of casualties for local residents, who played a prominent role in the fighting.[46]

It is hardly surprising that the Texans should exaggerate the size of Ampudia's army and the extent of the Mexican casualties; there was little they could do now but put the best face on things. While their version of events was not necessarily a deliberate attempt to conceal the truth, nonetheless it was a viewpoint skewed by their own vainglory and cultural prejudice. The reasons for their defeat were plain enough: although they had acquitted themselves well and more than held their own against a much larger Mexican force, their disrespect for authority and their chronic inability to act with any kind of cohesion had doomed their efforts and ensured disaster. Fisher's men, of course, had a different explanation, preferring to believe that victory had been stolen from them. Just as they were on the verge of driving the Mexicans from the town, they had been "tricked" into surrendering by the white flag. To the Texans, this was a decidedly more comforting analysis, and one which was all the more convincing because it confirmed their view that all Texans were bold and valorous, and all Mexicans base and contemptible. The Texans could never be beaten in a fair fight; only Mexican treachery and overwhelming numbers could have prevented them from winning the day.

Far from conceding defeat, the Texans defiantly insisted that they were the true victors at Mier. Green would later write: "the battle of Mier in its moral and political consequences to our country was a glorious triumph. . . . It was there that the people of Texas . . . [proved] themselves invincible to everything but duplicity and treachery; and it was there that the Texian made the name of his *rifle* and *death* synonymous terms throughout Mexico."[47] Another Mier combatant, writing from a Mexican jail shortly after the battle, demanded for his comrades "not the sympathy of the world alone—but more than that; I claim the highest admiration." Insofar as the battle of Mier had exacted a high price for the recent Mexican attacks on the Texas frontier, the military objectives of the Texans had been fulfilled. "The blood of our slaughtered countrymen of Fayette cried aloud from the ground for vengeance," he wrote. "The captivity of some of our best citizens appealed to Texians from the walls of the dungeons of Mexico for our effort to effect their ransom; the pride of having made that effort is the boast of my comrades."[48]

Fisher's men were confined to two buildings in the plaza, while the wounded on both sides were carried to the Purísima Concepción church. Fisher and Green were then taken to a building adjoining the church, where General Ampudia had made his headquarters. Fisher told him that the Texans were now prepared to surrender, but frankly admitted that there were men in his army who had only recently been released from Mexican prisons for taking part in the Santa Fe Expedition. According to the terms of their parole, they were to be executed if they took up arms against Mexico again. Fisher wanted assurances that they would not be harmed. The Mexican general promised him that these men would be given the same treatment as the others.[49] Satisfied, Fisher signed the articles of capitulation dictated by General Ampudia to Colonel Canales. The terms of surrender were as follows:

> *Agreeable to the conference I had with General William S. Fisher, I have decided to grant,*
>
> *1st. That all who will give up their arms will be treated with the consideration which is in accordance with the magnanimous Mexican nation.*
>
> *2nd. That conformably to the petition which the said General Fisher has made to me, all persons belonging to the Santa Fe Expedition will receive the same treatment and guarantees as the rest.*
>
> *3rd. All who desire to avail themselves of these terms will enter the square and deliver up their arms.*
>
> *Pedro d'Ampudia*[50]

Thomas Jefferson Green would later allege that the Mexican interpreter's translation was deliberately inaccurate, leading the Texans to
believe they would be treated "with all the honour and consideration
of prisoners of war."[51] Whether or not Green's version of the surrender
is correct is of little consequence, for even if the Texans were not formally prisoners of war, General Ampudia chose to regard them as such.
Indeed, Fisher's men were treated as well as and probably better than they
had reason to expect. The Texans may have seen themselves as knights-
errant on a glorious crusade, but the Mexican government could hardly
be blamed if it did not share this view. They were soldiers of a country
Mexico regarded as a rebel province, acting independently, wreaking
havoc along the Río Grande with plunder as their only apparent motive.
The punishment for insurgence and banditry was the same; Ampudia
would have been well within his authority to execute them at once.

The Mexican general spared the Texans at Mier because, as he saw it,
they were neither rebels nor bandits, but soldiers of a government with
which Mexico was at war. His country's claims of sovereignty notwithstanding, the Texas Republic had achieved a fair degree of legitimacy since
1836, and was now formally recognized by Great Britain, France, and the
United States. Its soldiers, therefore, deserved to be treated like those of
any warring nation, with dignity and respect. (Had he known they had
marched into Mexico against the orders of their own government, his decision might well have been different.)[52] Two years later, Ampudia would
have occasion to demonstrate that he had not lost his knack for dealing
with insurrectionists. Called upon to put down a revolt in Tabasco in
1844, Ampudia ordered the rebel leader executed and decapitated, only
this time he included a gruesome twist; the head was fried in oil before it
was placed on public display.[53]

This was the same General Ampudia who now extended to the Texans
all the privileges of prisoners of war and saw to it that they were treated
as well as the circumstances would allow. Ampudia asked the women of
the town to show the Texan wounded the same compassion as the Mexican soldiers injured in the battle.[54] Dr. Sinnickson administered to the
wounded and was given the medical supplies he required. Fisher and
Green were kept apart from the main body of prisoners and enjoyed the
same comforts available to Ampudia and his own officers. The two Texas
commanders would later write to the Mexican general expressing their
"warm gratitude" for his "kind consideration."[55] Ampudia's charity was
also extended to the three boys on the expedition, who were quartered
with the officers. John Hill, who had won praise for his bravery and marks-
manship during the battle, became a particular favorite of the Mexican

general. Ampudia supplied him with a new suit of expensive Mexican clothes to replace his own powder-scorched clothing.[56] Although the rest of the prisoners were cramped in their stone quarters and subsisted mainly on small portions of dried beef, some of the Mexican women took pity on them and were allowed to pass tortillas, red peppers, and *cabrito* (roast kid) through the gratings of the windows.[57]

The bells of the church pealed throughout the day to mourn the dead, as the townspeople returned to their homes. The bodies of soldiers killed on the rooftops were lowered to the ground by means of ropes and carried out to a ditch beyond the town. And in their makeshift prison the Texans argued among themselves, as they had done since San Antonio. They quarreled and they looked for scapegoats—Fisher for agreeing to surrender, even Dr. Sinnickson for bearing the white flag.[58] Every man had his own opinion about what should have been done to avert the disaster. The campaign ended as it had begun, with rancor and recriminations. But William Fisher, the old soldier, knew what had gone wrong, noting grimly that "we were utterly defeated, not by the enemy, but by ourselves." [59] The Texan invasion of Mexico had come to a sorry conclusion.

6

"Our National Calamity"

THE YEAR 1842 had ended with the Republic at the nadir of its fortunes. Texans looking back on the events of the past twelve months could find little to cheer about. The ill-fated Santa Fe Expedition in January, followed by the capture of San Antonio in the spring and fall, revealed the grandiose territorial claims of the Republic to be fraudulent; the Lone Star flag could fly safely no farther west than the Brazos River. With the country still reeling from this series of setbacks, things had gone from bad to worse. The mutiny of Somervell's forces on the Río Grande coupled with the so-called Archives War was indicative of the virtual collapse of governmental authority, while the defeat at Mier provided additional evidence, if any was still needed, that Texas could not rely on its military muscle for its salvation. Like Fisher's men at Mier, the people of Texas argued furiously and futilely among themselves, demanding to know the cause of their troubles. But as the Republic entered its seventh year, a remedy seemed as far away as ever.

Below the Río Grande, the mood was decidedly different. The defeat of the Texan forces at Mier was Mexico's greatest victory in the war to reclaim its errant province. While the centralists and federalists remained bitterly divided on most issues, Ampudia's victory brought nothing but praise for the Santa Anna regime. Even *El Siglo Diez y Nueve,* the opposition party newspaper in Mexico City, applauded the results at Mier:

The triumph of Mexican arms against the perfidious Texans is glorious for the nation and honorable for the military. . . . The sacrifices of our soldiers are now producing brilliant fruits: soon the great and generous nation that has been insulted by that hand-

*ful of adventurers will regain its territory and will have its laws
and government respected.*[1]

Buoyed by the news at Mier, General Juan N. Almonte, Mexico's minister to the United States, confidently predicted to American politicians in Washington that Texas was no longer in a position to offer Mexico any resistance.[2] In his despatches to Mexico City, Almonte indicated that the time was ripe for Mexico to reclaim Texas. Full-scale military operations should begin at once, he advised, before pro-annexation sentiment in Washington could be allowed to take root. Almonte predicted that the U.S. Congress, when it convened again in December, would once again take up the disturbing issue of annexation. "It is important that by that time," he wrote, "if the reconquest of Texas is not complete, operations should at least be well underway. If not, I fear there may be a reaction in favor of those adventurers and then it will be extremely difficult, if not impossible, to get public opinion [in the United States] again in our favor, as it is at present."[3]

There was no need for Texans to worry about an invasion from an angry Mexico, although there were many, Houston included, who took Mexican threats very seriously indeed. Santa Anna was still unable to attempt such a move, for there were now six thousand government troops bogged down in fighting against rebels in the Yucatán, and the meager financial resources of the country could not bear the strain of two wars. In spite of Santa Anna's promises to his people, he had no plans for a full offensive against Texas. He was, in fact, largely satisfied with events so far. Having captured the Santa Fe Expedition, occupied San Antonio twice, and convincingly defeated Fisher's force all within the space of little more than a year, the government's military record against Texas was impressive. Santa Anna was content to take credit for these victories and to gain from them as much quick political capital as he could. His policy was a popular one, but in the long term it was no policy at all. The stain of San Jacinto had not been removed, nor would it be until Texas was once more under Mexican control. These minor triumphs in themselves were not enough. They only raised expectations, leading the Mexican people to believe that the reconquest of Texas was feasible and imminent, a view which Santa Anna did nothing to discourage. Sooner or later, Santa Anna would have to fulfill his pledge to win back Texas, or face the consequences if he failed to do so.

While Santa Anna was trying to convince his people that an offensive war was possible, Houston hoped that recent events would show Texans the folly of such a course; all he could do now was wait and pray that they would profit by the tragedy. To his secretary of war and marine Houston wrote, "We have now too many prisoners in Mexico and I will never *sanction* any *addition* to our *national calamity*. . . . Texas cannot sustain such drafts upon the national character & continue to exist as a nation. Experience should make us wise. Surely disaster will learn us caution."[4]

At first it appeared that the defeat at Mier had taught his people nothing of the kind. Newspaperman Francis Moore was predictably truculent: "It is cheering to notice," his *Telegraph and Texas Register* observed, "that the late reversal of our arms during the campaign under General Somervell has not in the least dispirited our citizens, but on the contrary, has excited new ardor and a fixed determination to prosecute the war with vigor and energy."[5] General Thomas Rusk was reportedly raising an unofficial force of several hundred men from the areas of Nacogdoches, San Augustine, and Houston, while citizens in Fort Bend and Brazoria were also said to be ready to join another expedition bound for Mexico.[6] "[A]n army of two thousand or three thousand," Moore crowed, "could easily sweep the whole country from the Presidio to Matamoros." Throughout Texas, the War Party could still muster substantial support. "There is great excitement in Galveston against 'Old Sam,'" wrote one English traveler. "A storm is brewing and I suppose his opponents will not rest until they have a new expedition across the Río Grande."[7]

But it was clear in the days that followed that the mood of the country had changed. This time there was no action to back up Moore's loud talk. The invasion force against Mexico did not materialize, nor did war-hungry volunteers rush en masse to the frontier as they had done in the past. With nothing to show for their military efforts against Mexico but dismal failure, the people of Texas were growing weary of the firebrands' incessant call to arms. If defeat was still a difficult pill for Texans to swallow, they were growing accustomed to the taste. To be sure, Houston came in for his fair share of criticism for the mismanaged campaign, and the War Party continued to trumpet loudly for a policy of retaliation. On the whole, however, the people of Texas were coming around to Houston's way of thinking. In late March, an editorial entitled "A Volunteer Army; what one is and what it May Be," appeared in the Houston newspapers under the pen name "Marmaduke." The lessons of the Somervell and Mier fiascos had not been lost on the author, who observed: "the cause of this and perhaps future disasters [lies] in the utter repugnance of our people to submit to a moderate degree of restraint, obedience and self-denial."[8]

The Mier fiasco was a sobering experience for the Republic. The economic chaos of the past six years had been difficult enough, but if the "fighting Republic" could not hold its own on the battlefield, it was finished. The heady optimism that had once prevailed was gone; in its place was an atmosphere of gloom and despair. "Everything is doubt and uncertainty in the country, from the merchant to the farmer," wrote E. S. C. Robertson, who had joined the Southwestern Army of Operations but turned back with Somervell, to Isaac Van Zandt (the Texas chargé d'affaires in Washington, D.C.) that spring. "Unless something can be affected by mediation for the Country, our fate is uncertain, however, we have lost all hopes from that source."[9] The Texas correspondent for the New Orleans *Commercial Bulletin,* while concluding on a defiant note, nonetheless offered in the aftermath of Mier the following litany of woes:

We are all in confusion here—doubt hangs on the minds of all as to future events. The prudent and business portions of our community believe we shall be invaded both by land and sea in a short time. . . . Distrust pervades all classes of our community. Business is suspended. We have no money in trade—none in the national Treasury. No credit abroad, and it is utterly impossible for us to obtain any relief anywhere in case we are invaded by a powerful force. Many will continue to remove, as heretofore, to the United States, but a large majority will remain and prove victorious or die in defence of our homes.[10]

Van Zandt complained bitterly that these "outrageous and abominable slanders,"[11] which were reprinted in many American newspapers—the above report appeared in the influential Washington *Daily National Intelligencer*—totally misrepresented the state of affairs in Texas. But from his post in Washington the Texas diplomat was in no position to judge the veracity of such accounts, which may well have contained more truth than he realized or was willing to accept. These reports did further damage to the already dismal standing of the country in the eyes of many Northerners, who had never found much to admire in the slave-holding Republic, while the friends of Texas in the southern states were equally unimpressed by its latest military adventure. Wrote one Galveston resident: "There are people in N. Orleans who say, 'The Government of Texas is a joke and everything connected with the country is below par.'"[12] Samuel Swartwout, who had bought up lands along Galveston Bay, was naturally concerned about the effect that recent developments would have on his investments. To James Morgan, his agent in Texas, he wrote: "Your Country appears to be striding with giant steps and head-long impetuosity towards dissolution—Madness seems to govern in her councils and folly to push on her people blindly to destruction. Nothing is more common, even amongst the friends of Texas here, than the prediction of your speedy reconquest by Mexico. . . . Under these sickening and discouraging circumstances you must perish, and whilst this state of things lasts monied men in this country will shrink from all association with interest in your soil or peoples." [13]

The attitude in Europe with regard to Texas was much the same. According to Ashbel Smith, the Texas minister to England and France, it was widely believed that the days of the Republic were numbered. "Our national character it must be confessed does not stand high in Europe, but this we must attribute to ourselves," he wrote. The recent conflicts against Mexico "have done our national standing infinite harm. They have seriously impaired the high reputation we enjoyed for valor, and the confidence, at one time universal here, in our ample ability to maintain our independence." Moreover, these unfortunate events "have prevented the flow of emigration and capital to our country, which would otherwise have been immense." [14] Like Van Zandt, Smith found that the bad news from Texas did not make his job any easier. Smith attributed to recent events the sudden and unexpected reluctance of the Belgian government to enter into a treaty with the Republic, while at the same time negotiations for a sizable French loan were put on hold. [15] Keeping the French government abreast of affairs in Texas was Viscount Jules Edouard de Cramayel, the recently appointed acting chargé d'affaires in Galveston. In his dispatches to Paris, Cramayel offered a grim analysis of the Republic's misfortunes, warning French Foreign Minister François Guizot in early February: "The situation daily becomes more perilous and must inevitably lead to catastrophe." [16]

The cost of the Mier Expedition to Texas in terms of international respect and goodwill extended also to relations with Great Britain and the United States. Any chance that the major powers might be able or willing to exert pressure upon Mexico to accept Texas' independence now appeared exceedingly remote. The Mexican government could hardly be expected to listen calmly to any suggestions Great Britain and the United States might make regarding the recognition of Texas sovereignty. Any attempt to do so, according to Richard Pakenham, the British minister in Mexico City, "would be nothing less than an empty formality." [17] Realizing that nothing could presently be gained from mediation, the two major powers decided to let the matter rest for the time being.

Anxious to give the appearance of neutral bystanders in the conflict between Mexico and Texas, Great Britain and the United States were obliged to condemn the expedition, having earlier called upon Mexico to cease its border harassment against the Republic. Although conducted as a reprisal for Mexico's attacks, the Texan invasion could not fail to draw censure from the diplomatic community, which took note of the fact that while Woll's well-disciplined troops had respected private property in their capture of San Antonio, the Texas force on the Río Grande had behaved deplorably.[18] "I am instructed to remonstrate in strong language against Texas carrying on the war for retaliation by marauding parties," wrote Joseph Eve, the U.S. chargé d'affaires, to President Houston. "If she makes war, let it be open, manly, and according to the strict rules of modern warfare. Texas owes this to herself, and to the character of the Anglo-Saxon race."[19] Secretary of State Webster was blunter. Exasperated with these headstrong Texans, he delivered to Isaac Van Zandt, the Texas chargé in Washington, a scolding lecture in governance:

> *Sir; your affairs assume so many different* phases *that it is impossible one day to tell what will be the appearance on the next. If your Government would take the advice of its friends, to remain at home, unite among yourselves, confine your soldiers to your own territory, and to the defence of your own soil, suppress insubordination, prevent marauding parties upon the frontier and consolidate your energies, then Sir, we might be able to do something effective.*[20]

The Houston administration was anxious to make it clear that the lawless actions of the Mier prisoners should in no way be regarded as official government policy. To Van Zandt fell the unenviable task of explaining the fiasco in Washington. The citizens of the Republic were "liable to strong excitements," Van Zandt wrote to the fuming U.S. secretary of state; "it is but natural to suppose, that some irregularities will occur, and that attempts will be made at retaliation, by individuals suffering from the consequences of wrongs and injuries. These acts of individuals, though in a great degree excusable under such peculiar circumstances, should not be imputed to their Government."[21] Webster was in no mood for excuses, and this seemed to him a feeble one indeed. "[I]t is the business of Government to govern its citizens," he snapped, "and when it ceases to be able to do that . . . there is not much Government in force."[22]

Webster's irritation was hardly surprising. The secretary of state and the U.S. minister to Mexico, Waddy Thompson, had for the better part of a year worked to gain the release of the Santa Fe prisoners. Webster now found to his astonishment that a number had lost no time in taking up arms against Mexico in flagrant disregard of the terms of their parole. "I do not think that any application for the release of Individuals will be acceded to," Thompson informed Webster, "and after the violation of their parol[e] by so many of the Santa Fe prisoners I can not see any just ground of complaint against Mexico for not releasing any more prisoners."[23]

Equally annoying to Webster was the fact that he had recently rebuked the Mexican government—at Van Zandt's request—for the Vásquez and Woll raids into Texas. The secretary of state had already discussed the subject with Mexican minister General Almonte, and on January 31 Webster sent a note to Waddy Thompson, instructing him to persuade the Mexican government to abstain from these incursions; Webster added that a more forceful protest would follow in the near future if these attacks continued.[24] No sooner had this letter been dispatched than Webster was embarrassed to learn that Texas had engaged in a predatory raid of its own. Van Zandt's explanations notwithstanding, the news of the sack of Laredo and the invasion of Mexican soil by a band of men acting in defiance of their commanding officer made a mockery of the Texas claim that it was the aggrieved party in this war of harassment. Sensitive to Mexican charges that the United States was sympathetic toward the Texan cause, Webster immediately dispatched a second note to Thompson, this one adding that the United States would take exception to any Texan violations of Mexican territory as well.[25]

As in Europe, American concerns for the future of Texas had serious economic repercussions for the Republic. In Washington, the beleaguered Van Zandt was putting the finishing touches on a commercial treaty with the United States when unofficial reports of Somervell's troubles on the way to the Río Grande began to filter into the capital. It was only with great difficulty that Van Zandt managed to convince nervous senators "that the laws and constituted authorities [in Texas] were yet supreme."[26] The Senate subcommittee had in fact decided to recommend passage of the treaty when the reports of Fisher's mutiny and his defeat at Mier arrived in Washington. These new developments came, Van Zandt wrote, "like a blistering sirocco [and] blasted every effort of our friends, and paralyzed every movement in behalf of our treaty."[27] It was believed in Washington that Mexico would now seek revenge for this incursion and attempt to conquer Texas in earnest. If Mexico was successful, some senators feared, the terms of the treaty would then legally apply to the conquering nation. As a result, the most important articles of the treaty, which would have eliminated the duty on Texas cotton, were promptly deleted. Although ratified by the Senate, the altered agreement was of little advantage to the Republic, and Van Zandt advised the Houston administration to take no action on the matter, hoping that by the next session of Congress, the Senate might reconsider the treaty in its original form.[28] En route to his new post as the Texas minister to the Netherlands, William Daingerfield arrived in Washington in time to commiserate with his colleague Van Zandt. The Mier Expedition, "the result of our own folly and wickedness," had done incalculable damage to the Republic's prestige, he moaned, blaming the failure of the treaty on "[a]n entire want of confidence in the stability of our institutions."[29]

In a letter to Washington-on-the-Brazos, Van Zandt summarized the opinions of Washington policy makers as follows: "Texas is rent and torn by her own internal discords; she can [not] long stand under such circumstances; the chances are against her. She will either have to submit to Mexico or come under some other power."[30]

There was, of course, a possible solution to the Republic's misfortunes—annexation to the "other power" Van Zandt was referring to: the United States. Many Texans had always favored annexation, and they were now joined by level-headed citizens who were forced to admit that their experiment in nationhood had been a dismal failure. Mirabeau Lamar's vision of a mighty empire stretching from the Sabine to the Pacific appeared ludicrous in light of recent events. Peace and security were far preferable to lonely isolation. Annexation seemed to be the only answer.

Houston's own attitude on the question of annexation has been the subject of endless debate. Even his closest friends formed different opinions as to his true feelings on the issue. This is not surprising, for Houston always kept his own counsel; his most intimate friends were never confidants in any real sense. The President did indeed express many different and conflicting opinions to a great many people, leading some observers to conclude that he had no policy at all, or at best a very indistinct idea of what he wanted to accomplish and how to go about it. There is no doubt that Houston favored annexation throughout most of his first term, when the Republic had not yet recovered from its revolutionary turmoil. But as time went on he clearly flirted with Mirabeau Lamar's idea of a permanent Republic. He was not above letting his vanity prejudice his opinions, and on those occasions when he gave his imagination free rein—and he was certainly inclined to do so—he could see himself in epic proportions, as the founder of a vast and mighty nation. But the hard realities of governing a state on the verge of disintegration usually grounded such flights of fancy. It seems clear that by the fall of 1842, Houston had decided that annexation to the United States was not only desirable—it was a necessity.

The inability of Texas to stand alone had never been more painfully apparent than in the wake of the Mier Expedition. All Houston's efforts to stop an invasion across the Río Grande had failed. Texas, it seemed, could never be governed, nor could it continue to survive in a constant state of war. Even if the Republic remained free of Mexico, the mere threat of hostilities was enough to keep it an impoverished and thinly populated frontier. Immigration had ceased, and settlers were returning to the United States. Normal commercial relations with other countries were impossible, and barter was, as in 1836, still the principal means of exchange. Annexation would solve all of these problems. This last crisis only confirmed what Houston already knew; Texas had everything to gain by annexation, for it no longer had anything left to lose.

With Texans' morale at an all-time low, this seemed like a good time to once again test the annexation waters. Any proposal, however, must come from the United States, not Texas. Once before Texas had knocked at the door of Union and found it closed. This time any offer of annexation would have to be made by those who had the power to open it. There was much more than national pride at stake. Texas could not afford to throw itself at the mercy of the United States; to do so publicly would offend Great Britain and prompt Mexico to renew its efforts at reconquest. If the negotiations broke down or if an annexation treaty was rejected by the Senate, Texas would be worse off than before.

Houston was busy in the days after the disaster at Mier, as he set in motion a chain of events that were to have a profound impact on both the future of the Republic and the entire course of American westward development. Contacting anyone who could further the cause of annexation, the President wrote to Joseph Eve, the U.S. chargé d'affaires in Galveston, that the time was ripe to reopen the issue now that the majority of Texans were in favor of it. "Even the *oldest settlers*, even some of the original 'Three Hundred' are as anxious for [annexation] as any that I meet with," Houston explained to Eve.[31] Secretary of State Anson Jones instructed Van Zandt to drop broad hints in Washington, D.C., that Texas would consider a proposal to join the Union if one were offered, adding that Texans were "very unanimous" in their desire for annexation.[32]

Such overtures, of course, were nothing new; Houston had discreetly tried to reopen the annexation issue without success a year earlier. Now, he apparently decided to take a new approach. If Washington had hitherto been slow to see the advantages of annexing Texas, it must be made to see the disadvantages if it failed to act. Up to this time the Tyler administration, like its predecessors, had been reluctant to stir up the slavery controversy that annexation would cause. It was necessary to impress upon the United States that it was not Texas' only suitor. While Congress debated, Texas might be obliged to seek aid elsewhere. Great Britain was ready and willing to step in with offers of defense and commercial treaties. This was a disturbing prospect to most Americans; even northern Congressmen irrevocably opposed to the extension of slavery shuddered at the thought of Great Britain gaining a new foothold on the continent. By fueling these fears, Houston would prod the Tyler administration into action. It was Houston's private secretary, Washington D. Miller, presumably writing at the President's initiative, who first alerted President Tyler to the threat of British activities in Texas. Noting that Charles Elliot was a highly capable diplomat who had been sent to the Republic to thwart U.S. objectives in the region, Miller painted a dark scenario of British intrigue, and urged Tyler to make the cause of annexation his own. Though Miller explained that both Houston and the people of Texas wished to see the Republic annexed, the implication was clear that if Tyler procrastinated, the nation might have no recourse but to turn to Great Britain for assistance.[33]

As if to lend credence to these fears, Houston was at the very same time asking Charles Elliot for British aid to maintain Texas' independence. On January 24 Houston wrote a long, thoughtful letter to the British chargé d'affaires, in which he presented an entirely different analysis of recent events than the one which Miller had given President Tyler.[34] Annexation was not only possible, according to Houston; it was practically a foregone conclusion. There was unanimous support for annexation in both Texas and—here Houston was stretching the truth considerably—the United States. But what Texans really wanted was peace, and Houston confidently predicted they would lose interest in annexation once the threat from Mexico was removed. This was no doubt just what Elliot wanted to hear. If Great Britain wished to defeat annexation, the President suggested, it need only prevail upon Mexico to recognize the Republic's independence. This would end the state of war that had existed along the Río Grande for the past seven years, allowing Texas to develop and prosper (presumably through an alliance with Great Britain).

In the same letter to Elliot, Houston also discussed a more immediate problem: the new batch of Texans being held in Mexico. Drawing what little satisfaction he could from the fact that the bungled invasion had fulfilled his most dire prophecies, Houston ruefully observed: "The 'campaign of the people' is ended; and I think 'the eyes of the blind are opened,' but they will not see."[35] No doubt there were some men on the expedition, Thomas Jefferson Green being foremost among them, whom he would have gladly consigned to the dungeons of Mexico. But no one was more anxious to secure the release of the Mier men than Sam Houston, although his motives were no doubt more political than humanitarian. The prisoners would be a potent propaganda weapon in the hands of his enemies, who would gladly use them to discredit his pacific policy and whip up hostility against Mexico. There could be no peace as long as Texans remained incarcerated below the Río Grande.

Of particular concern for Houston was the very real possibility that the Mexican government might not choose to regard Fisher's men as lawful belligerents when it learned they had crossed the Río Grande without orders. Houston may have had little sympathy for them, but he knew the repercussions in Texas would be enormous if they were executed as outlaws. It was common knowledge in Texas that the Mier prisoners had acted in defiance of their government; several newspapers had already published reports of the mutiny against Somervell, and this information would soon make its way to Mexico City. Houston conceded that the Texans now languishing in Mexican jails had no one but themselves to blame for their predicament: "It is true the men went without orders," he told Elliot, "and so far as that was concerned, the Government of Texas was not responsible; and the men thereby placed themselves out of the protection of the rules of war."[36]

Houston would later regret this choice of words. The Mier prisoners would eventually learn of this correspondence with Elliot; ever suspicious of Houston's motives, they were quick to assume that he had washed his hands of the affair, and the President's enemies in Texas would soon charge that the Mier men had been disowned by their own government. The President went on to point out, however, that Fisher had signed articles of surrender with General Ampudia which would still have to be honored by the Mexican government. He told Elliot: "The moment that the men surrendered in accordance with the terms of capitulation, they became prisoners of war, and were entitled to all immunities as such. Upon this view of the subject I base my hopes for their salvation, if it should be speedily presented through the agency of Her Majesty's Minister to the Mexican Government."[37]

Houston's request that Elliot intercede directly on the prisoners' behalf exonerates him of the charge that he abandoned the Mier prisoners. Although there is no indication that the Mexican government ever intended to execute the Mier men as outlaws, Houston's prompt efforts suggest that he genuinely believed their lives to be in jeopardy. Had the President merely wished to give the appearance of solicitude, he might have formally petitioned either the British or the United States government to ask for clemency for Fisher's men, knowing full well that such an appeal, when sent through formal channels to London or Washington and then relayed to the diplomatic corps in Mexico City, would take weeks if not months—far too long to be of much help to the incarcerated Texans if Santa Anna intended to disregard the articles of capitulation signed in Mier.

But why did Houston ask this favor of Great Britain and not the United States? Curiously, and perhaps significantly, the President made no mention of the Mier Expedition prisoners to the American chargé in Galveston, Joseph Eve. One possible explanation is that Houston would quite naturally turn to Charles Elliot, a man whose talents he admired and with whom he was on the closest personal terms, for assistance in this rather delicate matter. The President might also have been hesitant to call upon the assistance of Waddy Thompson, the American minister plenipotentiary to Mexico, whose charity toward the Santa Fe prisoners had actually proven to be something of an embarrassment to the government of Texas. Finding the Santa Fe prisoners destitute following their release, Thompson had gladly paid their way back to Texas out of his own pocket. He was under the impression that he would be promptly reimbursed for these expenses, but was soon disappointed to find that the Houston government was reluctant to pay for the blunders of the previous administration.

Another important consideration for Houston in his decision to use British intermediaries to help the Mier prisoners was the fact that Great Britain enjoyed considerably better relations with Mexico than the United States did. Since the Revolution, Mexico had suspected the U.S. government of aiding and abetting the Texas rebels. In recent weeks U.S.-Mexican relations had taken a sharp turn for the worse, with the news of a bizarre attack on Mexican soil by an over-zealous naval commander, Thomas Ap Catesby Jones. While patrolling the western coast of South America with his squadron in October 1842, Jones received false reports that Mexico, with the aid of Great Britain, had declared war on the United States. Without bothering to check his facts, the commodore sailed into the port of Monterey, California, and trained his cannons on the fort in the harbor. Jones issued a proclamation claiming the entire area for the United States, while the bewildered inhabitants looked on. It was only after local authorities showed him the most recent copies of Mexico City newspapers, which contained not a word about war between the two countries, that he realized his mistake and rather sheepishly lowered his flag. Waddy Thompson had a difficult time explaining the matter to Santa Anna's government, which was understandably outraged, and a string of acrimonious messages coursed through diplomatic channels for several weeks.[38]

Nonetheless, the United States, and not Great Britain, was the likely candidate to intercede on the prisoners' behalf for a number of reasons, not the least of which was the fact that all but a handful of Fisher's men were natives of the United States. The Jones affair, while highly embarrassing to the Tyler administration, did not in the long run seriously impair U.S.-Mexican relations. (Santa Anna's government, once its initial anger had passed, proved surprisingly willing to drop the matter.) The Tyler administration had already shown that it was prepared to pressure Mexico into releasing filibusters who marched under the Texas flag, and the recent liberation of the Santa Fe prisoners was evidence that its demands were taken seriously by Santa Anna's government. Waddy Thompson, irritated though he might have been at not being repaid by the Texas government for the travel expenses of the Santa Fe prisoners, was well known as a friend to the Texas cause and was at all times ready and willing to act as the chief advocate and defender of Anglo-Americans incarcerated in Mexico. As late as December 29, Houston had acknowledged the Republic's debt to Thompson for his role in obtaining the release of his incarcerated countrymen. In a speech before the Texas Congress, the President took note of the American minister's "high reputation as a statesman and gentleman," adding: "Had those unfortunate men whom he thus assisted been citizens of his own country, he could not have evinced a more lively degree of sympathy and liberality in their behalf."[39]

The merits of American intervention notwithstanding, Houston clearly intended for the initiative in this matter to be taken by the British. The President's request for British assistance to win the release of the Mier prisoners may well have been a calculated attempt to arouse the jealousy of the United States, as the first step in his new strategy to give the appearance that the Republic could get along quite well without American aid. As previously noted, Houston had been searching since November for ways to make full use of Elliot's presence in Texas. The problem of the Mier prisoners seems to have presented him with just such an opportunity. While it may be argued that Houston was simply trying to avail himself of every possible means at his disposal to do what he could for the Mier men, it is evident from the correspondence emanating from Washington-on-the-Brazos in the weeks after Mier that Houston knew full well that the American government would take a dim view of

British meddling in the affairs of Texas. If it is true that after Mier Houston decided to court the British in order to arouse the suspicions of the United States, his request that Her Majesty's government intervene on the prisoners' behalf would appear to be very much a part of this policy.

Despite Houston's efforts, however, it was the American rather than the British government which took the lead in insisting upon clemency for the prisoners. Elliot forwarded the text of Houston's letter to Richard Pakenham in Mexico City who, realizing that this was a matter best handled by his American counterpart, brought it to the attention of Waddy Thompson. Although Thompson had not received any instructions from the State Department regarding William Fisher and his men, he had earlier been asked by Webster to do everything in his power to alleviate the sufferings of Texas prisoners in the Santa Fe episode. Accustomed to acting on his own initiative in any case, Thompson had already decided to take the matter up with the Mexican government, and he asked Richard Pakenham to join him in using their influence to protect the rights of the Mier prisoners. Pakenham declined, on the grounds that the attack on Mier had not been officially authorized by the government of Texas. Believing the Texans to be entitled to all rights as prisoners of war, Thompson paid a visit to Mexican Foreign Minister José María de Bocanegra and expressed his government's concern that the prisoners be treated in accordance with "the Laws of Civilized Nations."[40] Not surprisingly, Bocanegra's response was, by diplomatic standards at least, anything but civil. The foreign minister was "very much excited" by the American request, Thompson wrote his secretary of state. The Mexican diplomat curtly informed Thompson that "Mexico did not regard Texas as an independent power but as a rebellious province and that prisoners taken were not entitled to any of the privileges of prisoners of war, but that they were rebels and would be so treated, and that no suggestion on the subject from other Governments would be received or listened to."[41]

For all their considerable influence, there was in fact little either power could do to help the prisoners for the moment. Great Britain was Mexico's biggest creditor and trading partner, and the United States was currently trying to collect a debt of two and a half million dollars in unpaid claims.[42] Neither country could be seen to be too sympathetic toward Texas without jeopardizing its relations with Mexico. The plunder of Laredo and the fact that a number of the men had been prisoners on the earlier Santa Fe Expedition and were in violation of the terms of their release weighed against any appeals for clemency. The diplomatic corps in the capital would simply have to wait for tensions to subside before the matter could be brought up again with Mexico's leaders.

With Mexico deaf to the entreaties of the major powers on such important issues as mediation and the Texas prisoners, it seemed as though Great Britain and the United States could be of little help to the Republic in its time of crisis. But Houston was prepared to make the best of a bad situation, and determined to pursue a long-term diplomatic strategy designed to force both the United States and Great Britain to take a more active and productive role in the affairs of Texas. Houston knew that even if the Tyler administration sought to bring Texas into the Union, annexation would be a slow and difficult process. It would be several months before an annexation treaty could be hammered out and brought before the U.S. Senate. In the meantime Texas needed protection from its southern neighbor, which Great Britain, with its close ties with Mexico, could provide. Thus, Houston skillfully sought both the ultimate goal of annexation to the United States and the short-term benefits that would accrue to Texas by a courtship with the British. And if the United States for some reason failed to rise to the annexation bait, Texas would at least have a strong alliance with Great Britain which would be of invaluable benefit to the struggling Republic in the future.

Houston's overtures did not fall on deaf ears. "This is the first hint I have ever had of the President's ideas upon this Subject,"[43] Elliot wrote to Lord Aberdeen of Houston's avowed desire for an independent, pro-British Republic. Although the British representative knew Houston well enough to have once observed that he "sometimes says and writes what appears to be capricious and contradictory,"[44] it seems never to have occurred to Elliot that the President was capable of deceiving his friends as well as his enemies. Elliot was delighted with Houston's apparent willingness to deal with Her Majesty's government, and was soon expressing every confidence that Texas would establish itself as a permanent state on the continent.[45]

Viscount de Cramayel, on the other hand, did not share Elliot's optimism, fearing instead that the Republic's recent difficulties would actually force it to accept a closer relationship with the United States. The French chargé's suspicions were first aroused when William Daingerfield arrived in Galveston en route to assume his duties as the Texas diplomatic representative in the Netherlands. Cramayel noted that "his very obvious air of depression and anxiety, noticeable to everyone, made me the more inclined to suspect some secret motive for his journey."[46] Convinced that Daingerfield's plans to pass through Washington, D.C., were of far greater import than his ultimate destination in Europe, Cramayel invited the Texas diplomat to dinner in order to learn what he could about the reason for his voyage. Daingerfield readily admitted that Texas affairs were in a "deplorable" condition, adding that he saw no hope for the country unless France or Great Britain came to its aid. Cramayel, however, was unconvinced, believing that the Houston administration might now try to pursue an altogether different course. "By question after question," Cramayel later wrote, "I drew him to speak of the remedy of desperation to which Texians have always turned in moments of distress—*annexation to the United States*. From the open manner in which he replied and discussed the question with me, I could no longer doubt that he was actually going to the United States to seek once more the active protection of the North Americans and, as a last resort, to join the Union by means of annexation if they would consent." [47]

Thus, it is clear that the Houston administration's efforts to secretly revive the annexation issue while continuing to express a preference for Texas independence were not wholly successful. The French chargé had ascertained Houston's real intentions from the outset. Nonetheless, in order for Houston's diplomatic strategy to succeed, it was Great Britain, not France, which needed to be convinced of the President's sincerity. In spite of Cramayel's close relationship with Charles Elliot, the French diplomat seems never to have discussed his suspicions with his British counterpart—or, if he did, failed to convince him that Houston's avowed desire for an independent Republic might be less than genuine.

Meanwhile, the Tyler administration was beginning to look at annexation with a fresh sense of urgency. The U.S. President's bitter struggle with leading Whigs had led to his being expelled from the party, and he was now seeking to establish a party of his own. Tyler planned to salvage his political fortunes with the annexation of Texas, an issue intended to cut across established party lines and win him the support of both Democrats and Whigs in the southern states. With the South solidly behind him, Tyler hoped to ride the annexation issue to a second presidential term. On March 13, Secretary of State Anson Jones received a long letter from Isaac Van Zandt, who had already met privately with President Tyler to discuss the dangers of British activities in Texas. The President "listened with much attention and replied he would take the matter into serious consideration." Van Zandt further noted, "If the jealousy of this govt can be a little more excited . . . they would take an open and bold stand in our behalf." [48]

There would be times when Houston would seem to waver from this chosen course. No doubt the prospect of ruling over a separate republic never quite lost its appeal; annexation was, after all, not a matter of choice so much as a policy of expediency. Charles Elliot understood this. An independent Texas, he told Lord Aberdeen, "would be most agreeable to [Houston's] personal opinion, and ambition." [49] But Houston's love of power was tempered by a keen sense of pragmatism. Even had he wanted to establish a permanent new republic on the American continent, annexation was the clear choice for most Texans, and support for a marriage to the United States would grow rather than diminish in the months ahead. Houston did not want to embark upon a fool's errand if there was little hope that Texas could make anything of its independence; far better to take the credit for shepherding his Republic into the fold of the Union than to get the blame for its continued dissolution.

The Battle of Mier did much more than expose the inflated reputation of the Republic as a nation of warriors. It was, in fact, a turning point in the brief history of the Texas experiment in nationhood. The War Party, which throughout 1842 had blocked the President's every move, would become increasingly ineffective in the months ahead, unable to whip up popular support for an aggressive stand against Mexico. Texans had often turned adversity on the battlefield to their advantage; the Alamo and Goliad in 1836 and more recently the Santa Fe Expedition and the Vásquez and Woll raids had all served to instill in them an even greater military ardor. In the aftermath of Mier, many Texans seem to have experienced a similar surge of national pride and a desire to wreak a terrible vengeance upon their mortal enemy. But this time these sentiments passed quickly, giving way to a less belligerent posture and a more realistic assessment of the Republic's limitations. From the moment the news of the Mier debacle reached Texas, the Lone Star of the Republic dimmed perceptibly. Dispirited, Texans turned to the United States. Houston sensed the new public mood, and although international events constrained him from actually endorsing it, he had already decided on an appropriate course of action. The Lone Star would eventually have to be satisfied with a place among the Stars and Stripes, but as yet the twenty-six states of the Union were undecided about whether to make room for it. This would be Sam Houston's next challenge.

FOR FIVE DAYS the prisoners waited in Mier until, on December 31, General Ampudia ordered the Texans mustered in the square. In double file, flanked by Mexican infantry and cavalry, they were marched out of the village as a military band played. General Ampudia, his staff, and the Texan officers rode at the head of the column with one of the two cannons, while the second piece of artillery brought up the rear. Also riding alongside Ampudia was John Hill, for the Mexican general had taken a special liking to the boy. The wounded were left behind with Dr. Sinnickson and an interpreter.

The army followed the path of the river, stopping at little villages to camp along the way. The Texans were unaccustomed to long marches on foot, and few owned the proper footwear—a number wore high-heeled riding boots. After a difficult twenty-five-mile march on the first day, the footsore prisoners reached the outskirts of Camargo, a village along the river not much larger than Mier. Quartered in an open corral, they suffered from the cold, and to keep warm scraped away the coals of their dying campfires and slept in the warm ashes.[50]

On January 1 Ampudia entered the town to a hero's welcome. This was not a New Year's festival, as some of the prisoners first thought, but a ceremony that would be repeated in every town they passed along the river. Cheering crowds lined the streets into the square, where the officers stopped briefly for Mass in the church, after which the parade began again. The decaying stone houses were decorated in an odd fashion: from poles attached to the rooftops across the narrow streets, all manner of bright fabric fluttered in the breeze—scarfs, rebozos, even ladies' pink undergarments and men's silver-buttoned trousers. Paper banners with such slogans as "Eternal Honor al Immortal Ampudia" and "Gloria y Gratitud al Bravo Canales" proclaimed the victors of the battle of Mier. Three times around the square the Texans were marched as the bells of the church pealed wildly, before being quartered for the night in a large brick building on the outskirts of town.[51]

Two days later they reached Nueva Reynosa, where a similar welcome awaited them. On this occasion an old Indian and a troupe of young boys in traditional costume, wearing mirrors and ribbons on their heads and shaking rattles made of gourds, whooped and danced among the prisoners.[52] As always, the townsfolk came out of their adobe hovels for a look at the Texans. In each town, the public reaction to the parade was mixed. Some were jubilant at the sight of the defeated Texans, others simply curious, while many were moved to compassion when the desperate-looking prisoners passed by. Still others were interested primarily in the commercial benefits to be gained by the occasion. "There was no dearth of peddlers along our route," one prisoner wrote. "Our coming seemed to have been heralded far in advance, and every old palado [*sic*] that could scrape together a few eggs, tortillas, goat milk or goat cheese, got on the road to wait our coming, and those who had the money could buy, while the moneyless man had to resort to stealing."[53] Big Foot Wallace recalled that in some places the inhabitants, particularly the women, took pity on them and "gave us fresh water to drink, and sometimes more substantial refreshments. In others, we were hooted at by the mob, that were sure to collect around us whenever we stopped for a few moments, who would call us by all sorts of hard names, and pelt us with stones and clods of earth, and stale eggs." Wallace much preferred being on the road "with all its hardships and discomforts" to these brief sojourns in the small towns along the river. "While marching, I could, at any rate, breathe the pure, fresh air of heaven without being hooted at and reviled by the mob or rabble that always collected around us whenever we were halted on the way."[54]

None of the prisoners, however, complained about the treatment which they had received from Ampudia, and if the open corrals in which they were confined offered little shelter from the elements, better facilities were not available in these remote outposts. "Ampudia's deportment towards us was as liberal as could be expected," one prisoner recalled, "his own soldiers sharing our discomforts, and participating in all the deprivations to which we were subjected."[55]

At Matamoros, the principal town along the Río Grande, the celebration was somewhat more elaborate and sophisticated. The city was General Ampudia's headquarters, as well as home for most of the soldiers under his command. Before entering the town Ampudia's army stopped to prepare themselves for the parade. Musket barrels, swords, and buttons were polished until they gleamed in the sunlight. Shakos were dusted off, and the officers, who commanded extra burros to carry their belongings, put on their best uniforms. From their saddlebags they took out their ceremonial gorgets, neck-plates of gold or brass. The horses were groomed and the intricately designed leather saddles wiped clean. Miles outside town scores of villagers, some on foot or astride little burros, the women riding in oxcarts, went out to meet the column. Ampudia and his charges were escorted into town in this manner, amid the cheering and bell-ringing.[56]

After the parade the Texans were herded into three jails near the plaza, while their leaders and the three young boys were conducted to better quarters. Ampudia held a victory ball for his officers that night, and throughout the town the regular soldiers celebrated in their own way, parting with their pay at faro and monte gaming tables. Firecrackers and rockets rent the air and lit up the sky throughout the night. That Ampudia was sensitive to any charges of mistreatment of the Texans was evident when, apparently through some misunderstanding between Ampudia and the officer of the guard, Fisher and Green were abruptly taken to the common prison and thrown into a cold, dark room without bedding. Angry that officers would be treated in this fashion, Green dashed off a stinging rebuke to General Ampudia. Within an hour the cell door was opened, and they were taken back to their former, more comfortable lodgings.[57]

The Texans were quartered in Matamoros for six days, while Ampudia awaited instructions from the capital. The jails were as to be expected, dank and flea-ridden, but the food was palatable, and the prisoners were allowed to write home for the first time.[58] "During the week we remained in Matamoros," one of them later wrote, "we were treated with marked humanity by all the better classes of the population, native and foreign. The military not only supplied us most abundantly with wholesome and palatable food, but the citizens generously contributed large supplies of clothing, which we greatly needed."[59] Several American and foreign merchants furnished them with money and blankets. J. P. Schatzell, a German businessman, gave five dollars apiece to the men from Kentucky, where he had lived for several years (although many who were not residents of the state took advantage of the offer).[60] Schatzell also loaned a number of men on the expedition much larger sums of money; Thomas Jefferson Green received a draft of $400, funds which he put to good use in the months ahead to defray his expenses as a prisoner in Mexico.[61]

If the Texans grumbled at their accommodations, they were in reasonably good spirits and confident that such inconveniences would be temporary; they expected to be home soon. According to their interpretation of the articles of surrender, as prisoners of war they would be held in Matamoros or some other border town until they could be repatriated. The time was passed swapping stories of their recent adventure, and the tales with each telling became taller, the acts of heroism bolder, and the numbers of Mexicans killed at Mier greater. Firmly believing they had been robbed of victory, they boasted of how they had put Ampudia's men to flight.

But on January 13 they learned from General Ampudia that the Mexican government had no intention of allowing them to traipse homeward anytime soon; they were to be brought to Mexico City. There was no little amount of excitement when the news was announced. Those who had argued against surrender at Mier were furious, and recriminations broke out anew. Only the men who had taken part in the Santa Fe Expedition, who had already experienced the hardships of unending marches and months of grim captivity, knew what lay ahead of them.

The city was buzzing with rumors, no doubt picked up from newspapers in Texas, that General Thomas Rusk and another army of Texans were on the way to liberate the Mier men.[62] Ampudia ordered Colonel

Canales and his militia force to march the prisoners south immediately. To discourage any escape attempts by the Texans, the officers were to be moved on in advance of the main group. Fisher and Green were allowed to visit their men before setting out, and Ampudia reminded them that they were being held as hostages to ensure the good conduct of the others; they would forfeit their own lives if their men made a bid for freedom. Green and Fisher told Ewen Cameron, who as the "oldest and most experienced captain" had been unanimously elected commander in their absence, to use his own judgment and to do everything in his power to get his men safely back to Texas.[63]

Three days in advance of the main group, Fisher, Green, Adjutant-General Thomas W. Murray, and two other men serving as aides-de-camp set out for Monterrey[64] under a light escort guard. The rest of the prisoners were now placed in the command of Colonel Antonio Canales who, with five hundred *defensores* and an artillery piece, was ordered to march the Texans south. For the Mier prisoners the name Antonio Canales was a byword for treachery. It was Canales who had led the federalist forces against the centralists two years earlier and then made his peace with the government, leaving the Texans to fight their way out of the country. The Texans, particularly men like Cameron who had been betrayed at Ojo del Agua, never forgave the Mexican revolutionary for his role in the affair. It was said that the enmity between Canales and Cameron went back to the earliest days of the war, when Cameron's horse was stolen by one of Canales' soldiers. Spotting the horse one evening in camp, Cameron seized the culprit, and a furious argument followed between the federalists and their Texas allies. Canales stepped between the two men and ordered the Texan to surrender the horse. Cameron drew his pistol, saying he would shoot the first man to lay a hand on his property. For this incident Canales demanded that Cameron be court-martialed, but as a Texas mercenary he was tried by his own officers, who promptly acquitted him. More recently, Canales and his *defensores* in July had skirmished with and been repulsed by Cameron's men at Lipantitlán, on the Nueces River, no doubt adding to Canales' hatred of the Texas leader.[65]

Left behind in Matamoros were six sick prisoners and the three boys. John Hill was allowed to see his father before the Texans departed (his older brother, Jeffrey, had been among the wounded left at Mier). His story was to be one of the most remarkable chapters of the expedition. General Ampudia had taken the boy into his home, and soon after the main body of prisoners departed enrolled him, as Juan Cristoph Colón Gil de Ampudia, in a Matamoros school, where the boy quickly began to learn Spanish. In his dispatches to the capital, the general mentioned the youth's bravery at Mier and spoke highly of his character and intelligence. Such praise apparently piqued the interest of Santa Anna, and after several weeks in Matamoros Hill was instructed to proceed directly to Mexico City for an audience with the Mexican president.[66]

Under Colonel Canales the treatment of the main contingent of prisoners took a turn for the worse. It was rumored that Canales had insisted in Mier that the Texans be manacled for the march south, but had been overruled by General Ampudia. The prisoners now blamed Canales for the rough treatment they received from the *defensores* under his command, but it is more likely that these untrained militiamen were unaccustomed to and uneasy with their escort detail, and thus may have been more quick to use a musket butt or the point of a sword on stragglers than Ampudia's professional troops had been.[67]

With their chances of reaching Texas growing increasingly remote as they moved further south, many of the prisoners began to talk of escape. One week after they left Matamoros, most of the Texans had been won over to the argument that an attempt to overpower their guards must be made. They were quartered for the evening in a corral, with cavalry and infantrymen picketed outside. A loaded cannon was situated at the gate entrance. The large size of the guard made some of the men uneasy, but by four o'clock, when the dinner rations were brought out, the Mexican militiamen seemed to be taking little notice of the prisoners. It was agreed that Captain Cameron would give the signal to attack when the men drew their rations. There was some confusion among the officers about their orders, however, and at the last minute Cameron changed his mind and called off the escape.[68]

Green and Fisher were faring decidedly better. On horseback they made quick time to Monterrey, some 270 miles below the Rio Grande. Upon their approach to the city they could make out the gray outline of the Upper Sierra Madres rising up from the flat tablelands. Lying on the northeastern edge of the mountain chain, the city was situated in a picturesque basin of maguey and agave fields in the shadow of the Cerro de la Silla, an oddly formed peak that distinctly resembled a high Spanish saddle, for which it was named. Although Monterrey was regarded in Mexico City as a frontier outpost, in recent years it had grown and prospered as the capital of the state of Nuevo León. A fine, solidly built city of twenty thousand people, it was by far the largest and grandest of any urban center Green and Fisher had visited thus far.

Their quarters were infinitely better than the filthy cowpens to which their fellow prisoners were quickly becoming accustomed. In Monterrey they stayed at the home of an army colonel, where they were entertained in a high style which they had not known even in Texas. Fisher and Green purchased suitable clothes, Green having obtained an additional $300 from J. P. Schatzell's agent in the city.[69] The colonel's daughters entertained the Texas officers on the piano and guitar, and in the evenings Fisher and Green were guests at lavish dinners attended by Monterrey's prominent citizens. The Texans took great pleasure escorting the ladies around the dance floor; Green was particularly struck by the beauty and grace of these Mexican women, whom he described as "winged creatures," and who danced "with a bewitching, ethereal, gossamer touch."[70]

It was with genuine regret that Fisher and Green continued their march south after a six-day sojourn in Monterrey. Some days later they reached Saltillo, where they were quartered in some infantry barracks. Here they found five men who had been captured in General Woll's invasion of San Antonio, among them Norman Woods and two other survivors of the "Dawson Massacre." They were all in a bad way, particularly Woods, who had been delirious with pneumonia for more than two weeks. Since September they had been kept in towns along the Río Grande, too sick to make the long journey into Mexico. Even so, they had tried to escape in December, but the attempt had ended in disaster. Slipping away from their guards one night, they headed for the river. Woods, whose shattered hip had left him crippled, was easily recaptured. The others were caught a few days later, after two men tried to swim to safety but were swept away and drowned by the current.[71]

Woods pulled through, and he was considered well enough to march south with the main body of prisoners, which arrived one week later. They too had passed through Monterrey, where Canales was reassigned, and Colonel Manuel R. Barragán took charge of the prisoners for the next leg of their march to San Luis Potosí. Barragán's militia unit had recently been reinforced by a company of army regulars—known by the Texans as the Red Caps for the scarlet shakos they wore—apparently as a result of a second escape attempt that also had to be aborted. At their first encampment after leaving Monterrey, Ewen Cameron had again decided to charge the guards. The escape was to be made at daybreak, when the cavalry was out gathering the horses and the infantry would still be asleep. But at dawn the Texans found the soldiers awake, armed, and mustered outside their pen. Someone, they were certain, had tipped off Colonel Barragán. Many believed the culprit to be a runaway slave who had accompanied the army since Matamoros, who came and went among the prisoners as he pleased, who enjoyed their confidence and overheard their plans of escape.[72] Others blamed Captain Charles Keller Reese, one of the few officers who opposed the escape plan, who had refused to take the position assigned to him by Cameron.[73]

The officers were able to visit with the men only briefly before they were ushered again along the road toward San Luis Potosí. Barragán took up the same line of march the following day. The next time Fisher and Green would see the others would be four days later at the Hacienda del Salado, a *posada* that served as a way-station for travelers along the route from Saltillo to San Luis Potosí. Described by one American traveler as a "miserable place" inhabited by two or three hundred people, the Salado sat by itself in a desolate, barren valley with foothills on either side.[74] The prisoners were bivouacked in a stone corral, its walls some ten feet high, beyond which was another enclosure where the militiamen and the Red Caps bedded down for the night. Only Colonel Barragán, his aides, and the Texas officers were quartered in the main buildings.[75]

That evening a few of the captains obtained permission to see Green and Fisher. The men had been polled, and a majority were still determined to make an attempt to escape. Now that all the Texans were together, Captain Cameron wanted to charge the guards the next morning. In this he had the support of all but Captain Reese. It was Reese's opinion that nothing could be gained by a break at this point, for they were now some three hundred miles from the Río Grande. Green did not hesitate to side with Cameron. Fisher, on the other hand, was more cautious; but in the end he too gave his consent. Together with their aides, Fisher and Green would rush the small detachment that watched over them from a courtyard outside their rooms as soon as the attack began. The captains returned to the corral to pass the word among the others that the break would be made the next morning.[76]

The Black Bean Episode

EWEN CAMERON AND Samuel Walker were up early. It was not yet dawn, and in the cold gloom they shook themselves and beat their arms across their chests. The guards had given them some firewood, and with this and some debris which they had collected from the corral they built a small fire. Slowly the yard came to life as prisoners stirred, picked themselves up, and hurried over to the fire, stretching their benumbed hands eagerly above the flames. As the men gathered, they discussed their plans for escape. In half an hour Colonel Barragán would come through the open doorway separating the prisoners from the corral where the Red Caps were quartered. It was Barragán's custom every morning, when the breakfast rations were brought out, to look in on the Texans and to order them to prepare for the day's march. This would be the moment when they would seize the Mexican commander and rush the guard. The word spread quickly among the men.[1]

Captain Reese was also warming himself by the fire. As he had done the night before, he strongly advised against the escape. It was pointless to consider a bid for freedom so far from the Texas border, he argued; even if they managed to subdue the soldiers outside, they would be cut down by the local militia forces long before they reached the Río Grande. "You have sinned away your days of grace," Reese told the others. "What was courage and wisdom on the Río Grande would be madness and weakness here."[2] Cameron was becoming more than a little annoyed by Reese's persistent objections. He had warned him the night before to say no more on the subject, and now declared that "The break will be made this morning if I have to make it all alone and single-handed."[3] By this time most of the Texans had become suspicious of Reese, and there were rumors that he had already tried to alert the Mexican guards of Cameron's plans. Some accused him of cowardice; others believed he had escape plans of his own which he felt would be compromised if the entire body of prisoners rose up against the guard.[4]

This discussion was cut short when Colonel Barragán, earlier than usual, stepped through the doorway. With him were a few soldiers, who carried large urns of boiled rice into the center of the courtyard. The Texans made no move toward their meal, waiting for the signal from Cameron, but the big Scot remained immobile. There had not been enough time to inform all the men of the plan; some were still asleep. Barragán surveyed his charges for a moment. If the Mexican colonel noticed the prisoners' change of mood, the palpable tension that filled the yard, he gave no indication of it. He turned and walked back to the main house. The opportunity was lost.

Minutes later, Green, Fisher, and their small retinue emerged from the hacienda and rode off under a heavy cavalry escort. Some of the men interpreted this as a sign that Barragán had indeed been informed of the escape attempt, and had ordered Green and Fisher to leave ahead of the main body, assuming the Texans would not attempt a break without their officers. A few now urged Cameron to wait for another opportunity to present itself, perhaps during the night at the next encampment.

Reese's objections notwithstanding, the odds against effecting an escape at this point were not insurmountable. Green had learned, and no doubt passed this information on to the others the night before, that the main garrison of the Army of the North had been transferred from San Fernando de Rosas to Guerrero, farther south, leaving the roads leading to the northern towns along the Río Grande unprotected should the Texans decide to hazard an escape.[5] Barragán had only 100 infantry and the same number of cavalry to guard 209 prisoners, a force considerably smaller than that which had escorted the Texans under Colonel Canales.[6] Most important, in terms of the immediate success of their plan, Barragán's men had stacked their muskets just outside the corral in which the Texans were confined;[7] only two guards at the door stood between them and the means to overpower their Mexican captors. Whether it was these factors or the simple desire for freedom at any price which weighed in their decision, the overwhelming majority opted to join with Cameron in making a bid to escape that morning.

The men began to congregate around the pots of boiled rice. Cameron and Walker dipped their hollowed-out gourds into the pots and moved toward the doorway. In the outer enclosure the Mexican soldiers were preoccupied with breakfast. Of the events that followed, Big Foot Wallace later recalled: "We anxiously waited for the concerted signal from

[Cameron], and when it was given a 'yell was raised' that might have been heard for miles, and out we poured from our dens like a pack of ravenous wolves."[8] Cameron lunged for the soldier standing outside to the left of the doorway. Walker followed, wrestling the second guard to the ground, and the corral erupted as all the prisoners charged into the courtyard as quickly as the narrow doorway would allow. Startled infantrymen looked up from their breakfast to see the Texans racing pell-mell toward them and the guns nearby. Mexican soldiers were knocked to the ground and trampled in the mad rush. One Texan, wielding a slingshot fashioned from a coat sleeve, one end weighted with a stone, hurled it over his head and brought it down upon the skull of one of the guards.[9] Another tried to wrest a musket from the grasp of a Mexican soldier. The gun discharged, wounding the Texan in the hand and setting his clothes afire.[10] As more prisoners reached for the muskets, the Mexican soldiers, unable to stop the stampede, turned and ran. In a matter of seconds the yard was cleared of Red Caps. Two lay dead, a few were captured, and most had fled into the chaparral or the large buildings adjoining the corral. It had all happened so quickly that many Texans were still in the courtyard, jostling and pushing their way outside.

Beyond the enclosures Mexican officers tried desperately to rally their men. They managed to form a line behind the outer wall, which soon gave way as the Texans pushed forward. Big Foot Wallace charged into the fray with a bayonet he had yanked from an infantryman's musket.[11] Next to Samuel Walker a man dropped to his knees, the fragments of a musket ball lodged in his left eye.[12] Most of the Texans were now armed, while the others grabbed rocks and jammed them into the loopholes from which the Mexicans were firing. For the Texans, the prospect of freedom and the desire for revenge were two highly combustible elements that combined to produce an explosion of rage which swept all before it. Five minutes after Cameron threw his hat into the air the Salado lay abandoned by the Mexican guard.

Fisher and Green were less than a mile from the Salado when the break was made. Upon hearing the first shots, Captain Germán Romano, the officer in charge, halted the party. It was clear to both Mexicans and Texans that the prisoners were getting the better of the contest at the Hacienda del Salado. Men, women, children, infantry, and cavalry could be seen streaming from the buildings in a cloud of dust. Quickly Romano ordered them on from the scene at full gallop, with cavalry lances pointed at his prisoners should they have similar thoughts of escape. After going a few hundred yards he stopped on a small knoll and ordered the Texans to dismount. They waited here as the battle raged. Slowly the sounds of gun-fire diminished, then stopped altogether.

Green and Fisher were exultant, and were cheering the success of their comrades when a Mexican lieutenant rode up to the group with orders from Colonel Barragán. According to Green, Romano was instructed to execute the prisoners immediately and come to the assistance of the soldiers back at the Salado. As the cavalrymen prepared to obey this directive, Green countered that such an order did not take precedence over Romano's earlier instructions from José María Ortega, the governor of Nuevo León, who had ordered that the Texan officers be safely escorted to Mexico City. After some hesitation, Romano accepted this argument. Sending fifteen of his twenty-five men back to the hacienda to aid Colonel Barragán, the Mexican officer hurried the Texan officers south along the road to the capital.[13]

At the Hacienda del Salado, five prisoners and five Mexican soldiers lay dead or dying. Among the Texan fatalities was Dr. Richard Brenham, one of the commissioners of the Santa Fe Expedition. Having spent six months in a Mexico City prison, Brenham had been a particularly effective advocate for an escape attempt.[14] In a letter believed to have been written by Brenham some weeks earlier, he had vowed to take desperate steps to "releas[e] myself from this painful thraldom." Haunted by a premonition "that my career is shortly to be closed," Brenham had hinted at suicide if the prisoners could not be persuaded to make a bid for freedom.[15] Captain Archibald Fitzgerald would die the following day. A former British subject and veteran of the Napoleonic Wars, Fitzgerald had been captured by General Woll in San Antonio. Sadly, unbeknown to Fitzgerald, steps had already been taken by the British minister in Mexico City to secure his release.[16]

Cameron and his men set about collecting the equipment abandoned by the Mexicans. There were ninety mules and horses, 160 muskets and carbines, a dozen swords and pistols, and three mule-loads of ammunition—as well as $1,400 in silver coin. It was later reported in Mexico City that one of Barragán's men killed at the Salado was an officer, shot in cold blood after surrendering to the prisoners.[17] The Texans claimed that although there were some whose bloodlust was not yet satisfied and who wanted to kill their Mexican captives, their officers intervened, arguing that a massacre would seal the fate of the wounded Texans, who would have to be left behind.[18] Unable to join the escape, they would be at the mercy of Barragán's troops, who would soon be returning to the ranch.

By ten o'clock the Texans had buried their dead and were ready to begin their march homeward. The wounded were left in the care of Captain Reese and some twenty others, some of whom had refused to take part in the escape, pinning their hopes on an early release, while others, like Norman Woods, wanted to join Cameron but were too sick to undertake the long march home.[19] Cameron's men had only just left the Salado when Colonel Barragán came up on the road with a handful of cavalry. Speaking through an interpreter, the Mexican commander requested permission to approach. He was in no position to prevent the escape, the bulk of his force having fled in all directions, but Barragán nonetheless tried to convince Cameron that escape was futile, and guaranteed the Texans fair treatment if they would return peacefully to the ranch. Cameron heard Barragán out before declining the offer, and he and his men filed past, along the road to Saltillo, leaving the hapless Mexican officer to ponder his fate. But they had not seen the last of him. As the little army made its way north, Barragán and his cavalrymen were never far behind, always in view, waiting for the chance to alert other troops that would soon be dispatched to the vicinity as news of the escape spread.

The Texans soon left the Hacienda del Salado far behind them. They took turns riding the horses and mules, stopping only once that night at a house where they had camped with their Mexican guard two evenings before. After resting and feeding their mounts they were on the march again, and by daybreak had covered a remarkable distance of almost seventy miles.

But news of the escape was traveling with even greater speed. Approaching a farmhouse to obtain food and water, they found it occupied by Mexican soldiers and cavalry. Seeing the windows bristling with muskets, Cameron ordered his men to ride on. The Mexicans showed no inclination to come out of the ranch and pursue the Texans, and instead fired a volley at them, meant more as a warning than as an attempt to inflict casualties, for they were well out of range.[20]

The next morning, with a Mexican who had wandered into camp the night before acting as their guide, the Texans proceeded west until they struck the Monclova Road, where they turned north toward the Río Grande. Along the way they met an Englishman, who was able to provide them with interesting information concerning troop movements in the area.[21] At the moment, he assured them, their well-armed force was the strongest between Saltillo and the river. General Francisco Mejía, the governor of Coahuila, was assembling the local militia and intended to lead the manhunt himself, but he would not move until he had mustered a force large enough to meet the Texans. If Cameron marched his men speedily along the Monclova Road they would be several days in advance of Mejía or the army regulars. Their journey would then be a quick and relatively easy one to the Río Grande.[22]

But the English traveler was evidently unaware of the furious activity on the part of Mexican authorities to block the Texan escape. Mejía had learned of the break at Hacienda del Salado in the early morning hours of February 12. He immediately dispatched an express rider to Monterrey to inform Governor Ortega of the news, and set off with a handful of men for Venadito, a small ranch located on the Monclova Road, to intercept the Texans as they headed north. Mejía arrived at Venadito at eleven o'clock the next day and, after the arrival of more troops that evening, ordered spies to locate the Texans and observe their movements. In the days that followed, more soldiers and *rancheros* joined the search, providing Mejía with enough manpower to send squadrons across the state of Coahuila to cover all possible exits from the mountains. Governor Ortega would join Mejía on February 16, by which time the Mexican forces totaled 750 men.[23]

After the Englishman departed, the Texans continued along the Monclova Road, but it was not long before Captain John G. W. Pierson and several others began to doubt the wisdom of his advice. Pierson was convinced that the Englishman's assistance was a ruse to lead them into the hands of the Mexicans. There were others who, having marched through these same mountains during the Federalist War in the spring of 1840, also believed that a course through the mountains would lead them safely back to Texas. Cameron resisted their demands to leave the road, and kept to the route suggested by the English traveler. But by midnight their vigorous protests could not be ignored. Cameron, the hero of the hour not long before, found like Somervell and Fisher before him that his status as commanding officer counted for little to those intent on going their own way. Pierson declared that he was going into the mountains with his company, and any who chose to follow him could do so. Seeing that the majority sided with Pierson, and that, divided, they would have no chance against any sizable Mexican force, Cameron reluctantly agreed, although he intended to lead the army back onto the road later the next day. The Texans left the trail and headed into the mountains to camp for the night.[24] Of all the blunders, all the errors of judgment, all the simple downright bad luck of this ill-starred expedition, this was to prove the costliest mistake of all.

AT DAYBREAK THE Texans left the valley and began their ascent up the Sierra de la Paila. Bleak and forbidding, the mountains were entirely bar-

ren in this or any other season of the year, the brown slopes dotted only
with scrub bushes that offered neither shelter nor sustenance. The day
was a tedious and fatiguing one as the soldiers climbed high up into the
mountains, picking their way along the cliffs. Not a spring or waterhole
could they find anywhere, though channels of water had at one time
ploughed gullies, now dry, down into the valley below. They were soon
forced to deal with steep walls of granite that made the trek slow and
hazardous; often the horses and mules could only be made to maneuver
along the jagged rocks with a great deal of difficulty, and many were
lamed in the process. At the foot of one of these ledges the men made
camp for the night. Exhausted and too weak to give vent to their frustration that choice, not chance, had brought them here, they soon fell asleep,
while horses and mules wandered nearby to search the flinty soil in vain
for forage.[25]

When the sun came up over the mountains the next morning, it was
clear to everyone that the pack animals would have to be abandoned. Already valuable time had been lost bringing them this far into the mountains. To make matters worse, the previous day's march had led the Texans far from the road, and they were unable at this point to rejoin it.
While a scouting party went in search of water, the men began to prepare
for their journey. The mules and horses were rounded up and slaughtered, a task all the more unpleasant because each had to be killed with a
knife thrust to the heart to save ammunition. As one animal after another
slumped to the ground, more than a few men put their gourds to the
wounds and drank the blood of the animals for relief. The flesh was
stripped and roasted over small brush fires, for there was no timber to be
found anywhere. Those men whose shoes had fallen apart fashioned
crude sandals from the saddles. Here, also, the silver was divided up, with
each man receiving a share of seven dollars.[26] Most of the day was spent
preparing for the march ahead. "The scene here was awfully grand,"
Samuel Walker wrote in his diary, "so much so that language cannot fully
describe it. It presented a map of destruction and a set of men reduced to
the necessity of eating mules and horse flesh apparently in fine spirits &
willing to endure any hardships & make any sacrifice to regain their
liberty."[27]

Discovering a stagnant pool of brackish water in a basin two miles below, the men trudged down to the spot and filled their gourds. Not until
late afternoon was the group ready to resume its march. The Texans
clambered up a steep slope, the trek on foot made all the more difficult
with the added burdens of equipment and saddlebags. When they reached
the crest they looked down upon a range of mountains, each as barren

and as dry as the one on which they stood. Behind them, the basin where they had made camp could be seen below, littered with the carcasses of their animals. Encircled by jagged rock, it resembled a smoldering volcano, as thin columns of smoke from dying campfires curled skyward. Before them, "as far as the eye could reach, mountain after mountain, rose up, rough, rugged and broken, and the total absence of vegetation too surely indicated that no water was to be found in the parched-up valleys that lay between them."[28]

The soldiers grew increasingly discouraged as the day wore on. Weak and malnourished after six weeks of forced marches and inadequate food, they succumbed easily to fatigue. Even captivity now seemed preferable to such hardship. Three men abandoned the group after only a few hours' march, despite much urging from their friends, choosing instead to nurse their blistered feet in the rugged hills until their Mexican pursuers caught up with them.

Cameron and his men camped in a deep, heavily wooded ravine late that night, having covered by their reckoning some twenty miles. When they broke camp at dawn on February 16, two more soldiers were unable to continue. The group left them and followed the ridge of a mountain, and soon there were others, having come so far and endured so much, who began to fall by the wayside. By twelve o'clock three more men had dropped their packs and waved their companions on.[29]

But it was the absence of water, far more than the rigors of the march, which had begun to take the greatest toll. With their gourds empty once again, the men had been without water for twenty-four hours. It was dusk when the expedition found a trail winding through a narrow valley hedged by thickets of small pines. Many trees had been cut and hauled away, a sign that there were settlements nearby. But the Texans wandered on without seeing another living soul—or a drop of water. They had a little horse and mule meat left, but their throats were too dry to swallow it. They could not think of food in any case. The pangs of hunger were intermittent, a minor irritation compared to the searing pain brought on by thirst. Their tongues cleaved to the roofs of their mouths, tender and painful to the slightest touch; they would begin to swell up and turn black in another day or two. Their thirst was now so unbearable that few could sleep, and with the first rays of light they were on their way again.[30]

There was no longer any talk of reaching the Río Grande. Cameron and his captains agreed to split into groups and head in different directions to search for water. Cameron took the largest group of seventy men into the valley, while the others struck out into the mountains on either side, with instructions to alert the others with a smoke signal if water was found. The little groups set out on their own, growing more discouraged with each passing mile. It was not long before men dropped their rifles and packs on the ground and stumbled on. If they found clumps of palmetto or prickly pear, they tore the leaves from the ground and greedily chewed at the roots, but although the bitter juice moistened their tongues, it only made them nauseous and did nothing to alleviate their thirst.[31]

When darkness fell, no attention was given to where they should camp for the night. No campfires were built and no sentries were posted—it was just too much effort. None spoke, for parched and swollen tongues made speech impossible. Squad captains no longer gave orders; soldiers would not have obeyed them anyway. Each man curled up on a piece of earth, alone in his misery, haunted by refreshing visions of rippling brooks and streams that vanished as he knelt down to drink from them.[32]

Twenty-six-year-old John Alexander slept fitfully, dreaming that he was back home in Brazoria County at a great banquet with family and friends. All kinds of meats and vegetables were set before him but he pushed them aside. "I craved water, only water," he would later write, "and when this was forthcoming I emptied each jar as it was brought to me and called for more. Each draught seemed to inflame my thirst, and yet no one of the vast company seemed astonished at the amount of water I drank. My thirst was unquenchable."[33] This was Alexander's fourth day without water. When he awoke he dragged himself down the mountainside, almost oblivious to the sights and sounds around him, until suddenly he and his companions came upon a waterfall gushing from an outcropping of rock, which fed into a mountain stream. Here they spent the rest of the day, bathing and drinking and eating the horse meat, now spoiled, which they had left.[34]

Claudius Buster and John Toops, two stragglers from Cameron's main party, wandered off from the group and never found it again. They were lucky enough to find a rock filled with rainwater which enabled them to push on a little longer, but they were still too weak to go far, drifting into sleep each time they stopped for rest. They might have perished had they not happened upon an ox munching on scrub bushes on the mountainside. With the musket Buster had taken back at the Salado they killed the animal, drinking its blood before attempting to cut it open. The sharpest tool they owned was the flint of Buster's musket, and with this they succeeded, with some difficulty, in cutting through the animal's thick hide. The flesh proved too tough to penetrate, however, and they had to settle for a meal of roasted liver. By this time the two men were far from the main trails, and found that the inhabitants of the isolated ranches treated them with kindness and hospitality. With their share of the silver the two Texans purchased food and supplies, and continued to move in the direction of Laredo.[35]

The others were not so fortunate. The weather had turned oppressively warm during the day, adding to their suffering. Some, unable to move, threw their blankets on scrub bushes and crawled beneath them to wait for deliverance or death, indifferent to either fate. A few men scratched up the soil with their fingernails, wallowed like hogs in the cool dirt, and applied it to their inflamed mouths. Finally, they drank their own urine. Those who still had the strength staggered on as best they could.[36]

Well before dawn on February 18, the Mexicans abandoned their camp at Venadito, having learned from their spies that the Texans were coming down from the Sierra de la Paila into the Cañón de San Marcos. Leaving Ortega to establish a base of operations at nearby Boca de los Tres Ríos, twenty miles to the north, Mejía headed northwest with more than one hundred men. At the entrance of the canyon, Mejía came upon a dozen Texans who had gone in search of water. Too weak to resist, they promptly surrendered.[37]

That evening Cameron's party, which had by now dwindled to some fifty skeleton soldiers, spotted a thick funnel of smoke, which they believed to be a signal fire. Proceeding toward it, they discovered too late that they had stumbled into the Mexican camp. Despite their wretched condition, they insisted on the right to negotiate the terms of their surrender, offering to lay down the few weapons they still had if Mejía would treat them as prisoners of war. Although the Texan and Mexican accounts vary as to whether Mejía accepted these conditions, Cameron's men surrendered, and received their first taste of water.[38] The water was administered sparingly, for the Mexicans had but little themselves, a small drink measured out from a gourd for each man.[39] The next morning, the Texans marched twelve miles to Boca de los Tres Ríos. As leader of the escape, Cameron received close attention from his captors. His hands bound securely behind his back, he was kept apart from his men and guarded separately; on the trek to Ortega's camp Cameron and his guards marched two hundred yards in advance of the other prisoners.[40] Most of Cameron's men were unable to walk, and the Mexican cavalrymen were obliged to dismount and throw them across their saddles. At Boca de los Tres Ríos they rejoined Samuel Walker and his party, who had given themselves up earlier in the day.[41]

The Texans waited at Boca de los Tres Ríos until February 22, while the Mexican cavalry scoured the countryside. One by one and in small groups, the Texans were rounded up and brought in. Every exposed limb bore the marks of deep lacerations, but cactus spikes and rocks could draw little blood from bodies so dehydrated. Some were without hats or shoes, their clothing little more than rags. Big Foot Wallace described the Texans as they came into camp: "Our beards were rough and unshaven, and our matted and uncombed locks hung down in 'swads' around our faces, pinched and sharpened by long abstinence from food and water, from out of which our sunken hollow eyes glared with a wild and demoniac expression."[42]

The Mexicans slaughtered several head of cattle at the camp and cut the hides into strips with which to bind the prisoners in pairs. The paunches of the cattle, turned inside out, served as water vessels. While the Texans hardly needed to be bound, they were treated well and were given plenty of beef and corn to eat. After two men who had been allowed to drink their fill died a few hours later, the Mexican soldiers were careful to dole out small quantities of water for the prisoners until their strength returned.[43]

Buster and Toops made slow but steady progress by keeping away from the mountain trails that swarmed with cavalry. Finally they came down from the mountains and crossed the chaparral between the Sierra Madre and the Río Grande. Food and water were no less scarce here, but they moved quickly across the open prairie. Four days later they were standing on the west bank of the river. Proceeding along the river road in search of food before making the crossing, they came upon a deserted ranch house. In the corral they found the warm ashes of a campfire and scraps of beef and bones, signs that Mexican soldiers had been there only hours before. The two men built a fire and made a meal of the leftovers, but their dinner was interrupted by the rumble of horses: ten Mexican cavalrymen had spotted them and were galloping toward the ranch.[44]

After resting at their waterfall for a day, John Alexander and the others in his party headed north. They seem to have made no attempt to build a signal fire to notify Cameron of their discovery (Alexander makes no mention of it in his account of the episode), apparently believing that Cameron had changed course and headed for a mountain pass that lay to the northeast.[45] During the next few days they made little progress, and one by one the men in the group wandered off on their own in search of water, until only Alexander and Major George Oldham remained. They became fast friends and made a pledge to stay together. Along the way Oldham found a beehive and was stung repeatedly when he tried to scoop out the honey with his bayonet. It was some time before he was well enough to move on again, and not long afterward it was Alexander who fell ill, wracked by fever. Oldham cared for him, serving up a special broth of herbs for his friend to drink. At last the fever broke, and they pressed on.

When they reached the bank of the Río Grande, they dismantled an old stock pen, built a raft of the wooden poles, and floated safely across. Their troubles were not yet over, for by this time the citizens of Laredo had gotten word of the escape and were on the lookout for the men who had ransacked their homes. The pair skirted the town and by hiding in the bushes were able to avoid capture by the local militia. It was not until mid-April, nearly two months after winning their freedom at the Hacienda del Salado, that John Alexander and Major Oldham hobbled into San Antonio, their long ordeal finally over.[46]

In the meantime, the people of Texas had learned of the escape of the Mier prisoners at the Salado, but further details about their trek through the mountains were based more on wishful thinking than accurate information. According to one account, the Texans had marched quickly to the Río Grande and captured the town of Camargo after a fierce battle with local Mexican troops. Another version reported that the Texans had failed to capture the town but in their weakened condition had still managed to kill "seven or eight hundred" Mexicans while sustaining only slight casualties. Captain Cameron had avoided capture and was now said to be marching with well over one hundred men into Apache country.[47]

It would be several weeks before Texans would learn the sad truth of the fate of the Mier prisoners. After three days the Mexican officers called off the pursuit, although fifty escapees were still at large. The prisoners were now marched south back to Saltillo, a six-day journey. Along the way more Texans rejoined their comrades. Some had traveled as far as the Río Grande, but during the next few weeks all but a handful would be recaptured. Only four men were known to have reached Texas. Eight others were believed to have perished in the mountains.[48]

Fearing another escape attempt, the guards beat a number of the men severely for untying the leather thongs that chafed their wrists. The straps were eventually replaced with iron handcuffs, and at each ranch or waterhole where they camped for the night the prisoners were ordered to sit or lie in the dirt, not allowed to stand without permission. Such precautions were unnecessary, as many were still so enfeebled that they needed mules to carry them on the day's march.

On March 1 the prisoners arrived on the outskirts of Saltillo. Here they waited for several hours for General Mejía to arrive before making their entrance into the city.[49] After capturing Cameron's men, Mejía had marched to Cuatrociénegas in search of more prisoners, and wanted the privilege of escorting his captives into the city, where another parade had been organized to greet them.⁵⁰ A short, stocky, handsome man, the governor of Coahuila was described by one American traveler as "a very clever, gentlemanly and rather polished sort of fellow."⁵¹ Mejía did not have long to enjoy his moment of victory. By this time, word of the escape at the Salado had reached Mexico City. Since October Santa Anna had been in semi-retirement at his estate near Veracruz, having left the day-to-day business of the capital in the hands of General Nicolás Bravo. When the news of the escape and the subsequent recapture of the Mier men reached Mexico City, Bravo sent word to Saltillo that all the prisoners were to be executed. Mejía refused to carry out the edict, and promptly resigned.⁵²

Mejía's action would have bought the Texans no more than a few extra days of life had he been alone in his concern for their welfare. Before the order to execute all the Texans could be enforced, however, Waddy Thompson and Richard Pakenham, the U.S. and British ministers in Mexico City, learned of the escape. Technically, the men were no longer American citizens, but since their relatives back home had petitioned the United States government to intercede on their behalf, their plight had become a major concern for Thompson. He had already helped to gain the release of the Santa Fe prisoners and was presently working to aid those captured by General Woll in San Antonio. Now, upon hearing of the recapture of Cameron and his men, he decided to call on José María de Bocanegra, the Mexican foreign minister.

The American minister to Mexico had been at his job for one year. At the time of his appointment, he seemed an astonishing choice; few men seemed less likely to foster amicable relations between the United States and Mexico. The former South Carolina congressman was a well known and outspoken advocate for Texas and the extension of slavery. In 1836 he had played a large role in bringing about the U.S. recognition of Texas independence, which he saw as the first step toward annexation. A minister to Mexico who advocated nothing less than the dismemberment of that country could hardly expect a warm reception. By all indications Thompson would make himself persona non grata in the capital the moment he arrived.

But Thompson proved to be a pleasant surprise for the Mexican government. Unlike many members of the American diplomatic corps, Thompson did not share the typical Anglo-Saxon's haughty disregard for cultures different from his own. After his confirmation by the Senate he began to spend his spare time studying Spanish, learning enough to make himself understood by the time he reached Veracruz. He quickly became quite fluent, and was able to deal with Mexican officials without the aid of interpreters. In time he developed a high regard for the Mexican people, and his firm position on annexation seemed to soften as he came to appreciate the Mexican point of view on this sensitive issue. He managed to maintain a good working relationship with Mexico's leaders, and if they did not always agree and were frequently at odds, there was at all times an easy dialogue that was often absent when less capable ministers represented American interests in the Mexican capital.[53]

In spite of Thompson's good intentions, a number of problems soon arose to test both his patience and his diplomatic skill. Relations between the two countries were never good—they had almost gone to war in the 1830s over the issue of Mexico's unpaid claims—and were certain to deteriorate still further now that Americans were looking westward, eager to expand their empire. Mexico, of course, was not a little alarmed by the growing threat of U.S. expansionism. Support for the annexation of Texas, particularly in the southern states, seemed to be growing in spite of Mexico's claim that it still owned this territory. What was more, it was clear that it was not just Texas but the entire southwest which excited the American imagination. Mexico's hold over this vast desert was tenuous; there were perhaps no more than fifteen thousand Mexicans living above the Río Grande. Many Americans believed that it was only a matter of time before their country took title to the property—as long as Great Britain did not grab it first. In the past, Mexico had always been able to count on the northern antislavery forces in Congress to block this westward push. But as Manifest Destiny gained momentum, it transcended sectional lines, firing the heart and quickening the pulse of Americans everywhere.

Although the U.S. government insisted it had no expansionist designs, Mexican leaders remained unconvinced, particularly in the aftermath of the seizure of Monterey, California, by Commodore Jones. Although it continued to maintain a strictly neutral posture in the ongoing struggle between Mexico and Texas, Washington was likewise embarrassed by Americans, especially those in the southern states, who made no secret of their sympathies with their neighbors across the Sabine. Mexico complained bitterly that Texas was supplied with volunteers, money, and arms from the United States. Secretary of State Webster could only reply that these were the efforts of private citizens, which his government was powerless to prevent.[54]

The dust kicked up by the Jones affair had not yet settled when Thompson paid his visit to Foreign Minister Bocanegra. This may not have been a very good time to ask a favor of the Mexican government, which was, in any case, becoming increasingly exasperated with Thompson for his efforts to aid Americans who marched into Mexico under the Texas flag. When Thompson once again insisted that the Texans be treated with clemency, the Mexican foreign minister flew into a rage. Thompson later wrote in his autobiography, *Recollections of Mexico:* "it was the only instance, in all my intercourse with him, that his conduct was not dignified and courteous." During the course of this meeting, Thompson recalled, the following dialogue occurred:

> He said to me: They are not American citizens, and you have, therefore, no right to interpose in their behalf. I replied: They are human beings and prisoners of war, and it is the right and the duty of all nations to see that Mexico does not violate the principles and the usages of civilized war—more particularly it is the duty of the United States to maintain those laws and usages on this Continent. He replied with much warmth, that Mexico would listen to no suggestion upon the subject, from any quarter. I rose from my seat, and said: Then, Sir, shoot them as soon as you choose, but let me tell you, that if you do you will at once involve in this war a much more powerful enemy than Texas—and took my leave.[55]

Thompson's protests may not have been quite so strident as this account, which was published three years after the fact, suggests, for the American minister had no wish to provoke a rift in U.S.-Mexico relations over the Texas prisoners. Thompson had recently negotiated a new payment schedule to collect from Mexico two and a half million dollars in American claims, and he did not want to do anything which might jeopardize that agreement. While the U.S. minister regarded the execution "with unmixed horror," his dispatches to the State Department stressed the need to tread lightly, and reveal his concern that the Texas problem might well undermine his efforts on behalf of his own government.[56]

British minister Richard Pakenham likewise endeavored to pressure the Mexican government to adopt a more lenient policy toward the Texan prisoners, and he had occasion to do so in an audience with Santa Anna on March 12, one week after the Mexican leader's arrival in the capital. In this interview, Pakenham found the Mexican President determined to stand by the initial decision to execute all the prisoners. The British minister pointed out that international public opinion would not look favorably upon an act of such "excessive severity," but his remarks seemed to have little effect, and the Mexican President gave him no reason to hope that the lives of the captured Texans might be spared.[57]

But the interposition of the two diplomats seems to have had a greater impact than Pakenham realized, apparently prompting the Mexican President to reconsider the edict. Up to this point the Texans had been treated well, and the government could not be criticized for its handling of the Mier affair. Mexico could ill afford to upset relations with its powerful northern neighbor, particularly at a time when annexation sentiment was gaining ground and Americans appeared to be looking for any excuse to take California. Santa Anna knew that American sympathies lay with Texas, and he had to be careful to do nothing that might further strengthen the ties between the two countries. Nor was the Mexican President unmindful of the need to maintain good relations with Her Majesty's government, which Santa Anna was counting on to take an aggressive stand against American expansionism in the region. A brutal response to the escape attempt, therefore, would do Mexico's cause little good.

These arguments aside, the deaths of the five Mexican soldiers at the Hacienda del Salado, Santa Anna believed, demanded some sort of retribution, and on March 13, the day after his meeting with Pakenham, he issued new orders: only one out of every ten prisoners would be shot.[58] The prisoners would draw lots to determine their fate. The *diezmo* was a common enough form of martial punishment in Mexico and had, in fact, been used before with Anglo-American prisoners.[59] In Mexico City, the government pronounced the sentence "harsh but just," adding that it "serves as a warning to all those who might still dare to attempt an invasion" of Mexican territory.[60] Moreover, the government was quick to point out that the decree was in full accord with the rules of war, quoting from the work of Swiss legal scholar Emerich de Vattel to support this position. In his treatise *The Law of Nations* (which would later be used by American politicians in defense of the annexation of Texas), Vattel had argued that while all prisoners deserve to be treated with humanity, quarter may be denied in those cases when the enemy has committed "some enormous breach of the law of nations, and particularly when he has violated the laws of war." Vattel did not specify what might constitute "a crime deserving death," and indeed went on to state that in order for a punishment to "be justly inflicted, it must fall on the guilty."[61] Nonetheless, while the arbitrariness of the *diezmo* may have been shocking to Anglo sensibilities, the Mexican government took the view that the sentence was, in fact, an act of clemency, since all the prisoners who had risen up against the guard at the Salado shared the responsibility for the deaths of five Mexican soldiers.

Waddy Thompson disagreed. Although gratified that his intercession had helped to save the lives of more than 150 Texans, he was by no means satisfied with this new edict. The decimation of the Mier prisoners was "a cold-blooded and atrocious murder," he believed, and a far greater act of cruelty than the slaughter of the Alamo defenders or Fannin's troops at Goliad. They "were not on parole," he argued, "and had a perfect right to escape if they could." [62] In spite of his personal feelings, Thompson did not deem it wise to press the issue and suggested to Secretary of State Webster that if the United States wished to issue a stronger protest, it should come not from the U.S. minister to Mexico but from President Tyler himself. Quite clearly, however, Thompson hoped his government would not take the matter any further, and he pointedly advised against any action which might upset the agreement with the Mexican government to resume payments of outstanding American claims. "I do not choose to furnish this Government with any pretext for not complying with the terms of the late [claims] convention," he wrote Webster, "as the first payment and a very considerable one will fall due on the 29th instant." The hostilities between Texas and Mexico had proven to be a much more troublesome issue than Thompson had ever anticipated when he accepted the post as U.S. minister. He complained to the secretary of state: "I find that much the most painful, responsible and expensive of my duties here do not grow out of the relations of my own Country with this,—but from this Texas war." [63]

IN THE MEANTIME, the Texas officers were marching deep into Mexico. During the course of their journey they were joined by sixteen men who had refused to take part in the break with Cameron at the Hacienda del Salado. Every so often their guards were replaced by fresh troops and new officers. Some treated the men kindly, but others were eager to take advantage of them, engaging in petty swindles to rob them of what little money they had. [64] Fisher and Green found that there was a price for each of the privileges which as officers they had enjoyed while in the custody of General Ampudia. The horses provided for them at Mier were taken away. If the Texans wanted a pack mule to carry their equipment, they were obliged to hire one from the *leperos* who followed them along the route. Sometimes the thirsty prisoners were even deprived of water, or had to pay for it, for some of the Mexican officers had a special arrangement with the *pulque* vendors in the towns they passed along the way. In this manner the funds which the Texans had received from friends and benefactors in Matamoros dwindled quickly. By mid-March they reached the outskirts of Mexico City, stopping briefly at the archbishop's palace at Tacubaya, Santa Anna's suburban retreat, where they were billeted in an open courtyard on the palace grounds.

Upon their arrival at Tacubaya, the Texans received several visitors, including British minister Richard Pakenham and two men attached to the United States legation. It was from the two Americans that the Texans first learned of Houston's letter to Charles Elliot, asking the British government to intercede on their behalf. As noted earlier, Elliot had made a copy of this request and forwarded it to Pakenham, who in turn discussed its contents with Waddy Thompson. A few days later, William Reese, one of the young boys traveling with the Texas officers (and the brother of Charles Keller Reese) was allowed to go into Mexico City to meet with Thompson. During this interview Reese inquired further about the letter, perhaps at the request of Thomas Jefferson Green, who was inclined to look with a jaundiced eye upon anything connected with Sam Houston. Thompson may have been unaware of the intense hatred which many of these men held for their President, and when pressed for details, he freely related the letter's contents: how Houston conceded that the men had marched into Mexico without orders, thereby placing themselves outside the rules of war, but said that they were nonetheless entitled to proper treatment. Houston's purpose in sending the letter, as Thompson must have made clear, was to request diplomatic aid to alleviate their situation, but the prisoners chose to see it another way. Thomas Jefferson Green came to the extraordinary conclusion that this was a deliberate attempt by his old enemy to take his revenge for their insubordination. By disavowing any responsibility for their actions, Green charged, Houston was giving the Mexican government a carte blanche to mistreat them. There is no evidence that Santa Anna ever saw the letter, and even if he had, it was common knowledge that Fisher's men had invaded Mexico without the consent of Somervell, their commanding officer. But Green refused to believe otherwise. Having condemned Houston for doing all in his power to prevent an invasion of Mexico, he now condemned him for its failure.[65] If the prisoners were harmed in any way, he raged, the blame would lie with the President of Texas, and no one else.

Green's anger may well have been heightened by fears for his own safety, since it was Green who had snatched Santa Anna from a boat under sail bound for Mexico at Velasco in 1836. Green had good reason to be worried. Santa Anna had already seen a list of the prisoners and was no doubt aware that this was the same Thomas Jefferson Green who had violated the terms of surrender after the battle of San Jacinto. He had not forgotten that he had been thrown into chains, compelled to endure the taunts of an angry mob, and almost killed as a result of Green's sedition. For all Green's talk about the rights of the Texans as prisoners of war, the treatment of Santa Anna in 1836 had been less than exemplary. But the Mexican President made no effort to single Green out for a special fate. Green, Fisher, and the others would soon be on their way toward the Castle of Perote, their ultimate destination. Evidently, Santa Anna felt this was punishment enough.

FOR THREE WEEKS Cameron's men languished in their old quarters in the Saltillo jail. Occasionally a prisoner who had managed to elude capture would be reunited with the others, and he would add new anecdotes to a story that always had the same unfortunate end. The conditions in the Saltillo jail, as before, were poor indeed. The Texans petitioned the new governor, José Juan Sánchez, for extra rations; in addition to their one meal per day they now received bread and coffee in the evening. Sleeping without blankets on a cold floor, one young soldier contracted pneumonia and became deathly ill. When visited by a local *padre*, he refused to be baptized. Had he accepted the Catholic faith, some of the men believed, he would have received the medical attention he needed, but he was left in his worsening condition and died soon afterward. Three days after his body was removed, five sick prisoners summoned a priest and received the sacraments. If their purpose was to gain favor with the Mexicans, they were disappointed. Their conversion brought them no special treatment, but it did earn them the lasting censure of the other Texans.[66]

Special army hearings were now being held to investigate the circumstances of the break at the Hacienda del Salado. Alfred Thurmond, who served as interpreter, and two other men who spoke Spanish were brought before the committee and grilled for two days. The presiding officer would later report that the governor of Nuevo León had been guilty of negligence by providing an escort for the prisoners that was insufficient and untrained. The report also concluded that Colonel Barragán's failure to maintain discipline among his troops was in part responsible for the escape. Barragán was relieved of his duties shortly thereafter.[67]

In Saltillo, a new officer, Colonel Juan D. Ortiz, was ordered to march the Texans south with a cavalry unit and a company of regular infantry which had been brought up from the garrison at San Luis Potosí. The march began as before, along the same route toward the Salado. Two days after leaving Saltillo the handcuffs of all the prisoners were examined. The sick had been allowed to march without irons, but now they too were manacled.[68] Some of the Texans saw ominous signs in the extra security measures, convinced that some action would be taken to punish them for the escape and for the Mexican soldiers killed at the Salado. Others saw little cause for concern. By now they had heard of Mejía's defiance of the execution order, and since there had been no word overruling the governor's decision they no longer feared a firing squad. Ortiz allayed the fears of many; along the way he cheerfully told his charges to walk briskly, for the sooner they arrived in Mexico City, the sooner they would be liberated and sent home. Later, when he saw that the prisoners were bothered by the dust kicked into their faces by the horses alongside them, the colonel ordered his cavalrymen to fall back to the rear.[69]

On March 25 the prisoners marched a short distance back to the Salado. The weather was clear and warm that day, but as they neared the ranch in mid-afternoon a sandstorm came up. The sky suddenly became dark and the wind howled down the plain as the Salado, which had been in sight only seconds before, vanished in a sheet of dust. They braced themselves as the storm hit, blasting their faces with such fury that they could only see a few feet in front of them. Each prisoner tightly clenched his hat with his one free hand, leaned into the wind, and slouched forward to the Salado.[70]

As they entered the ranch, the prisoners noticed that it was already occupied by a company of thirty Mexican infantrymen.[71] To escape the fury of the storm, the Texans quickly sought refuge under an open shed which ran alongside the outer wall of the enclosure where they had earlier been confined. Once they were underneath the shelter, the wind began to die down. Just as abruptly as it had begun, the storm was over and the dust settled to earth.

Shortly after their arrival, Colonel Domingo Huerta, who had been ordered to carry out the execution, summoned the prisoners out into the courtyard.[72] Above them, on the walls of the enclosure, stood a number of infantrymen. Alfred Thurmond was called to the front of the group to interpret as the officer read from a dispatch in his hand. They huddled closer, some expectantly believing that this was the order for their release. When Thurmond announced to them that one out of every ten men was to be executed, the initial reaction was one of mute disbelief. "So entirely unexpected was this murderous announcement," said one, "that a stupor seemed to pervade the whole assembly, not a word escaping from the lips of any for more than a minute."[73] But all at once some of the men let loose shouts of rage and tried to free themselves. The guards came at the

Texans with their musket butts, pushing and shoving them back inside the shed. Seeing that any attempt at resistance was useless, the prisoners quietly submitted to their fate.[74]

Minutes later two Mexican subalterns entered the yard carrying a bench and an earthen pot. The Texans were marshaled out of the shack and ordered to line up, as Huerta poured 159 white beans into the pot. On top of these he poured 17 fatal black ones, and shook the jar gently. Many Texans thought they noticed that the black beans were not evenly mixed with the white, which they interpreted as an effort to cause the officers, who were called first, to draw the fatal beans on top. A white handkerchief was placed over the jar to cover the color of the beans.

As the leader of the escape, Ewen Cameron was the first called forward. Cameron thrust his hand down to the bottom of the jar and pulled out a white bean. He reportedly called out "Dip deep, boys," as he stepped back into line.[75] The other captains followed. All drew white beans except Captain Eastland.

The rest of the men were now called forward to take their turns in the lottery. As each man drew, his bean was handed to the officer, who entered the name and color of the bean on a list. If the color was black, Colonel Huerta tucked it away in his vest pocket. If white, it was left on the bench. The bowl was then shaken, and the next man called forward.[76] One prisoner recalled: "During this scene which was sufficient to test the fortitude of the men, they were perfectly composed, and apparently indifferent as to the results when they went to the jar to decide whether it was life or death to them. There was no shout of gladness or marked change of countenance by those that fortune favored, and those more unfortunate appeared to exhibit the same composure; there were several Mexican officers much affected by the scene they were witnessing, there is but little doubt would have rejoiced could it have been countermanded."[77] Another prisoner recalled, "Several of the Mexican officers seemed deeply affected, shedding tears profusely, and turning their backs upon the murderous spectacle. Others again leaned forward over the crock, to catch a first glimpse of the decree it uttered, as though they had heavy wagers upon the result."[78]

Big Foot Wallace related that there was but one exception to the stoicism with which the Texans met their fate. One prisoner, overcome with emotion, was "wringing his hands and moaning audibly, and continually telling those near him that he should draw a black bean." When his name was called he stood rooted to the ground, unable to step forward, until the guards shoved him and the man to which he was chained up to the table. Two soldiers forced his hand into the jar, and he was told that if he drew more than one bean he would be executed with the others. "At last the poor fellow was forced to withdraw his hand, and his presentiment proved too true, for in it he held the fatal black bean. He turned deadly pale as his eyes rested upon it, but apparently he soon resigned himself to his inevitable fate, for he never uttered a word of complaint afterward. I pitied him from the bottom of my heart."[79] As for Wallace himself, he had been watching the proceedings intently, and it seemed to him that the black beans were larger than the white. When called forward he dipped his hand into the jar, scooped up a handful of beans and rolled them with his fingers, determined to find the very smallest of the ones left. Withdrawing his hand, he held out a bean that looked neither black nor white but an indeterminable grayish color. Huerta took it from him, examined it, and judged it to be white.[80]

When all seventeen black beans were drawn, the manacles of the victims were knocked off and they were separated from the group and taken to a courtyard on the opposite side of the wall. A few others were allowed to accompany the condemned men. Henry Whaling, described by his friend George Washington Trahern as "full of hell and jolly as could be," insisted on a last meal.[81] The Mexican cooks served up a meal of mutton stew and beans, and all the condemned men were given double rations. Few could eat except Whaling, whose appetite was unaffected by his predicament. "I'm going to take a good square meal," he said. "It's the last I'll get."[82] After gorging himself he called for a cigar, and this too was given him. Others called for pen and paper to compose letters to their families. Robert Dunham scribbled this terse and poignant message:

Dear Mother,

I write to you under the most awful feelings that a son ever addressed a mother for in half an hour my doom will be finished on earth for I am doomed to die by the hands of the Mexicans for our late attempt to escape. . . . [It was ordered] by Santa Anna that every tenth man should be shot we drew lots. I was one of the unfortunate. I cannot say anything more I die I hope with firmness may god bless you, and may he in this last hour forgive and pardon all my sins . . . farewell.

Your affectionate sone, [sic]

R. H. Dunham[83]

A priest who had accompanied the men on the march from Saltillo was present to sprinkle holy water on the ground and administer last rites; only two availed themselves of absolution. "I confess not to man but my God," Dunham said.[84] He was asked by the men to give a prayer, but a Mexican guard prevented him from doing so. They knelt in the dust and prayed silently.

There were now only a few minutes of daylight left. A log had been positioned along the outer wall of the corral. Nine of the condemned men took their seats upon it, blindfolded, facing their executioners. The remaining eight waited inside the house. The main body of Texans was kept under heavy guard on the other side of the wall, only a few feet away. William Preston Stapp gave the following account of the execution as he listened from the courtyard:

> *The wall against which the condemned were placed, was so near us we could distinctly hear every order given, in halting and arranging the command for the work of death. The murmured prayers of the kneeling men, stole faintly over to us—then came the silence that succeeded, more eloquent than sound—then the signal taps of the drum—the rattle of muskets, as they were brought to aim—the sharp burst of the discharge, mingled with the shrill cries of anguish and heavy groans of the dying, as soul and body took their sudden and bloody leave.*[85]

Another volley followed, then another. The execution was clumsily done. The firing continued for several minutes, a series of volleys being needed to dispatch the victims. A few soldiers positioned on the wall turned to witness the execution. One fainted, dropped his gun, and was grabbed by the others before he fell off the wall. When at last the victims had ceased to stir, their bodies were stacked against the wall, and the remaining eight men were brought out to take their places on the log. After each blast of musket fire Henry Whaling could be heard cursing his executioners. Though wounded more than a dozen times, he continued to unleash a string of defiant profanities. The tirade was finally ended by Huerta, who stepped up to the wall, placed his pistol to Whaling's temple, and fired.[86]

It was now dark and the victims were left where they had fallen, to be buried the next morning. Sentries were posted to keep away the dogs and other animals that might come to gnaw on the limbs of the dead. But not all the victims had succumbed to the barrage. James L. Shepherd, seventeen years old, had somehow survived. A musket ball had ripped open his cheek and fractured his arm, but he had never lost consciousness. Later that night, when the sentries had fallen asleep, he crawled away from the scene of the execution and disappeared.

It was not until the following morning that the guards detailed to bury the bodies made the startling discovery that one was missing. Shepherd was wandering alone in the mountains, attempting to make by himself the same arduous journey that he and all the prisoners had failed to make together. Four days later Shepherd was recognized near Saltillo and handed over to the authorities. By order of Governor Juan José Sánchez he was taken beyond the town and shot.[87]

1. The Somervell and Mier Expeditions

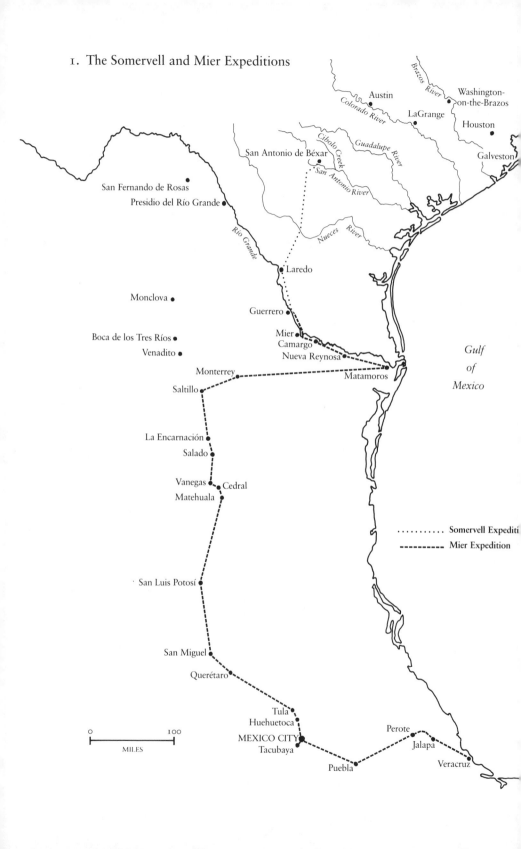

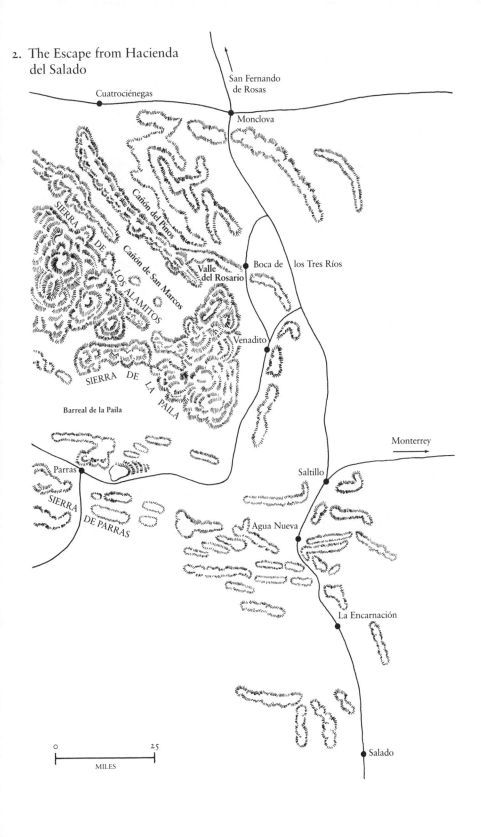

2. The Escape from Hacienda
del Salado

San Fernando
de Rosas

Cuatrociénegas

Monclova

Cañón del Pinos

SIERRA DE LOS ALAMITOS

Cañón de San Marcos

Boca de los Tres Ríos

Valle
del Rosario

Venadito

SIERRA DE LA PAILA

Barreal de la Paila

Monterrey

Parras

Saltillo

SIERRA DE PARRAS

Agua Nueva

La Encarnación

0   25
MILES

Salado

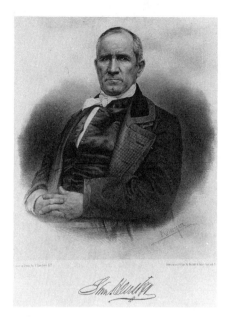

Sam Houston, President of the Republic of Texas. The University of Texas at Austin, Eugene C. Barker Texas History Center.

Antonio López de Santa Anna, President of Mexico. The University of Texas at Austin, Eugene C. Barker Texas History Center.

Thomas Jefferson Green, second-in-command of the Mier Expedition. From Green, Journal of the Texian Expedition against Mier (1845). The University of Texas at Austin, Eugene C. Barker Texas History Center.

Pedro de Ampudia, victor of the Battle of Mier. The University of Texas at Austin, Eugene C. Barker Texas History Center.

The Mier Expedition descending the Río Grande. This and other sketches by Charles McLaughlin, a Mier prisoner, first appeared in Thomas Jefferson Green's Journal of the Texian Expedition against Mier *(1845). The University of Texas at Austin, Eugene C. Barker Texas History Center.*

Killing their horses for sustenance on the Sierra de la Paila. McLaughlin sketch from Green's Journal. *The University of Texas at Austin, Eugene C. Barker Texas History Center.*

John C. C. Hill, the youngest member
of the expedition. Hill remained
in Mexico after his release and went on
to become a successful engineer.
San Jacinto Museum of History
Association.

Ewen Cameron, leader of the attack on
the guard at Hacienda del Salado. The
University of Texas at Austin, Eugene
C. Barker Texas History Center.

José María de Bocanegra, Mexican foreign minister. Courtesy Nettie Lee Benson Latin American Collection,
University of Texas at Austin.

Samuel H. Walker. Three years after his
escape from Molino del Rey, Walker
won fame for his exploits in the Mexican War. Reproduced from the Collec-
tions of the Library of Congress.

Drawing the beans at Hacienda del Salado. McLaughlin sketch from Green's Journal. *The University of Texas at Austin, Eugene C. Barker Texas History Center.*

The execution of the Black Bean victims. McLaughlin sketch from Green's Journal. *The University of Texas at Austin, Eugene C. Barker Texas History Center.*

Waddy Thompson, U.S. minister to Mexico, 1842–1844.

Wilson Shannon, U.S. minister to Mexico, 1844–1845. From United States Magazine and Democratic Review 25 *(August 1849).*

Paving the road to the Archbishop's Palace at Tacubaya. McLaughlin sketch from Green's Journal. *The University of Texas at Austin, Eugene C. Barker Texas History Center.*

Escape from the Castle of Perote. McLaughlin sketch from Green's Journal. *The University of Texas at Austin, Eugene C. Barker Texas History Center.*

8

"There Is No Hope of Release"

IN THE MORNING the Texans were assembled in the courtyard, and as they filed out of the ranch they passed the outer wall where the victims of the execution still lay, their "stiffened and unsepulchred bodies, weltering in blood . . . their rigid countenances, pallid and distorted with agony . . ."[1] The prisoners now began their long march to the capital, leaving the bleak frontier settlements behind them as they headed down into the central plateau. Although the men were still chained in pairs, conditions improved as they traveled through this more fertile, more heavily populated region of Mexico. The sick were allowed to ride in oxcarts, and the prisoners were well fed and provided comfortable quarters. They rarely slept out of doors, but spent the nights in warehouses and abandoned buildings in the towns they passed. Along the way Colonel Ortiz allowed them a day of rest and the luxury of a bath at a nearby stream. When they reached the city of San Luis Potosí, the irons which they had worn for nearly a month were removed.[2]

But the march was never an easy one, and the weak would not survive. Many were still in wretched health since their ordeal in the mountains. Five men who had never fully recovered were left in an army hospital in San Luis Potosí, where they soon died. Pleurisy claimed another on the way to Mexico City. This discouraging attrition rate may have helped to instill a sudden religious fervor in four men, who asked to be baptized in the Catholic Church. Although they were unfamiliar with the religion and had never heard a mass in their native tongue, there is no reason to doubt that this was a genuine effort to obtain some measure of spiritual comfort in their time of trial, since they were aware that their new-found faith conferred no special privileges, and the other prisoners would have nothing more to do with them. One disapproving prisoner noted that the converts "seemed extremely sanctimonious and devout after the ceremony, preserving as profound a silence, touching the mysteries of their new faith, as entered apprentices of Masonry."[3]

Their journey took them through Querétaro, San Miguel, and many other small towns. Frequently the townspeople, though beggarly poor themselves, raised small sums of money, enough perhaps for each prisoner to buy an extra plate of frijoles or a cup of pulque.[4] When they stopped in Tula, another escort was waiting to take them on the final leg of the march to Mexico City. On April 24, one month after the execution at the Salado, the Texans reached the Indian village of Huehuetoca. As they approached that evening a storm blew up, as sudden and as fierce as the one which had greeted their entry to the Salado ranch.

In the middle of the night an express rider arrived from the capital. Ewen Cameron and Alfred Thurmond were ushered into an adjoining room, where Thurmond was given another grim order to translate. Ewen Cameron was to be shot the next morning. A heavy guard was placed on him to prevent any communication with his men.

At dawn the Mexican escort pushed the Texans quickly onward, leaving Cameron and Thurmond with a contingent of cavalry. A short time after their departure Cameron was taken out behind the building and made to stand against a stone wall. The dismounted cavalry primed their *escopetas* and took aim at close range. As Thurmond later told the story after rejoining the others, Cameron refused to accept a blindfold, but bared his breast for his executioners and called on them to fire. He was struck by eight musket balls and died instantly.[5]

The Texans offered more than one explanation for Cameron's death; some believed that since only seventeen men were executed at the Salado for the punishment of 176, another victim was required to make up the balance for the decimation to be complete.[6] Others were inclined to believe that it was Colonel Canales, with his great hatred for Cameron, who requested that the Scot face a firing squad, black bean or not.[7] Neither explanation squares with the Mexican government's official version, although the Santa Anna regime was less than forthcoming about its motives for issuing this new death sentence. Percy Doyle, who had recently replaced Richard Pakenham as the senior British diplomat in Mexico City, demanded an explanation from José María de Bocanegra, but failed to receive a satisfactory answer.[8] In a subsequent conversation with Minister of War José María Tornel, however, Doyle learned that the death sentence had been carried out because Cameron had for several years been "one of the most active Partizans in the warfare going on between the two countries," and had been responsible for inciting the Texans to rise up against their guards. Tornel added that Cameron had shot the Mexican officer at the Hacienda del Salado—an allegation hotly denied by the prisoners who met with Doyle upon their arrival in Mexico City— and even suggested that the Texan had led several Indian attacks upon the Mexican frontier.[9] While Cameron may not have been guilty of all the crimes ascribed to him, certainly the Mexicans had good reason to hate the Texan leader. One of the prisoners noted that Cameron was "well known to the enemy to have been an indefatigable officer on the frontier of his country."[10] While his marauding activities against *rancheros* living below the Nueces River had won him praise in Texas, the Mexican government denounced such depredations against its own citizens. It was Cameron's notoriety as a brigand, not a soldier, coupled with his prominent role in the attack at the Hacienda del Salado, which seems to have sealed his fate.

Whatever the reason, Cameron's death was a great loss to the men who followed him. He was perhaps the only man on the Mier Expedition to emerge as a bona fide leader, which, given the unruliness of its participants, was no small accomplishment. While Fisher and Green were both men of considerable education and refinement, only Cameron, the stone-mason who could just barely read and write, typified the rank and file. Like every other military chieftain of Texas, Cameron was sometimes challenged and disobeyed, but those who had abandoned his leadership and ventured into the mountains above Saltillo sorely regretted their decision. His Nueces cowboys, who knew him best, had followed him with near-fanatical devotion for eight years. To the Texans he embodied the spirit of an untamed frontier; to the Mexicans he was a renegade who despoiled the land that was rightfully theirs. He was certainly both.

TWO DAYS LATER the prisoners entered the Valley of Mexico. On either side of the road could be seen the occasional field in cultivation, but Mexico City's environs were largely marshlands, for at one time most of the valley floor had been under water. Now the lakes upon which the Aztecs had once built their floating gardens were receding, although the city was still bordered by the shallow waters of Lake Texcoco on the east, Lake Chalco and Lake Xochimilcho to the south.

At sunset they reached the convent at Santiago Tlaltelolco, two miles from the northern *garita*, or entrance gate, to the city. Here they had a splendid view of the valley and, to the southeast, the two snow-capped volcanoes Popocatépetl and Ixtaccíhuatl. The spot where they now stood had once been the great Aztec marketplace, and it was from here that Cortés had directed his last assault upon the city. The capital of Mexico was built on a master plan that borrowed its symmetry from the Aztec builders of Tenochtitlán, with wide streets laid out along a rectangular grid. Since independence some of the public buildings and roads had fallen into disrepair, and by 1843 its population of 150,000 was only one-third that of New York City. But there was no city in the western hemisphere that could match the massive solemnity of its churrigueresque architecture, even in decay, nor rival the beauty of its surroundings. Nor did any city so completely dominate the life of a nation. What London was to England and Paris to France, Mexico City was to Mexico, and more—its cultural, intellectual, political, and religious epicenter. The Texans had marched some eight hundred miles since laying down their arms in Mier. They had at last reached the heart of Mexico.

A few weeks before the main body of Mier prisoners reached Santiago, John Hill, the youngest of the Texans, had arrived in Mexico City. After spending several weeks at the Archbishop's Palace, Hill received a summons to appear before Santa Anna. A Mexican officer escorted the boy across the Zócalo to the National Palace, an enormous building covering ten acres, which housed not only the residence of Santa Anna but also the executive offices of cabinet members and public servants, as well as the courts of justice. The youth was taken before Santa Anna, who asked him if the stories he had heard of the boy's bravery at Mier were true. Hill ingenuously replied that he did not know how many Mexicans he had killed, but that he had fired fifteen or twenty times during the battle. Then the Mexican president made a suggestion that took Hill completely by surprise, offering to adopt the boy and assume the responsibilities of guardian until he reached his majority. Hill replied that this was a decision that could only be made by his father; nonetheless, his sumptuous surroundings and the lavish treatment he had received may have done much to weaken his attachment to the cabin in Fayette County he called home. He told Santa Anna that if his father gave his consent, he would remain in Mexico.[11]

This was not the first time Santa Anna had offered to adopt a child of Texas. A similar incident is believed to have occurred after the siege of the Alamo in 1836. Among the few known survivors were Suzanna Dickinson and her fifteen-month-old daughter Angelina, who were rescued from the smoking ruins after the battle and brought to Santa Anna's tent. The young woman clutching her baby no doubt made a touching scene, and stirred the same emotions within the man that he evidently felt for the youth who had distinguished himself at the Battle of Mier. Santa Anna suggested he take the child back to Mexico with him and raise her as one of his own. Having just witnessed the slaughter of her husband and the rest of the Alamo defenders, Suzanna Dickinson must have felt that Santa Anna would make a highly unsuitable surrogate parent. She indignantly refused.[12]

The Hill family was much more agreeable. Asa Hill, who soon arrived in Santiago with the other prisoners, apparently believed his son's prospects were brighter here than in Texas and allowed him to take advantage of Santa Anna's offer. John Hill remained in Mexico City, living at the home of General Tornel while he pursued his studies at the prestigious College of Mines. Not long after his initial meeting with Santa Anna, Hill paid another visit to the National Palace, and orders for the release of his father and brother were promptly issued.[13] When Albert Gilliam, the newly appointed U.S. consular officer in California, passed through Mexico City in 1843, he found that Hill had adapted quickly to Mexican life. En route to his post in California, Gilliam had occasion to meet Hill, who gave him a tour of the College of Mines. Gilliam recalled that "as he was conducting us from room to room, it was observable that he was forgetting his native tongue, by being often very much in want of English words to express himself."[14] Hill went on to become a successful engineer; he died in Monterrey in 1909.

On the national scene, all seemed to be running smoothly for Santa Anna. With the army behind him, he had dissolved the pro-federalist Congress and appointed a Council of Notables to write yet another constitution. This one would give the Mexican leader and his centralist regime decidedly more power than the last. Local government would be curtailed by dividing the country into eighteen departments which would, for all intents and purposes, take their orders directly from the capital. Santa Anna quickly took steps to silence any possible opposition. A number of key federalists who were expected to cause trouble were jailed and would not be released until after the new constitution went into effect.[15] Waddy Thompson believed that the Mexican leader, though far from popular, was firmly in charge. "No other man in the country has the energy and the prestige, which are necessary to govern it," he wrote to the new secretary of state, Abel Upshur.[16] With no one powerful enough to challenge Santa Anna, he remained secure.

But there was trouble ahead. Mexico still owed two and a half million dollars in claims to the United States, although by Santa Anna's own admission there was barely enough money in the national treasury to cover one quarter of the government's operating costs.[17] As always, the greatest drain on the treasury was the army. The rebellion in the Yucatán demanded top priority, while the garrisons stationed across Mexico were needed to quell any other local uprisings that might occur. The demands of a swollen military budget would have to be met, for Santa Anna needed the loyalty of the officer corps if he was to stay in power. But the support of the army could be purchased only at the expense of the clergy and *hacendados*. From these groups, the government imposed a "forced loan" of $270,000 to pay its first quarterly installment to the United States.[18] Unwilling to cut military expenditures and unable to maintain the support of the nation's economic elite, Santa Anna's regime faced a number of important domestic challenges that could not be solved by the promulgation of a new constitution alone.

While Santa Anna must have been aware of these disturbing undercurrents, he chose to ignore them. For all his keen political acumen, the day-to-day business of running a country seemed to hold little interest for the Mexican leader. He spent most of his time on his country estates, tending to his gamecocks, returning to the capital only when political events absolutely required it. Immensely skilled in the practice of seizing power, Santa Anna often appeared indifferent to the responsibilities of high office. This trait, and not his cruelty nor his avarice nor the many other flaws—real and imagined—that Texans and Mexicans alike have attributed to him, was Santa Anna's greatest shortcoming. Rather than take charge, he preferred to delegate authority to loyal but less talented subordinates. Rather than address the economic woes that beset the country, he tantalized the people with the empty promise of subjugating Texas. Rather than establish an agenda for Mexico, he let it drift. A personality cult was no substitute for responsible government. It was a state of affairs that could not continue indefinitely.

SHORTLY AFTER THEIR arrival at Santiago, the prison commandant called in the Texas officers and informed them that they would be provided with new suits of clothing and put to work on the roads of the city. Indignant, the officers insisted that they were prisoners of war, not common felons, and as such could not be required to perform manual labor. They relented only when Waddy Thompson, on one of his visits to the prison, informed them that they had no choice in the matter; moreover, many of the men were still wearing the same clothes they had been captured in back at Mier, and considered manual labor a modest price to pay for the chance to replace their threadbare garments with new suits of clothing. Big Foot Wallace, for example, had lost his hat, and his head was covered by a large red handkerchief wrapped about it like a turban. He was missing one shoe, for which he had substituted a leather thong tied around his foot. Much of his coat and trousers had been left behind on the cactus thorns of the mountains above Saltillo. He was no expert with a needle and thread, but his jacket was a crazy quiltwork of whatever bits of cloth he could find and stick together. The trousers, however, were absolutely beyond repair. He was compelled to leave his shirttails hanging out in the interests of decency, to hide the gaping holes and the extremities thus exposed.[19]

The prisoners were given simple flannel convicts' uniforms, white with green and red stripes (the national colors), coarse cotton shirts, and sandals. All the prisoners were furnished with footwear except Wallace, whose feet, so the story goes, were so large that his sandals had to be custom-made, thereby giving him his curious nickname.[20] In their new attire the prisoners received shovels and picks and were marched to Tacubaya, five miles to the west, on the outskirts of the city. Here they were chained in pairs again, with heavy irons ten feet long attached to the ankle, so that to keep them from dragging along the ground they had to be carried with one hand or hooked onto the belt while walking.[21]

At Tacubaya, the Texans were told that they would be working on the road leading from Santa Anna's suburban residence to the town. Here they were placed in the charge of a splendidly caparisoned young captain, barely out of his teens, no doubt a graduate of the Chapultepec military academy nearby. He addressed the men with great courtesy, telling them that he would do everything in his power to make their task an easy one. Cooperation, he stressed, was the key, promising them fair treatment for a fair day's work. As proof of his sincerity the Texan officers would be his overseers; it was their job to make sure that the work was completed on schedule. Having explained the grading of the road, its width, and the method of construction, he galloped away, leaving a pair of soldiers to stand guard and the Texans to their task. A handful of industrious men grabbed picks and pestles and proceeded to put their backs into the work, but most headed straight for the cool shade of an ash grove, to spend the day in happy retirement.[22]

Several weeks passed and remarkably little work was done. The Texans were quartered at Molino del Rey, the King's Mill, a powder mill and foundry located a little more than a mile from Tacubaya. Each morning their guards, whose only concern was that the prisoners not escape, marched them down to the road, and for the rest of the day the Texans could do largely as they pleased. They operated in shifts, with a few dozen men laboring for the sake of appearances, while their friends lolled about nearby. The young officer rode by occasionally to inspect their progress, growing more exasperated with each visit. In his presence the Texans would pound away at the rocks with inspired vigor, but the moment he was gone they returned to the trees along the roadside.

Finally the patience of the Mexican authorities came to an end. One day the prisoners reported to work to find the young captain gone and another in his place with strict instructions to get results. The Texan officers were told that they would no longer be exempt from work detail; supervision of the road work was now entrusted to a group of convicts and about twenty soldiers who were brought up from Santiago. The new officer informed the Texans that there would be no malingering. To illustrate his point and as a warning to the rest, two prisoners were taken out of line and clubbed to their knees. The Texans seized shovels and picks and started after the guards, and a full-scale riot was averted only when the officer ordered his men to release the pair.[23] But the message was clear; a road would be made, and the Texans would build it.

These heavy-handed methods proved only slightly more successful. Although threatened with severe punishment, the Texans still found numerous ways to delay construction of the road. A stream that coursed one mile from the road provided a source of supply for the stone, and the Texans discovered that much time could be wasted going to and from it, when they were not under the constant supervision of their overseers. By cutting slits in the bags, or by frequent stumbling, they returned to the road with the bags almost empty. Tools were hidden, lost, deliberately broken, and sometimes even sold. At times the prisoners approached their work with such lethargy "that it was hard to perceive whether we were stationary or moving."[24]

Some of the men reported sick, but discovered that medical treatment was in no way preferable to work on the road. For most maladies, the prisoner was stripped naked and not allowed to move from his hospital bed. He was given only cornmeal gruel and a liberal diet of castor oil. The results were fairly immediate, and most patients were eager to return to work.[25]

At the end of two months barely one hundred yards of road had been completed, work which by the Texans' own estimate should have taken them about ten days. The Mexican authorities adopted new measures to increase productivity, improving the quality and quantity of their rations, and allowing them to cook the food themselves. The chains of the better laborers were taken off, and mules and carts were brought in to carry the stone from the creek bottom. With these incentives, the Texans began to make progress.[26]

MEANWHILE, THE MARCH of Green and Fisher had reached its close. By late March their small group, still ignorant of the fate of the others, had reached Perote, their final destination. The little village of Perote was situated in a flat, narrow valley high in the mountains, some seven thousand feet above sea level, lying 160 miles from the capital and about the same distance to Veracruz.[27] To the north loomed the imposing Cofre de Perote, to the south another series of high peaks, although they were usually hidden from view by a thick blanket of clouds. Dense forests of pine and fir draped the mountains of this volcanic region, but the valley floor, which was covered by gray lava, seemed barren and lifeless. The climate was as dismal as the countryside. In the shadows of these mountains, at such a high altitude, Perote received little sunlight and was cold year round, making bone-chilling winds and freezing rains as common in summer as they were in winter.[28] In June, one of the Texas inmates would write to his friends at home: "this is the most disagreabel climate on the Globe. It rains nearly every day . . . in fact it is colder here at this time than it is in Texas in December."[29]

Less than a mile from the village sat the castle of San Carlos de Perote, a solidly built structure of whitewashed volcanic pumice rock. Built in a deep excavation which served as a dry moat, the fortress did not appear particularly imposing from a distance, but as the Texans approached, they could make out the cannon that filled every embrasure along the rampart. Built by the Spanish in the 1770s to guard the principal trade route from Mexico City to the coast, Perote Castle still stands, and still serves as a prison today, looking much the same as it did when Green and Fisher approached it in the spring of 1843.

Outside the fortress walls a twelve-foot parapet built of squared cedar logs, reinforced on either side with adobe brick and a sloping embankment of earth, served as a defense perimeter. Projecting from each of the four corners of the castle itself was a large bastion, with guns trained on all sides, so that any point of the main wall which came under attack could be defended. Perote's walls rose 60 feet from the bottom of the moat, which was itself 20 feet deep and 150 feet wide. A subterranean duct from the mountains provided the castle with an ample fresh-water supply. From the mouth of a lion carved in stone a steady stream of water poured into two main reservoirs. A small tank nearby was used for bathing. Underneath the prison was a much larger reservoir, which could be opened to flood the channel in time of war.[30]

Impressive in size, Perote was equipped to hold a garrison of two thousand men. Although the regular complement of infantry and cavalry was much smaller, rarely exceeding five hundred soldiers, the officers' families lived on the grounds, and troops en route to other military posts around the country were often quartered at the fort for short periods of time.[31] One American soldier billeted at the castle during the Mexican War described Perote as "almost a town in itself."[32] A handful of Mexican inmates performed menial jobs about the fort, but Perote was first and foremost a military installation, and could hardly be compared to the country's more notorious prisons, such as the Acordada in Mexico City. To the extent that Perote served as a detention facility, it was used primarily to keep political and military prisoners. Federalists and other enemies of the centralist government spent time here as they waited for the political climate to change. One of the fort's most distinguished inmates was General Matías Peña y Barragán, imprisoned for his defeat at the hands of rebel forces in the Yucatán.[33] The castle was also the retirement home for General Don Guadalupe Victoria, the former President of Mexico, who died shortly after Green's arrival. Santa Anna and his wife, Doña Inés, were frequent visitors, spending the night at the fort when traveling from the capital to Manga de Clavo, their estate near the coast.[34]

The new inmates passed by the guardhouse and crossed the bridge over the moat, beneath an archway into the castle, as a bell clanged to announce their arrival. Inside the fort was a complex of two-story buildings which housed the officers' quarters, soldiers' barracks, storerooms, carpentry, wheelwright, and other workshops, and stables. These buildings formed a square, in the middle of which was a cement-paved central plaza. Here the prisoners were introduced to Lieutenant Colonel Isidro Pombo, the *mayor de la plaza,* a sinewy officer with a bad limp who walked with a cane.[35] The plaza was the hub of activity in the castle during the day, but work stopped whenever new prisoners were brought in. Off-duty soldiers milled about near the barracks, while the women and children who operated the garrison stores also came out for a look. Scattered here and there, crowded around the windows of the carpentry and wheelwright shops, were careworn, hungry-looking men in striped uniforms who watched the Texans file off as their names were called.[36]

On the interior side of the main walls ran a series of high arches around the length of the fort that supported the uppermost ramparts. Green, Fisher, and the others were conducted to a big, empty room on the upper level, about seventy feet wide and twenty feet long, with an arched roof. The cell was drafty and dark; the only light was admitted through a small aperture in the wall at the far end of the room and a narrow grating in the door. A previous inhabitant had described the cells of Perote as follows:

> *The walls of our dungeon are smoke-stained black and brown. The limestone plaster is still visible in only a few places. White saltpeter, which forms everywhere, is the only adornment of our damp abode. Forming along the cracks in the walls and ceiling, it solidifies into formations of various shapes. With a little imagination one can see animals, human profiles, Saturn's rings, the Milky Way, the isthmus of Panama, and other things. The floor, half brick and half limestone mortar, is full of holes and not too easy to walk on. In one corner . . . there is a barrel; one can easily guess its purpose without my describing it. In the opposite corner there is another barrel that contains water, our daily beverage. On wooden pegs, protruding rocks, or on cords we hang our clothes, tools, and other things.*[37]

The next day the new inmates had an opportunity to speak with the more than forty other Texas prisoners at Perote, who occupied two cells just down the corridor. The men captured by Adrian Woll in his attack on San Antonio had called Perote home since December. Although a few were ill with dysentery, generally they were in good health. Only one man had died since their arrival, in a tragic incident a few days earlier. Shields Booker was sitting on a bench in the yard with a Mexican lieutenant, who earlier in the day had disciplined one of his men for drunkenness. As they were talking the soldier came out of the guardhouse with a musket and fired at his superior. The bullet hit Booker instead, passing through his neck. He died twenty-four hours later, and his body was taken out and buried in the moat (only Catholics were buried in the castle cemetery).[38]

The new inmates of Perote quickly settled into the routine of prison life. Every morning at seven o'clock breakfast was brought in, consisting of coffee and cornmeal gruel sweetened with brown sugar.[39] At nine o'clock they were counted and turned over to Captain José Guzmán, the daytime officer of the guard. Those with the necessary skills were assigned to the carpentry and wheelwright shops, for which the government paid them twenty-five cents a day. Some were given the unpleasant task of carrying out the refuse from the barracks and stables in wheelbarrows, while others were employed as sweepers, or put to work repairing the fortifications around the prison.[40] Green and Fisher were also told to join in the work detail, but as officers they adamantly refused. General José Durán, the commandant of the fortress, called them in to complain that these were his orders, but he made no attempt to carry them out. Although Green and Fisher were repeatedly warned that they would be punished if they did not report to work, the matter was dropped.[41]

At noon the prisoners received their only substantial meal of the day. Sometimes their rations consisted of the worst kind of beef, with offal, gristle, meat, and bone all tossed into a pot of boiling water and spiced with salt and red pepper, with small portions of onions and rice. On other days they got no meat at all, only potatoes or frijoles.[42] Guzmán, who served as the prison quartermaster in addition to his duties as officer of the guard, provided the prisoners with enough to keep body and soul together, but little more. The cattle brought into the fortress were invariably scrawny and often sickly. Cows that were to be slaughtered the following day were tied to a stake in the courtyard below the prisoners' cells. By counting the rings on the horns the Texans ascertained that these animals were well past their prime. One cow that could barely stand was inspected by the Texans and found to have a large swelling, a snake-bite, on its neck. When they brought it to Guzmán's attention, the officer assured the prisoners that he would not give them the snake-bitten part.[43] The prisoners complained of the quality and quantity of their rations, but it is unlikely that the soldiers who guarded them or the townspeople beyond the fortress walls fared much better. Those who had managed to obtain money from friends back home, or who still had a little of the money which they had received in Matamoros, were able to supplement their small rations of beef with lard, onions, and red peppers. They could also buy coffee, sugar, eggs, donkey milk, and fruit.[44]

In the evenings another dish of gruel was doled out to each prisoner before they were counted at six o'clock and herded back into their cells. A sentinel was placed at each door for the night. To pass the time some prisoners danced and sang, others played cards, and a few kept diaries of their captivity.[45] Occasionally they got hold of American newspapers, usually the New Orleans papers—the *Daily Picayune,* as well as the *Commercial Bulletin* and *The Tropic*—but their most reliable source of news came from Waddy Thompson and the other foreign dignitaries of Mexico City, who kept them informed of their chances for release.

The most pressing problem which the prisoners faced on a daily basis was money. Everything but their meager rations had to be purchased, including such items as pens and paper, and even tapers to provide light to read and write by in their dark cells.[46] Some of the prisoners were paid for their work, and occasionally, on national holidays, the commandant provided them with small gifts of money. These funds were never enough to cover their expenses, however, and the prisoners had to rely upon the charity of friends and relatives. One prisoner wrote: "the condition of most of our men have been Eleviated by their friends in the United States by sending them money as for myself sence the 25th December 42 I have been destitute of money not one cent to buy soap to wash my skin Cloth is out of the question we are all Lousy as pigs."[47] Wrote another: "I have not got a single shirt to my back nor scarcely anything in the shape of pantaloons. Nor have I any prospect of getting things. Those who received money from their friends in the States can get along verry well but those that have none suffer."[48]

The days dragged by slowly and uneventfully. To relieve the boredom they took no small amount of satisfaction in annoying their overseers. Some drew charcoal caricatures on the walls of their cells and the prison yard of Guzmán and Pombo, whom the Texans nicknamed "Guts" and "Old Limpy."[49] The turnkeys found these drawings highly amusing, but the targets of such humor flew into violent rages when they spotted them. When these two officers were on duty, the Texans were always on their guard, careful not to be too flagrant in the rules they broke. They quickly learned the habits and daily routines of both men. Neither man could be considered cruel. If they pursued their tasks with an undue amount of zeal, it was because they appreciated the advantages of higher rank; any neglect of duty on their part, and they would find themselves sharing the uncomfortable lot of the rank and file. The Texans soon learned just how far they could go in exasperating their overseers without bringing trouble for themselves.

Every petty act of insubordination took on the aspect of a major triumph against tyranny. Like their fellow prisoners at work on the Tacubaya road, the Perote inmates were poor hands at manual labor. Every day some of the men were hitched to a wagon with rawhide harnesses, twenty-five men in a team, to haul rocks from the mountainside to the fortress. They often pretended to lose control of the wagon, sending it crashing into the sides of the houses of Perote, which infuriated local homeowners as much as their guards. On one occasion the Texans succeeded in demolishing the wagon completely by swerving from the road into a tree.[50]

Ironed together in pairs, the Texans soon found ways to make their chains less burdensome. Two prisoners might take a rock and hammer a link in their chain against the paving stones of their cell floor, taking pains to muffle the sounds to escape detection from the guard at the door. When they had occasion to leave the room during the day, one of them could hold both pieces of the chain in one hand, as if it were unbroken.[51] For one *medio*—about four cents, a considerable sum—the prison blacksmith could be bribed to replace the iron rivets on their leg irons with leaden ones, which could be more easily removed.[52] Since prisoners found with loose bolts or broken chains were sent immediately back to the blacksmith, the Texans devised elaborate methods to escape detection. Using tools stolen from the carpentry shop, they managed to cut the bolts on their leg irons in such a way that the bolts could be replaced without appearing to have been tampered with.[53] So proficient did they become at devising ways to rid themselves of their "jewelry," as they called their chains, that after lock-up each evening they routinely discarded them, but the sound of guards at the door always sent them scrambling to put the chains back on.[54]

Disciplining the willful Texans proved to be a problem. Corporal punishment was never used systematically, and beatings seem to have been the exception rather than the rule. A particularly recalcitrant prisoner might have to wear hobbles—an iron or wooden crossbar attached to his leg-irons—or spend a day or two in the solitary confinement of the *calabozo*.[55] By far the most effective means of punishment was to deny the Texans the simple comforts that made prison life a little easier. Of these, perhaps the privilege which they appreciated most was the opportunity to adjourn to a sunny spot in the prison yard every morning and scour each others' heads for lice. The seventy-year-old castle was swarming with vermin. No matter what precautions were taken—every day the hard stone floors on which they slept were doused with boiling water, and those that had extra clothes changed and washed them regularly—each prisoner awoke from a night's sleep with skin literally crawling with the milky-white creatures. To better perform this ritual of prison life the Texans cropped their hair short and kept their fingernails long. In the morning each man got down on all fours to hunt for the animals in the scalp of a friend. Only the biggest of the creatures were visible, however, and the next day the entire process had to be repeated.[56]

Though a terrible nuisance, lice also provided the prisoners' best source of entertainment. According to Thomas Jefferson Green, the Texans became dedicated louse-racing enthusiasts during their incarceration. A circle eighteen inches in diameter would be drawn in charcoal on a piece of wood, with a small ring in the center. The bugs were then set loose, to wander toward the winner's circle amid the shouts and demonstrations of trainers and wagerers. Cash bets were sometimes made, but as money was in such short supply, the most common wagers were *tlacos*, square pieces of soap worth a cent or two, or an "old soldier," a used chaw of tobacco (for fresh tobacco was in shorter supply than money). Tobacco was chewed, loaned to friends, and chewed again. When at last it lost its flavor, it was dried and smoked in a pipe.[57]

Mescal was another luxury that could be taken away if the prisoners became troublesome. A sutler store on the grounds, run by a lieutenant's wife and daughter, sold liquor to soldiers and inmates alike, and the Texans were regular customers. On certain days the store was forbidden to sell to them, as punishment for some infraction, but they always managed to get their hands on mescal in spite of the prohibition. Some of the women were willing to break the rules for their Texas friends, or a soldier might buy mescal in town and sneak it into the castle in a cow's intestines, curled up like a snake in his shako. He could then make the rounds of the cells, charging the prisoners for each mouthful.[58]

There were, however, limits to this kind of fraternization. Once in a while a prisoner overstepped the bounds of acceptable familiarity, and the line between captive and captor was brought sharply back into focus. On one occasion, a fight broke out in the laundry house between Isaac Allen, one of the Bexar prisoners, and a Mexican lieutenant. Only when Guzmán arrived on the scene were the two men finally separated. The Mexican officer claimed to have caught Allen in a compromising situation with his wife, one of the laundrywomen. The Texan countered that his intentions were innocent enough: he had merely kissed the woman to thank her for washing his shirt. Yelling loudly that he was the innocent victim of the officer's rage, Allen dropped his pants to reveal the handle of a shoemaker's awl planted firmly in his backside. Guzmán ordered Allen to report to the infirmary and promised that the lieutenant would be reprimanded for his behavior.[59]

Like all prisoners, they lived for mail days. Three times a week the Veracruz–Mexico City stagecoach passed through Perote. Although mail service to and from the United States was expensive and notoriously poor (there was, of course, none to Texas), a few letters did manage to reach them. Waddy Thompson and the U.S. consul in Veracruz sometimes received letters through the diplomatic mails and forwarded them to Perote. But frequently there was only a short note from Thompson, urging them to keep their spirits up, and more often than not there was nothing at all.

They wrote long, touching letters, always with the knowledge that these notes might never reach their destination. Samuel Maverick, one of the Bexar prisoners captured by General Woll, told his wife, "Hardly a night now passes but it presents the most vivid pictures of events and scenes connected with the past. They are all pleasant and happy scenes, but in no point of view are they so gratifying to my constant heart as the fact that you, dear Mary, are always there." More concerned with her welfare than his own, he urged her to "be on the lookout for sickness" and "exercise on horseback, visit and do everything to keep your health and spirits good." [60]

At times they painted an all too rosy picture of their confinement to allay the fears of family and friends at home. In a letter to his wife, Jane, Norman Woods wrote: "We have plenty to eat, good clothes to wear, coffee twice a day, meat once, [and] good flour bread. I am coopering and make about one well bucket a week." [61] In these breezy and cheerful letters, Woods wrote optimistically of his hopes for an early release. In letters to his brother, Henry Gonsalvo Woods, who had managed to escape the slaughter and capture of Dawson's men, he was more candid. His shattered hip had never healed properly, leaving him crippled and in constant pain. His one great worry, however, was the effect his long absence would have on his family. From his prison cell he tried to manage his affairs as best he could, giving precise instructions as to which bills to pay, and which ones to collect. [62] To Henry, who was not married, he wrote: "I wish you to act as a brother to my family, and see my children schooled. This subject bears heavyer upon my mind than any other, but being satisfied that you will pay my family every possible attention relieves my mind in no inconsiderable degree." [63]

In their letters they also poured out their frustration and their rage. To the Mexican government they sent protests deploring the food and living conditions. Samuel Maverick even lodged a formal complaint against Captain Guzmán, demanding his immediate removal, which he sent to Foreign Minister Bocanegra via Waddy Thompson (the American minister wisely pocketed these angry missives, knowing they would have anything but a positive effect on attempts to win the prisoners' release). [64] One Bexar prisoner scribbled this anguished note in his semi-literate prose: "When we shall guet out of this snap God only knows. My only hope is an exchange of prisners . . . things growes daily more gloomey . . . they treat us worse evry day." [65] On another occasion the same prisoner wrote: "The Mexicans point me out and say I am the worst one in the Castle—I have worn hobels two weeks, binn beat with there spades and muskets, calaboosed and every means to cow me they can think of. . . . There is no hope of release." [66]

Yet it was the humiliation of their confinement, and not the physical hardship that they found so difficult to bear. If prison life was by no means comfortable, neither was it unendurable. But their freedom, which they considered their birthright as Americans, they held sacred, and the loss of it touched them deeply. "Inhale a small quantity of the air of Liberty for me," a prisoner asked a friend in Texas. "I have almost forgotten the smell of it." [67] Steeped in the rhetoric of democracy, they were fiercely proud of their heritage, which they believed endowed them with qualities that set them apart from all other men. To be sure, their understanding of what Jefferson meant by inalienable rights was confused at best. There was nothing enlightened or idealistic about their faith in republican principles. Instead, these ideas bolstered and served to justify their already virulent brand of racial prejudice. They believed, as did so many Americans, that democratic institutions were a unique product of Anglo-Saxon culture. And they were no less convinced that those who labored under tyrannical rule were plainly inferior and incapable of change. Far from being created equal, all men got the kind of political system they deserved. As for the Mexicans, they were stunted by centuries of servitude and oppression, a race not to be pitied but despised.

Enslavement, of course, challenged this deep-seated ethnocentrism, and defied the order of things as they were supposed to be. The conviction that they were superior to their captors in every respect was a far greater torment than any kind of physical abuse. Every indignity suffered at the hands of a race they regarded as no better than the black slave or the red savage was galling to their Anglo-Saxon pride. Wrote one irate prisoner, "The overseers . . . often beat the Texans with sticks with as little ceremony as they would beat negroes." [68] Another complained to Thompson when a guard hit one of the men: "What then must be the deep agony of an American to be struck by one of these imps of darkness . . . ? Sir, it is insupportable. The blood of an American cannot brook the degradation." [69] Never questioning for a moment that their cause was just, they often succumbed to maudlin self-pity. One prisoner composed a poem entitled "The Texian Captive's Dream," which he managed to send on to Texas, where it appeared in the Brazos *Planter*. The last lines read:

> *Grim murder with his clanking chain*
> *And rapine, manhood's foulest stain*
> *And theft, and every other crime*

Known in this t'ribly vicious clime
Have all their agents seated round
My pallet on the cold, damp ground
They look on me with fiendish leer
And shake their chains with hellish sneer
What have I done? Why am I here?
I've fought in freedom's sacred cause
For freeman's rights, and freedom's laws
So please the Lord I will again
Despite the tyrant and his chain[70]

There was much time to think and dwell upon the circumstances of their imprisonment, and the longer they waited, the angrier they became. Every day brought its insults—some petty, some serious, but all burned into memory—and every day they vowed revenge.

As the weeks, then months went by, their frustration grew. They began to feel abandoned by their government, by their friends and families. "I could rite you much but it appears that you like the rest have forgotten a frend in distress," wrote one prisoner.[71] Complained another, "what is the Texians doing that they don't get us out of this scrape? Does our Congressmen take up all their time passing laws regulating roads and canals or custom house duties that they cannot give one moment's thought towards their suffering countrymen in the Castle of Perote?"[72] Wrote one prisoner in a letter to his father, "we look to Heaven for mercy and to our country for redress."[73]

But only Santa Anna held the power to unlock their prison doors and send them on their way, and this was something which the Mexican President, all rumors to the contrary, had so far shown little willingness to do. He could fly into fits of rage at the very mention of the expedition, as he recalled the sack of Laredo, the violation of Mexican territory, or the attempted escape at the Hacienda del Salado. He had ordered the decimation of the prisoners without regard for international public opinion, and made no apologies for it. At the same time, however, he was not unwilling to grant dispensations on an individual basis, and he chose to do so for reasons both personal and political. When the spirit moved him, he could be most generous toward the Texan invaders. John Hill was not the only prisoner to enjoy Santa Anna's hospitality; there were several men who, through the intercession of friends in the United States, obtained their release by special order of the Mexican President. One fortunate inmate at Perote was given his letters of transit and instructed to proceed to Manga de Clavo, Santa Anna's country estate. He arrived still wearing his prison stripes and filthy from work on the chain gang, and was wined and dined by Santa Anna and his family for two days before leaving for Veracruz.[74]

The Mexican President was not one to forget past favors. Finding the name of Orlando Phelps on the list of Mier prisoners, Santa Anna recalled that after the Battle of San Jacinto, he had been held at the plantation of a Dr. James Phelps. Shackled, ill-treated by his guards, and despondent over his defeat, he had attempted suicide by an overdose of laudanum. The Texas doctor had pumped the narcotic from Santa Anna's stomach and cared for him until his health returned. When told that the Orlando Phelps on the list of prisoners was the son of the man who had saved his life, Santa Anna issued an order for his release. Phelps was brought to Mexico City, where he was given new suits of clothes and a room at the National Palace. A short time later the Mexican President paid his passage back to Texas.[75]

Santa Anna also felt obligated to repay a debt of gratitude to Andrew Jackson. Not long after his suicide attempt at the Phelps plantation, he had accepted an invitation from then-President Jackson to visit the United States, where the disgraced general was treated with infinitely more courtesy and respect than he would have received in his own country at that time. As a result, two Perote prisoners, one of Fisher's men and another captured by General Woll, were given their freedom when Jackson brought them to the attention of the Mexican President.[76] Jackson was also one of a number of American statesmen who petitioned Santa Anna to release George B. Crittenden, son of the Kentucky senator. Although John J. Crittenden was a Whig and ally of Jackson's enemy Henry Clay, Jackson confidant Francis Blair had lived next door to the Crittendens in Kentucky. At Blair's request, the ex-President promptly sent a letter to Santa Anna. "I do not visit the sins of the father upon the son," he told Blair.[77] When news of Jackson's special relationship with Santa Anna was reported in the American press, the Hermitage was inundated with letters from the relatives of Perote prisoners begging the aging ex-President to use his influence on their behalf. Jackson estimated that he had received at least one hundred such letters. After the release of these men, however, Jackson was reluctant to press the Mexican President's generosity, although he continued to forward the many appeals which he received at the Hermitage on to Waddy Thompson.[78] In March 1844, he would write to Santa Anna in an unsuccessful attempt to gain the release of all Texans held in captivity in Mexico.[79]

Statesmen friendly to Mexico also exercised some influence. The British, who enjoyed the best relations with Mexico of all the major powers, managed to convince Santa Anna that a few of the Mier men born in the British Isles were not, in fact, Texas renegades and enemies of Mexico, but loyal subjects of the crown.[80] Prominent members of the Whig party in the United States, who were strongly opposed to the annexation of Texas, seem to have been given particular preference. Daniel Webster had been instrumental in arranging the release of George Crittenden after the battle at Mier,[81] while Henry Clay and John Quincy Adams were both successful in petitioning the Mexican government for clemency for certain constituents.[82] But while it helped to have friends in high places, these politicians could intervene in an unofficial capacity only. Once having secured the liberation of a fortunate few, they, like Jackson, could do no more.[83]

One of the San Antonio prisoners, Judge James W. Robinson, who had served as lieutenant governor of the provisional government of Texas in 1835, decided not to wait for the influence of friends back home to win his freedom. Accordingly, he took pen and paper and wrote to the Mexican President himself. Robinson made the startling and wholly unfounded observation that Texas could be induced to return to Mexican control in exchange for a measure of home rule. A mediator should be sent to Texas to work out such an arrangement. That mediator, of course, should be Robinson himself. Santa Anna pondered over the letter for some time, presumably aware that Robinson might be motivated only by a desire to cut short his stay at Perote, which appears to have been his sole intention. Nevertheless, the Mexican leader found the proposition an interesting one and sent for Robinson, drafting a letter outlining a peace plan based on the prisoner's suggestions for the Texan to take back to Sam Houston.[84]

Not long afterward, Santa Anna received another letter from a Perote prisoner. The Mexican President must have been surprised to see that the sender was none other than the man most responsible for his own captivity after San Jacinto: Thomas Jefferson Green. Perhaps, Green wrote, his conduct at Velasco Beach in 1836 had been misunderstood. It had not been his wish to keep Santa Anna from sailing back to Mexico; he was merely carrying out the orders of the interim government. (Acting President Burnet, who had been threatened with lynching if he did not hand Santa Anna over, might have disagreed on this point.) Far from delivering Santa Anna to the mob, Green insisted that he had actually rescued him from it. "I had informed those on shore that if any offered violence to you it should be over my dead body."[85] Green went on to list other kindnesses of which Santa Anna might not be aware. He claimed to have paid out of his own pocket some $3,000 in transportation costs when the Mexican

President and his aides left Texas.[86] He had even taken the coat from his back when he heard that the general was in need of warm clothing, although he doubted that Santa Anna was ever told who owned it. "My reward," he concluded magnanimously, "was in believing the coat did you service."[87] Of course, Green hastened to point out, he was only mentioning these charities now to set the record straight, not to win liberty for himself. He added, however, that a meeting between them could prove worthwhile, a none too subtle hint that he might be induced to undertake a mission similar to Judge Robinson's.

This ingratiating letter, so very different from Green's earlier boastful accounts of the Velasco incident, failed to produce the desired result. For the next few weeks Green would wait for the stagecoach to bring some word from Santa Anna; he would never receive a reply.

"A Mysterious Silence"

TACUBAYA WAS A small village of country homes with a commanding view of the Valley of Mexico, situated four miles from the capital and less than a mile from Chapultepec Castle. Santa Anna's residence was the former summer palace of the Spanish archbishops, a rambling, two-story mansion surrounded by gardens of rosebushes and fruit trees. Whenever Santa Anna journeyed from the capital to his suburban residence, the Mexican overseers were notified well in advance and lined the Texans up in respectful formation along the roadway. His entourage included one hundred cuirassiers in full dress uniform. If the Texans looked quickly they could see Santa Anna in the shadows of his carriage as it hurtled past in a swirl of dust and then disappeared behind the wrought-iron gates that led into the gardens of his estate. When visiting Tacubaya, he never ventured beyond the walls of the palace, but would occasionally come out onto his veranda, where he could see the prisoners laboring on the road.[1]

Although the hopes of the Texans were frequently raised by rumors that Santa Anna intended to release them, their freedom remained a dim prospect so long as hostilities between Mexico and Texas continued. Indeed, relations between the two countries had steadily worsened since the beginning of the year. No sooner had Fisher's men laid down their arms at Mier than the Texas Navy undertook a freebooting enterprise of its own. For reasons of economy, Houston planned to sell the navy and had ordered Commodore Edwin Ward Moore, who was then in New Orleans, to return to Galveston. The independent-minded navy man had other ideas, and set sail instead for the Yucatán, having already agreed to hire out his two ships to Mexican rebels there. Moore engaged the Mexican fleet on two occasions, inflicting considerable damage, although no ships were lost. With Sam Houston and Santa Anna both accusing him of piracy, Moore finally dropped anchor in Galveston, but only because the rebel Yucatán government could no longer afford the monthly stipend. To prove his innocence, Moore demanded a court-martial and was acquitted of the major charges against him, but his exploits did the prisoners' cause little good. "My rule is," Houston wrote to a friend, "when my hand is in the lion's mouth, do not strike him on the nose!" [2]

But the President could not blame his enemies for all his troubles with Mexico. In the fall of 1842, even before Somervell received his instructions to cross the Río Grande, Houston had issued a commission to Charles Warfield, authorizing him to raise a small force to attack Mexican wagon trains along the Santa Fe Trail. With the government desperate to win some sort of victory against Mexico, no matter how small, a convoy of Mexican wagons out in the desert seemed an easy target. In January of the following year, two weeks after learning of the disaster at Mier, the President sanctioned a similar expedition under the command of Jacob Snively. But even these modest enterprises proved unsuccessful. Unable to raise a sufficient force, Warfield joined up with the Snively Expedition, which skirmished with Mexican troops but could find no caravan on its way to St. Louis. Fed up and tired of waiting, the expedition began to break up; a large portion of the command suffered the indignity of being captured by U.S. troops when it allegedly crossed over into American territory. [3]

But the allegations stemming from the President's handling of the Mier affair soon proved to be the biggest embarrassment to the Houston administration in the spring of 1843. Scarcely two and a half months after he had written to Charles Elliot asking Her Majesty's Government to intercede on behalf of the prisoners, Houston's private correspondence with the British chargé d'affaires had become public knowledge. Having learned through Waddy Thompson that Houston did not regard them as legitimate prisoners of war, the Mier men charged that the President was therefore personally responsible for all the indignities and privations which they had suffered at the hands of their Mexican captors. [4] Despite Charles Elliot's repeated assurances that Houston's letter was never intended to prejudice the Mexican government against the prisoners, the British diplomat was unable to silence the President's detractors, and this "extremely unjust and injurious insinuation" became more grist for the anti-Houston rumor mill in Texas. [5] The letter became so controversial that Elliot, fearing it might be stolen from him and fall into the wrong hands, took the highly unusual step of forwarding the original to the Foreign Office in London for safekeeping. [6]

Initially, Houston decided that the best course of action would be to ignore the charges against him, and he advised Elliot to do the same. "You can say nothing, nor will I; but let matters pass," he told the British representative in May. Claiming to be unruffled by the controversy, he wrote: "Pray don't let [the attacks in the press] affect your serenity. I am as cool as a shoemaker's lap stone in an open shop at Christmas."[7] But in fact the President was furious that his correspondence with the British representative had been made public. Believing that Waddy Thompson had deliberately misrepresented the contents of the letter in order to embarrass him, he instructed Isaac Van Zandt to demand a full inquiry into the matter in Washington.[8]

Elliot was at first skeptical of Houston's accusations. "I find it easier to believe that these released prisoner's [*sic*] misconceived General Thompson, than that He afforded them any ground to misrepresent General Houston's plain and kind purposes on their behalf."[9] Nonetheless, Elliot soon came to the conclusion that there was enough evidence to be suspicious of Thompson's motives, and ten days later he was reminding Percy Doyle that there must be "no relaxation of your just reserve respecting the exhibition of my private letters to General Thompson."[10]

Thompson's discussions with the Mier prisoners on this subject were highly embarrassing to the President of Texas, creating a controversy that would not soon go away. Even nonpartisan newspapers often supportive of the administration were growing impatient at the President's refusal to publicly respond to his critics' allegations, not to mention his inability to bring the prisoners home or to alleviate their suffering. The Houston *Morning Star*, which unlike most of the major newspapers in Texas was not a mouthpiece for either the administration or its opponents, flatly condemned the President and urged him to give a full account of his actions concerning the Mier prisoners:

> He has preserved, during the whole period since their captivity, a mysterious silence, and we fear, by this means, has encouraged the Mexican despot to aggravate their cruelties and sufferings. We cannot believe that Gen Houston is fully aware of the extent of the injury thus inflicted upon his captive countrymen, and we will still indulge the hope that he will relent, and make a public and explicit declaration that he considers those prisoners entitled to all the rights and privileges of prisoners of war. The country demands this—our captive countrymen now groaning in slavish chains implore for it—the great cause of humanity requires it. Let the President, therefore, even at this late period, atone in some degree for

past neglect, and accord justice to his oppressed and suffering fellow-citizens.[11]

For the present, Houston refused to publicly discuss the subject. Convinced that little could be gained by an acrimonious debate in the national press, the President continued to hope that quiet pressure from the major powers might ultimately secure the prisoners' release. Houston endured the criticism with his characteristic thick skin, but occasionally the sniping managed to get under it. A "gasconading course," he complained to a friend, "would represent the ravings of a poor impotent maniac chained to his ward."[12]

As the debate over Houston's correspondence with Elliot continued, reports of the decimation of the Mier prisoners began to reach Texas. The news could not have come at a worse time for the administration. "Such lamentable atrocities," French diplomat Viscount de Cramayel believed, "are the more deplorable when directed against a people like the Texians, as they will fail utterly to achieve their only conceivable purpose. Among people accustomed to regarding the life of a man as a plaything and the chances of war as a game, such acts of barbarity, far from intimidating them, serve merely to stimulate their reckless character and are greeted almost with joy as an excuse in advance to follow their own inclinations and exact bloody retaliation."[13] Charles Elliot agreed, and worried that the episode would spark a new wave of anti-Mexican feeling, leading to renewed calls for an invasion of the Río Grande Valley. If this "shocking event" was intended to intimidate the citizens of the Republic, he wrote Lord Aberdeen, it demonstrated an "extraordinary ignorance" of the Texan character, and could be expected to "influence these people to the highest degree."[14] During a visit to New Orleans shortly afterward, Elliot found that the public reaction there to the news of the decimation was much as he had predicted. The execution at the Salado, combined with the exploits of Commodore Moore, had caused "considerable excitement in this City, and probably more or less, throughout the whole Southern part of the Union."[15] The *New Orleans Bee* called the decimation "the most inhuman piece of butchery that has been perpetrated by a government professing to be civilized within the present century."[16]

In Texas, however, the kind of outcry that Elliot expected was surprisingly restrained, contrasting sharply with the reaction to the mistreatment of the Santa Fe prisoners the year before. There were, of course, the rather predictable denunciations of Santa Anna and promises of vengeance. The Houston *Morning Star* wrote: "The names of these murdered heroes will be registered with those of Fannin, Travis, and their

Spartan bands. A nation's tears shall bedew their graves—a nation's gratitude shall embalm their memory. It cannot be that their fiendish murderer will long evade the just punishment for this attrocious [*sic*] violation of every law human and divine." [17] But for the most part, the public outcry was limited to these rhetorical outbursts; one Galveston resident reported only that the news of the decimation had created "a gloom indeed here." [18]

No doubt the fact that the Texas Congress had recessed until the fall denied the President's most vociferous enemies a forum for their views and kept them out of the headlines. Moreover, a great deal of confusing, contradictory, and erroneous information had been published about the fate of the Mier prisoners following their escape, and it was some time before the reports of the execution were finally confirmed. The four men who had managed to make their way back to Texas could furnish no information as to the whereabouts of their comrades, but their successful escape fueled rumors that the bulk of Cameron's force would soon be arriving on the west Texas frontier. These hopes were not easily extinguished; although the first reports of the recapture of most of the prisoners appeared in Texas newspapers in early April, accounts of Cameron's exploits with the Apaches persisted for several weeks. This misinformation was not fully laid to rest until mid-May, when news of the decimation was finally confirmed. [19]

But perhaps the most important factor which helps explain the relative absence of public indignation toward the execution was that the country's attention was at that moment diverted by the arrival of Judge Robinson, who brought with him from Mexico a peace plan that promised to bring an end to the hostilities between Mexico and Texas. The proposals which Santa Anna had outlined in his meeting with Robinson were as follows: Texas must acknowledge the sovereignty of Mexico, in return for which it would be guaranteed almost complete autonomy as an independent department; no Mexican troops would be stationed within the borders of Texas; and its residents could initiate their own laws and elect representatives to the national Congress, advantages not extended to the other Mexican departments. [20]

Such a plan was, of course, out of the question; Texas had severed its ties with Mexico in 1836, and under no circumstances would it consent to a proposal that brought it back, even nominally, under Mexican rule. Upon his arrival in Galveston, Robinson made the purpose of his mission known to the press, which responded to the Mexican government's proposals, predictably, with a universal howl of indignation. Robinson then proceeded to Washington-on-the-Brazos, to meet and discuss the terms with President Houston. That Houston granted Robinson an audience at all was considered tantamount to treason as far as many Texas patriots were concerned.[21] But if Texans had no intention of relinquishing their independence, the prospect of peace was an alluring one, and in the weeks ahead support for establishing a dialogue with Mexico grew steadily. Instead of fueling the fire for reprisals, Robinson's unexpected diplomatic mission opened the door for a possible reconciliation between the two countries, creating a climate of opinion in Texas which was decidedly in favor of a more moderate policy.

The prisoners themselves took a dim view of Robinson's diplomatic errand. Believing that his sole object had been to gain his freedom, they were enraged to find that Robinson had actually laid the plan before the people of Texas. In a lengthy letter which appeared in the Houston *Morning Star*, one Perote prisoner begged his countrymen to ignore the proposals, denouncing Robinson as "an emissary of the devil," who would "attempt to hood-wink and lead them blindfold into purgatory."[22] Another prisoner called Robinson "the worst man that Texas ever had within her borders—say to him for me that his blood shall atone for his conduct towards us. His conduct is the sole cause of our lengthy confinement here in this hell I might call it."[23]

Although the Mexican government was offering a similar arrangement to the Yucatán rebels in an effort to bring an end to the insurrection in that province, Santa Anna could have been under no illusions about the willingness of Texas to return to Mexican rule. Whatever reaction he expected from Houston, his own motives seem clear. The Mexican President could not continue to assert that the reconquest of Texas was imminent. His government had made this promise for two and a half years, and was losing credibility the longer it remained unfulfilled. If Texas could not be taken by force, a face-saving alternative was needed. The arrangement he now offered Houston seemed to be a way out of this dilemma.[24]

Also a factor in Santa Anna's decision to suggest an armistice at this time was his fear that the United States might soon try to annex Texas. Mexico still insisted that the Republic was a province in rebellion over which it would ultimately reassert its control, but this convenient fiction would crumble if Texas became a state in the Union. While the United States was keeping quiet about any annexation plans, Mexico was suspicious enough to put the Tyler government on notice that an attempt to take its territory would lead to war.[25] Such threats were given little serious attention in Washington; since Santa Anna seemed reluctant to commit his army to an invasion of Texas, he was in no position to risk an armed conflict with the United States.

Great Britain, which was as anxious as Mexico to keep Texas out of American hands, urged Houston to at least consider Santa Anna's proposals. Charles Elliot did not expect the President to be wholly satisfied with the plan, but apparently believed that Mexico might make further concessions at the negotiating table that could lead to a formal declaration of Texas independence.[26] Even Waddy Thompson, who was becoming more and more sympathetic to the Mexican cause, saw merit in the proposals. The American minister believed that such an arrangement would only be temporary—privately he had been assured as much by Mexican cabinet members—and might well be advantageous to Texas in the long run. Peace would bring immigrants from the southern states pouring once again across the Sabine. Trade would resume, with Texas enjoying access to the Mexican market for cotton. Texas would soon be in a position to dictate the terms of its future, choosing to remain independent or annexing itself to the United States.[27]

The President himself professed to be startled and amused by Santa Anna's offer. To U.S. chargé Joseph Eve he remarked that he found the proposal "a curiosity . . . and that is about as much as can well be made of it."[28] But Houston had apparently decided from the outset that it would be wise to at least show some interest in the plan. Eager to silence the critics of his conduct toward the Mier survivors, Houston was mindful of the fact that Mexico would have to send the prisoners home if a peace could be established. It was this concern for the Texans incarcerated in Mexico, according to Washington D. Miller, which prompted the chief executive to first consider the Mexican peace initiative. "If my recollection serves me," Miller wrote some years later, "the President at once conceived the idea that [Santa Anna's proposals] might be turned to good account in securing the liberation of the prisoners still in Mexico."[29]

There was, however, another, more important consideration: an armistice would give Houston the time he needed to pursue an annexation agreement with Tyler and Secretary of State Upshur. The willingness of the British to mediate in any peace talks with Mexico would lend credence to the growing suspicion in the United States that Texas was drifting under British control. An armistice arranged by Great Britain would be the very thing to put the United States on notice that it could not take Texas for granted. The Tyler government would now have to realize that Texas was perfectly capable of going its own way. In one stroke, Houston could solve his most nagging domestic political problem and take a decisive step toward fulfilling his diplomatic strategy.

Houston sat down with Robinson to compose a reply to Santa Anna, which Robinson duly transcribed and signed in his own hand.[30] The

Mexican peace proposals, the judge explained in the letter, with considerable understatement, had not elicited the enthusiasm he had hoped for among the people of Texas. He went on to say, however, that negotiations might still be possible if a way could be found to ease the tension between the two governments. If Santa Anna would agree to an armistice and release the prisoners currently being held at Perote and Molino del Rey, Robinson suggested, the terms could then be considered by the people of Texas in an atmosphere "free of passion and excitement."[31]

The Mexican President was quick to respond to Robinson's letter. He contacted Percy Doyle, and informed him that he would agree to a temporary cessation of hostilities. This news was in turn relayed to Houston through Charles Elliot in Galveston, and on June 13 Houston issued a proclamation declaring a one-year armistice. During this time representatives from the two countries would meet at a designated spot on the Río Grande to hammer out a permanent peace treaty. The Texas delegates would then proceed to Mexico City to negotiate for the release of the prisoners taken in San Antonio and Mier. It was, by all appearances, a momentous step; for the first time in seven years, Texas and Mexico were formally at peace. And for the first time since their capture, the Mier prisoners had reason to be hopeful.

Not everyone was happy with the armistice. In Mexico, the Veracruz *Censor* blasted the proposed armistice as "dishonorable," objecting to any accommodation with "the double-dealing Anglo Saxon Americans."[32] Houston, of course, had considerable difficulty selling the armistice to the citizens of the Republic, many of whom were pathologically suspicious of any Mexican peace overtures. A convention demanding the President's removal was called in LaGrange.[33] Houston's critics insinuated that he had struck a corrupt bargain with Santa Anna and sold the country out to British interests. The anti-Houston New Orleans *Daily Picayune* demanded that the Texas President be "impeached at once, either as a traitor or an imbecile. One or the other of the charges can certainly be sustained."[34]

But on the whole Mexico and Texas both had reason to be satisfied with this new turn of events. The armistice provided a much-needed boost to the economies of the two countries. When the news reached London, the Mexican bond rating, always desperately low, immediately jumped ten points.[35] Ashbel Smith reported that the armistice had done Texas "a world of good" in promoting its credibility in the eyes of European leaders.[36] Equally beneficial to both countries was the reopening of commercial relations. "The Mexican trade through Corpus Christi is active and quite brisk," Washington D. Miller observed after the armistice had been signed.[37] "The American spirit of enterprise," Viscount de Cramayel noted, "nearly paralyzed last year by the threat of invasion and unfortunate circumstances, seems to begin to revive in Texas. No sooner is there some hope for peace or at least an armistice to provide respite from anxiety than commerce picks up, and a progressive movement is noticeable in the small city of Galveston."[38] The Houston *Morning Star* even went so far as to suggest that the armistice would usher in a new era of peace between Texas and Mexico. Commenting on the rebuilding of the fort at Corpus Christi, the newspaper predicted the development of "an immense and valuable trade," and suggested that the two countries would soon "be inclined to view each other in a very different light, from that dimed [*sic*] by the cloudy atmosphere of war."[39]

Houston's popularity also improved now that most Texans realized that peace would bring the prosperity they wanted. The President's principal antagonists, if not effectively muzzled, seemed at least to have lost much of their influence. Of Francis Moore, the editor of the *Telegraph and Texas Register,* one Texan observed, "Surely that man is demented. . . . His reckless and injurious course would seem to justify the suspicion— But I venture to predict that his days will not be long in the land—His voice will soon cease to be heard—it is even now almost without an *echo.*"[40] "The general sentiment of this community approves of the Armistice," O. M. Roberts, an East Texas attorney, wrote to Washington D. Miller. "Surely we needed rest,—rest from anxiety, rest from excitement,—and rest from dissentions. External aggression having ceased, our internal diseases will be healed for want of the customary stimulant."[41] Even the *Picayune* correspondent in Texas had to admit that the people were "lauding Sam the First to the skies."[42] Dismayed that many Texans remained loyal to their chief executive in light of recent developments, another New Orleans paper complained that "the treachery and imbecility of the Executive . . . do not seem to have excited among the people of Texas the indignation which they ought."[43]

The impeachment convention met as planned that summer, but it was a failure; only a few delegates from the western counties bothered to attend.[44] So well received was the news of the armistice that it had even garnered support for the President in these traditionally anti-Houston districts. "The people in this section go almost *en masse* for the Executive," wrote one Austin resident; "they say, let us have peace, if it can be had on honorable terms—Many of us in this neighborhood (who you know are the *very first* settlers of Texas,) have spent, or rather wasted, more than twenty years amidst every species of hardship and privation, war, turmoil and confusion and we are not ashamed to confess that we want repose."[45]

Houston himself seemed to adopt a much more optimistic outlook in the summer of 1843, although the birth of his first son in May may have had something to do with his buoyant mood. At any rate, it was with no small amount of satisfaction that the President was able to write to George Hockley that month, "You will admit that but one foolery is stationary with us, and that is *to make war without means*." [46] In July he wrote to Ashbel Smith: "The Armistice has cheered our people, and the vicious, traitorous, and factious are confounded." [47] And to a friend in Texas he expressed similar sentiments: "Our Mexican relations have assumed a more promising aspect. Let us never dispair [*sic*] of the Republic; but like true citizens obey the laws, love order, be industrious, live economically, and all will soon be well. Noisy, non-productive and disappointed men, who hate labor and aspire to live upon the people's substance, have already done us great injury abroad. At home they are too well known to be feared." [48]

Thus, in spite of the difficult obstacles which had presented themselves in the first six months of 1843, the Houston administration could look forward to the remainder of the year with a realistic sense of confidence and optimism. For the first time in its short history, the country was at peace, and what was more important, it was clear that most Texans preferred it that way. "The publication of the armistice," one contemporary historian wrote, "dispersed the warlike preparations of Texas. The people were pleased with the change: ignorant of the moving causes, they saw a prospect of peace." [49] Moreover, the recent harvest, the most abundant seen in Texas since independence, augured well for the economic recovery of the Republic. [50] Commodore Moore's exploits had briefly breathed new life into the anti-Houston party, but the population as a whole had been won over to the policy of retrenchment which Houston had advocated at the start of his presidency. Even the recent news of the decimation of the Mier prisoners did not seem to dampen the overwhelming desire for peace. Texans would soon be going to the polls again to elect the members of the Eighth Congress, and this time they would elect men the President could work with. As Houston had predicted, the majority of Texans had learned their lesson; disaster had indeed taught them caution.

WITH THE NEWS of an armistice between Texas and Mexico, the rumors that the prisoners would soon be liberated were revived during the month of June. As encouraging as this new development seemed, it was certainly premature to suppose that their release was imminent. The initial peace talks on the Río Grande were not even scheduled to begin until the fall. Some of the men were growing exasperated with Waddy Thompson's repeated assurances that they could expect their freedom any day. "Thompson wishes to Create an impression that he is much interested for our welfare, altho' . . . he is perfectly *Mexicanized*," wrote one soldier whose hopes had been raised once too often. "I think now he is a good hand at 'Wind Work' only."[51]

Still, the fact that a dialogue had been established between the two countries was a necessary first step, and the prisoners immediately felt the effects of improving relations. The Texans at Molino del Rey petitioned Santa Anna for a day of rest to celebrate the July 4 holiday, and to their surprise the request was granted. A committee was created to procure refreshments and edibles, and all hands contributed what little money they had. The fund was tallied, but it was only enough to supply some meat and a little liquor, hardly the kind of celebration they had in mind. Someone suggested they invite the Mexican officers, who proceeded to dig deeply and generously into their own pockets. A large quantity of mescal was made available, as well as assorted fruits and meats. The prisoners looked forward to their finest meal on Mexican soil.[52]

A room in the powder mill was consigned for the celebration, and those men with artistic talents sketched in charcoal the portraits of Washington, Jefferson, and other famous Americans on the stone walls. The Mexicans even agreed to bring a brass cannon from the armory, to fire off a salute for every state of the Union. The arsenal was pitifully stocked, however, and the prisoners had to be satisfied with the nine cartridges that could be found.

At two o'clock the guests arrived, and Mexican and Texan sat down together. Spread out before them on three tables was a feast so inviting that the customary pre-dinner toasts were postponed (under these circumstances appetite took precedence over protocol). For several minutes the group ate in silence, but at length a few of the Texans made attempts to communicate with their guests. The Mexicans smiled politely, and tried some greetings of their own in stilted English. A marvelous détente seemed to be in the making, as stiff formalities began to melt away with each cup of mescal.

The liquor flowed freely—too freely—and by the time Judge Fenton Gibson, who had been asked to give a speech for the occasion, was presented, the affair was clearly getting out of hand. A number of the men were drunk, and the rest were rapidly approaching the same state. Amid wild cheers and applause, some of the prisoners offered suggestions for his oration, which included denunciations of Santa Anna in particular and the Mexican people in general. The Mexican officers half-rose from their seats in anticipation of insult. The drunken members of the assembly were quieted, and the guests assured that the speech would not give offense.

Judge Gibson opened his address innocuously enough, with a review of the American Revolution and the fight for independence. The men thundered their boisterous approval. As he chronicled the achievements of George Washington, his listeners beat their fists and chains loudly upon the tables. Waxing philosophic, Gibson then launched into a lengthy discourse on the subject of freedom and, in a thinly veiled reference to more recent conflicts, went on to explain how its foes were destined to be crushed underfoot by the sons of liberty. At this the men hooted and hollered with alarming enthusiasm. It was a spirited oration indeed; without intending to do so, Gibson was whipping the men into a frenzy. Plates were swept away and crashed to the ground. Patriotic songs were sung, not one at a time, but several at once. Some prisoners leaped upon the tables and danced. Pandemonium broke loose. Shouting above the din, the judge tried to continue but was drowned out. Disgusted, the Mexican officers withdrew. Their exit was barely noticed.[53]

THE TEXANS AT Molino del Rey made no attempt to escape because they still expected to be released soon. But in the hot month of July, Samuel Walker decided he had waited long enough. Although not a model prisoner, he was a reliable worker, and for this reason his chains had been removed. Getting out of Molino del Rey posed little problem. The powder mill was not designed as a prison, and in recent weeks the vigilance of the guards had grown terribly lax. Some prisoners managed to get passes to go into Tacubaya, provided a guard went with them. On these outings their first and only stop seems to have been the local cantina, and on several occasions it was the prisoners who brought the guard home.[54] Walker was waiting only for money from friends in Texas when Willis Coplan wandered off on the night of July 30. For twenty-four hours the guards did not know he was missing (in the next three weeks he would travel eight hundred miles, only to be recaptured at the Río Grande, near Matamoros).[55] Walker believed that once Coplan's escape was discovered, all the men would be rechained, and the guards were not likely to take their duties so casually again. He resolved to make his escape immediately.

The following evening Walker and two friends, James C. Wilson and D. H. Gattis, strolled by the sentinels shortly before sunset and continued walking to a far-off corner of the wooded grounds. They scaled the walls, letting themselves down with torn blankets which they had earlier smuggled out of their cell. It was nightfall by the time they reached Mexico City, and they passed through the deserted streets of the capital without stopping. In the morning they hid in bushes a few miles away, where they waited until dusk to begin their hike toward the coast. They had only just started out when they were stopped by two maguey farmers, but Walker gave them a dollar and they were allowed to move on unmolested. The next day their hiding place was discovered by four men who marched them to a nearby village and handed them over to the alcalde. Here they were locked in a one-room jail for the night and told they would be sent to Mexico City at daybreak. The alcalde did not think to leave a sentry at the jail door, however, and they quickly went to work to get the door open before dawn. Unable to pick the lock, they managed to dig away some of the dirt underneath the door and, using a wooden plank, succeeded in prying it off its hinges. By the time the guards came for them at sunrise, the three Texans were well on their way.[56]

They hiked through the mountains, staying clear of the roads and the goatherds who could be seen roaming the hillsides. But it was impossible to pass through the country entirely unobserved, and once again they were apprehended, this time by some suspicious *rancheros*. Walker and his friends passed themselves off as English mineworkers, and were asked to produce some sort of identification. Wilson found in his pockets a wrinkled piece of paper, on which a fellow prisoner had written the verses to an old ballad, "When Shall We Three Meet Again." "They told him to translate it," Walker later recalled. "He told them that he could not translate very well, but he would satisfy them that the passports were genuine. He commenced and translated a pretty good passport out of the song ballad."[57] Wilson soon fell ill, but Walker and Gattis continued on their journey, traveling only through remote Indian villages. They reached Tampico on August 12, and with the aid of the U.S. consul and other foreign businessmen they signed on as hands on American vessels. Wilson, when he was well enough to travel, also returned home safely, by way of Tampico.

Six other men, emboldened by Walker and his friends, also decided to take their leave of Molino del Rey. The discovery of these escapes sent the Mexican cavalry galloping along the roads of Tacubaya. Descriptions of the men were printed on handbills and tacked up in nearby villages and in Mexico City. But the furor over their disappearance was not quite so great as might have been expected. Anxious to avoid the blame for their neglect of duty, the guards reported that some of the escapees had died in prison.[58]

By the first week in September, after four months of work, the Tacubaya road was completed. There were those who, in spite of everything, were still optimistic, having convinced themselves that as soon as the road was finished, they would be allowed to go home. The hopefuls received an extra boost when the men were visited by Santa Anna's private secretary, who told them that the government was satisfied with the work.[59] Again their expectations proved unwarranted. A few days after the completion of the road, they received the news that they were to march immediately to the Castle of Perote.

TIME WAS MOVING too slowly for Thomas Jefferson Green, who had by now abandoned any hope of hearing from Santa Anna. Both his father—a judge on the Tennessee Supreme Court—and his brother had made frequent appeals to Washington on his behalf. Green himself had written to President Tyler, as well as many prominent politicians, all without success.[60] He sounded out his fellow officers at Perote on the prospect of an escape, and surprisingly the most enthusiastic about such an enterprise was Captain Reese, who had refused to take part in the Salado escape. Reese had expected clemency for his good conduct, and while at Perote had written letters to Minister of War Tornel requesting parole. Receiving no answer, he now decided that his only chance for a speedy liberation lay with Green.[61] William Fisher, on the other hand, was not so keen on the plan. Sensitive to the charge that he had been wrong to surrender at Mier, Fisher did not like the idea of escaping without his men. He would not leave until the last of the Mier prisoners was free.[62]

Green and Reese eventually decided to take part in an escape operation already underway by a number of the San Antonio prisoners, who had for several weeks been working in their own cell on a tunnel through the walls of the fortress. It looked for a time, however, as if there would be no need for an escape. The prisoners of Perote got wind of the same rumor their friends had heard in Tacubaya—on Santa Anna's saint's day, they would be released. Waddy Thompson wrote to tell them to make preparations for going home. The guards, too, were congratulating the prisoners on their good fortune. So certain were the Texans that they would be released that work on the tunnel stopped completely.[63]

When it became clear that the Snively Expedition had destroyed any hope of freedom, work on the hole resumed. At the far end of each cell there was a funnel-shaped opening, only four by twelve inches in size on the outside, but widening through the eight-foot-thick walls so that in the cell it was about two feet square. Efforts had been made to widen this aperture in one cell, but the stones around it on the outer wall were too secure, and it was necessary to bore diagonally through the pumice rock, which over the years had become quite soft in the damp Perote climate. There was a shutter on the opening inside the cell to keep out the cold night air, and after some work it was possible for a man to crawl up into the hole, lying flat on his stomach, and chisel through the rock with the shutter closed. Several men worked in the carpentry shop making artillery carriages, so chisels and other tools were fairly easy to come by. When a man finished digging, the fragments were gathered up and buried under a loose pavement in the floor, to be disposed of later in the latrines. Every man planning to make the escape through the wall would start with at least two weeks' rations. To avoid suspicion, small quantities of sugar, chocolate, fat bacon, and other items were bought over a period of several weeks, as well as pieces of rope which, when tied together, would be used to lower the men down the wall.[64]

Shortly before lockup at six on the evening of July 2, Green, Reese, and Dan Henrie, another Mier prisoner, exchanged places with three Bexar men in the cell next door. Green left in William Fisher's care a wry note addressed to Santa Anna. Since the climate of Perote, he explained, was "not suiting my health, I should, for the present, retire to one in Texas more congenial to my feelings." [65]

It was raining the night of the escape, and the men were not asked to line up for a head count outside the doorways of their cells, as was the custom on clear evenings. In the dim light of the cells it was difficult to see the faces of the prisoners, and the switch went unnoticed by the guards. Later that night, to divert the attention of the sentry outside, a group of prisoners kept up a vigorous game of monte near the door. To keep the sentry interested in the card game, the Texans gave him some tlacos which he passed through the grill, telling the men how to bet for him. A jug of mescal was handed round, and poured into an eggshell and passed through the gate for the guard. To drown out the noise of the digging, the other men sang and danced, keeping up a constant racket in their chains.

Behind a curtain at the far end of the cell, the prisoners were finishing their last-minute preparations. But as they scraped away the outer crust of the wall they found that the hole was still too small, and additional work was needed to widen it. It would take another two hours of hard digging to remove some obstinate pieces of stone and mortar before the opening was finally big enough.

At nine o'clock the first of the prisoners was lifted by his comrades feet first into the hole, and with painstakingly slow effort squeezed through the wall of the fortress. One by one the prisoners made their descent, but the escape hit a snag when a prisoner got stuck, unable to move any further in either direction. After some confusion his cellmates slid a rope into the tunnel and with considerable difficulty pulled him back into the cell. Undeterred, he disrobed and squirmed naked back into the opening, pulling his clothes in after him, and eventually managed to wriggle through. Three hours would pass before all sixteen men were safely outside, standing on the bottom of the moat. The Texans adjusted their packs and clothing and stole across the moat in single file. On the far side of the moat was a flight of narrow steps, invisible in the dark, and they felt their way along the bottom until they found it. Once over the moat they ran to the outer wooden wall, clambered over the sharpened points of the logs and slid to the ground. Here they split up into small groups to make their way to the coast.

The next morning, at nine o'clock, Captain Guzmán and his turnkeys opened the doors to the cells and ordered the prisoners to form up outside. The Bexar prisoners did not file out with their usual promptness, offering a number of different excuses to remain in the cells a little while longer. When Guzmán in exasperation entered the room and demanded to know the reason for the delay, he saw that fully half of them were missing. One of the prisoners wrote in his diary that evening, "it is almost impossible to describe the mingled emotion of surprise, mortification and fear detected in his face, the vains [*sic*] in his neck swelling and appearing as though he was laboring under some dreadful malady." [66]

Sorties were immediately dispatched to cover the area. Some of the escapees did not get far. One man fell off a cliff and broke his arm, and was brought back to the castle within a few hours. His comrades were soon overtaken by the cavalry. During the next few weeks eight of the sixteen men, including Isaac Allen, were back in irons at Perote.

Fortunately for Green, he had American friends in Mexico City who had supplied him with a map of the surrounding countryside and made arrangements for him to be helped along the way. From Jalapa, where he spent six days at the home of an elderly Mexican hostile to the centralist regime, Green was escorted the remainder of the way to the coast by bands of *ladrones*. The bandits led Green and his companions down little-used mountain trails by night and hid them in bushes during the day, out of sight of the Mexican cavalry. In Veracruz they were secreted away in a posada owned by a Frenchman during an outbreak of yellow fever. One night they slipped down to the harbor to an American steamer, shortly before it set sail for New Orleans.[67]

By September Green was back at his home in Brazoria County, where he was greeted with much fanfare as a prodigal hero. Sam Houston, who must have thought he was rid of Green for good, cannot have been pleased.

"A Fragile Peace"

GREEN WAS SAFELY back on Texas soil by the time the prisoners from Molino del Rey reached the gates of Perote Castle on September 21. Although the stark, grim walls of the fortress left them dispirited, the next few weeks would prove to be fairly pleasant ones for the new inmates. For one month the prison authorities allowed them to remain unfettered and gave them no work to do, permitting them to spend several hours each day with the Bexar prisoners, all of whom were anxious to hear of the Texans' adventures at Mier and the Hacienda del Salado.[1] "Our rations are good," wrote one of the Mier prisoners, "coffee and bread in the morning, Beef, soup, Rice, bread at noon, coffee & bread for supper. . . . Officers & soldiers seem to allow us all the privileges they can."[2]

The Mier prisoners were not the only new residents of Perote. Owing to reasons of ill health, General Durán had quit his post as the prison commandant a few days before the Texans arrived.[3] The new governor was General José María Jarero, a strict, elderly officer who had the habit of whacking prisoners on the side of the head with his cane if they were slow to remove their hats in his presence.[4] Though the prisoners grumbled at his discipline, he seems to have taken an active interest in their welfare, issuing them new clothes, shoes, and sometimes small sums of money.[5] He even allowed the Texans to join in the amusements provided for the garrison. On one occasion, a company of equestrians put on a demonstration in the castle moat, but their horsemanship failed to impress the prisoners. "It was rather a poor performance to us, but it appeared to tickle the Mexicans considerable," one Texan sniffed.[6]

The fort was the scene of considerable troop activity throughout the fall, due in large part to the ongoing rebellion in the Yucatán, with various regiments billeted at the castle en route from one post to another as military circumstances required. In early October a new garrison arrived, and with it a new set of officers entrusted with the task of guarding the Texans.[7] Shortly afterward, the Mier prisoners were ordered to take part in a work detail engaged in sweeping and cleaning the fort. A lively but civilized argument ensued between the men and the officer of the guard, with the former citing their rights as prisoners of war, the latter insisting that a precedent had already been set by the road work done in Tacubaya. The next morning the officer visited them again, and again the recalcitrant prisoners told him they would take no part in such degrading menial labor. Without another word the officer retired, and the doors of the cells were relocked. Satisfied that they had made their point, the men waited for their breakfast rations to be brought in, but the doors stayed shut all morning. Noon came and went and still the Texans remained cooped up in their cells. Some of them shouted through the grate, demanding food and water. No response came from the soldiers outside the door. By mid-afternoon, as the sunlight receded from the narrow windows, the stale air was becoming unbreathable. The prisoners shuffled silently about in the darkness. When it became clear that there was to be no food that day, they settled down with empty stomachs and went to sleep. It was not until the next morning that the key turned in the lock and the door swung open. The buckets of warm cornmeal and coffee were brought in. And the Mier prisoners went to work.[8]

The Texans had been at Perote only a few weeks when some of the men began to complain of severe headaches, which were quickly followed by wracking fever chills. Soon others came down with the same symptoms. They were suffering from typhus, although the prisoners often described the disease as "jail fever," believed to be caused by a lack of ventilation and proper food and the shock of prison confinement. During the month of October the sick list grew. In the prison hospital the patients were allowed a few days of rest, and then ordered back to the work detail. They suffered relapses almost immediately. Any suspicions that the Texans were shirking soon faded. Those who were well enough continued to go about their duties, but they worked listlessly and without humor. One by one even the hardiest prisoners begged to be allowed to report to the hospital. By the end of the month the disease had reached alarming proportions. There was even talk among the men that they were being poisoned.[9] To check the spread of the contagion the prison hospital was moved to the village, but the epidemic quickly spread to the guards and the townspeople of Perote.

The carrier of this particular strain of typhus was the louse, of which the moldy walls of Perote held such an abundance. The disease was transmitted through the feces of the animal, infecting the victim through skin abrasions that were the result of constant scratching. But the causes of typhus were unknown in 1843, and at no time did the doctors strike at the source of the disease. A strict delousing program might have contained the contagion, but this was not implemented. Instead, prison authorities curtailed the consumption of water, supplying the men with hot coffee and even brandy. Fruit was forbidden, and chili con carne and soups were added to vary the otherwise unimaginative menu. Wooden planking was brought in to keep the men from sleeping on the cold, damp floors, and the doors of their cells were kept open all day to provide better ventilation.[10] Still the epidemic raged.

Daily the oxcarts passed over the drawbridge on their way to the hospital in the village, with their cargoes of men, nauseated and delirious with fever. At one time there were eighty-six Texans there. The prisoners who returned to the fort looked little better than those who had recently come down with the disease. Gaunt and ghostly pale, they had not fully recovered, but hospital beds were needed. And sometimes the oxcarts would come back from the hospital with a body wrapped in blankets and bound up with twine, ready for a grave in the castle moat. The hospital in Perote resembled a madhouse. Feverish patients screamed and writhed in pain as blisters rose up on their bodies. In their delirium they tried to rip them off and had to be restrained by doctors and orderlies. Tied to their cots, they could lie there for up to three weeks, completely insensible, unable to see or hear.[11]

Given their lack of knowledge about the disease and the limited resources at their disposal, the doctors appear to have made every effort on behalf of their patients. Big Foot Wallace described his doctor as "one of the best-hearted men I ever knew."[12] Another prisoner wrote that the inmates "were well cared for, the physicians and nurses being attentive, and every thing appropriate of necessity or comfort being provided them."[13] Not all the Texans were satisfied with their treatment, however. One prisoner reported: "the fact is that not a Blanket, Shoe, shirt or even a piece of bread was left to an invalid by the Mexican attendants at the hospital."[14] But the epidemic did not discriminate; according to one prisoner "thousands" of Mexicans died of typhus that winter.[15] The soldiers at the fort who came down with the disease received no better treatment than the Texas inmates, and when no more hospital beds were available, the orderlies laid them out on the floor in the filth and vermin.[16]

To be sure, the suffering brought out the best and the worst in human nature on both sides. Guards and prisoners alike cast greedy eyes upon the belongings of the sick. There were sordid scenes of guards taking money and valuables from bodies still warm, of prisoners urging delirious comrades to will their valuables to them if they died. One Texan refused to give a dying comrade twelve cents for food.[17] Fights broke out among the prisoners. When word of the epidemic reached Mexico City, a concerned Santa Anna asked General Jarero for a status report on the disease and its effects on the Texas prisoners. Some of the inmates, at Jarero's request, signed a statement to the effect that they were being well treated, but their cellmates believed this was done only to curry favor with the commandant in the hope of obtaining better treatment.[18] The camaraderie born of their confinement was wearing thin.

IN THE MIDST of this misery there was for the prisoners one bright ray of hope. Since the summer Texas and Mexico had enjoyed peace, and now the Texas commissioners were preparing to leave for the Río Grande to discuss a permanent treaty with Mexican officials. The armistice had held for the past six months, but not without some difficulty. Mexicans living above the Río Grande were not free from harassment and persecution. Since Mexico still claimed Texas as its own, it regarded any acts of violence against the Mexican population there as violations of the armistice. Sparsely populated south Texas had long been a trouble spot. The activities which had won for Ewen Cameron and his "cowboys" such notoriety had not abated with their enlistment in Somervell's army. Numerous gangs continued to prey on Mexican *rancheros* living above the Río Grande.[19] In the fall of 1842, in apparent retaliation for the Vásquez and Woll incursions, Anglo-Texans had burned Mexican homes near Victoria, forcing the Mexican residents to flee for safety below the Río Grande.[20] The following year seven Mexicans from Camargo obtained letters of safe passage from the mayor of Victoria to visit relatives in the area. On their way home, after purchasing supplies in the town, they were followed by one of the many gangs that prowled the Nueces Strip, a particularly cold-blooded bunch of outlaws known as the "Men-Slayers." The travelers were robbed of their goods, then tied up and shot; only one survived to tell of the slaughter. No attempt was ever made to bring the culprits to justice.[21]

The Mexican government, although it was unwilling to break off the armistice and renew hostilities, vigorously protested the treatment of its citizens in the Nueces Strip. Banditry had become such a serious problem that Houston was obliged to put the entire area under martial law, giving the task of law enforcement to Jack Hays and his ranger company, who had had the foresight not to cross the Río Grande with Fisher's men the year before.[22] Houston could not do much more than insist that the government of Texas was doing everything in its power to protect all citizens living in the area. Nonetheless, the depredations against Mexicans in the Republic continued.

To further complicate matters Great Britain, which was doing all it could to bring the two sides together, was involved in a petty dispute with Mexico that temporarily resulted in the rupturing of diplomatic relations. Ironically, the Mier Expedition was indirectly the cause of the affair. When the Texans were captured at Mier they had no flag to surrender to General Ampudia; however, a British flag the Texans had taken from Indians along the Río Grande was found among their possessions after the battle and sent on to the capital as a trophy of war (the Indians were believed to have come into possession of the flag when a wrecked British vessel was washed up along the Texas coast).[23] At a ball at the National Palace on September 11, the anniversary of Santa Anna's victory against the Spanish in 1829, British chargé d'affaires Percy Doyle spotted the banner displayed on a wall with other flags taken in battle. He insisted that the flag be taken down that evening, but as the incident had already drawn the attention of others at the gala, to save face the Mexican government offered to deliver it to the British legation the next day. Unsatisfied, Doyle stormed out of the palace in protest, accompanied by the other British subjects present. Upon learning that the flag was still hanging on the wall at month's end, Doyle took the extreme step of suspending his diplomatic functions. Protocol and pride were eventually satisfied, and although the episode did not disrupt plans by Texas and Mexico to send representatives to the Río Grande, it was not until a new British minister arrived a few months later that proper diplomatic relations between Great Britain and Mexico resumed.[24]

As a precondition for the negotiations, Houston wanted Santa Anna to free all Texas prisoners. If Mexico was really interested in achieving "a successful and happy termination of existing difficulties," Secretary of State Anson Jones wrote to Charles Elliot, "I cannot but express the hope that our unfortunate prisoners now detained in captivity will be forthwith released. So long as they are detained, and accounts of their sufferings (perhaps exaggerated) continue to reach their friends and countrymen here a state of public feeling will be constantly kept alive, which I much fear will be fatal to every effort at pacification."[25] Houston also stressed this point in his own meetings with the British chargé d'affaires, who communicated the President's concern to his counterpart in Mexico City. "Pray strenuously endeavour to persuade General Santa Ana [*sic*] to release the Texian prisoners," Elliot wrote to Percy Doyle. "No measure would be better calculated to allay angry feeling, and support the influence of the [British] Govmt. for useful, and modern results."[26]

Santa Anna, however, appears to have had no intention of releasing the prisoners so soon. When Percy Doyle broached the subject some months before the flag episode in an audience with the Mexican President, Santa Anna replied that the sack of Laredo was a far greater crime than the offenses of many Mexican felons, who like the Texans were compelled to labor in chains on the roads of Mexico.[27] No doubt the President was also aware that the Texans represented a valuable bargaining chip not to be disposed of lightly; if the prisoners were set free, Houston might very well lose interest in the armistice talks. Still suspicious of the sincerity of the Texas government, the Mexican President would hold onto the prisoners to test Houston's willingness to come to the negotiating table.

Santa Anna did not wish to appear unconciliatory by rejecting the request of the Texas government out of hand. Instead he avoided the issue, replying that he would release the Texan prisoners only when all Mexican prisoners in Texas were freed, some of whom, Santa Anna said, had been held since the Revolution. As a dilatory tactic this was indeed a transparent one, for there were no Mexican prisoners in Texas. Some Mexican soldiers captured at San Jacinto in 1836 had chosen to remain in Texas, but they were now private citizens.[28] Nonetheless, on September 4 the Houston government issued a proclamation officially releasing any Mexican soldiers being held against their will (it had issued an identical one in 1837).[29] But the order came too late to have any effect. By this time the date scheduled for the negotiations on the Río Grande was only weeks away, allowing Santa Anna to ignore the Texas edict, as he had probably intended to do all along.

To represent Texas at the armistice talks Houston chose two close friends, Samuel May Williams and George Hockley. The former was the most prominent merchant and financier in the Republic, who had on more than one occasion loaned Houston money when he was short of funds. Hockley's friendship with the President was of long standing. Having served as an aide when Houston was governor of Tennessee, Hockley had been rewarded with a number of political jobs after following his former chief to Texas on the eve of the Revolution. The two men had quarreled over Houston's war policy in 1842, when Hockley quit his post as secretary of war, but were now reconciled. Both Hockley and Williams belonged to the ever-shrinking number of Texans who favored a strong and independent Republic, opposing annexation to the United States.[30] They would therefore be acceptable to the Mexican government and could be counted on to work strenuously to achieve a peace.

What they failed to realize—and what Houston failed to tell them— was that the administration's primary objective remained the annexation of Texas to the United States. Nor did they know just how close the two governments were to reopening negotiations to discuss the matter. It had not gone unnoticed in Washington that Great Britain had helped arrange the armistice between Texas and Mexico. Although Charles Elliot in Galveston and Percy Doyle in Mexico City had served as little more than intermediaries in bringing the two sides together, Houston did not mind exaggerating their efforts, and made it a point to publicly applaud Her Majesty's government for its assistance.[31]

Reports of the Houston administration's close cooperation with the British government were causing quite a stir in the southern states of the Union. Elliot's friendship with the President quickly became a major news item, as newspapers across the United States reprinted stories from the anti-Houston presses in Texas and New Orleans.[32] Elliot was described as a shadowy figure who was plotting to destroy slavery in Texas and, with Houston's help, to turn the country into a British satellite. So great was the outcry among slaveholders that both Houston and his secretary of state came forward to publicly defend Elliot and to declare that the British diplomat had at no time discussed with them the possibility of abolishing slavery. In spite of these disavowals, the rumors of British intrigue in Texas, once started, could not be contained. No sooner had William Murphy, the new American representative sent to replace Joseph Eve, arrived in Galveston than he reported that President Houston was completely under British influence.[33]

Murphy was particularly startled by the contempt which the Houston administration was now showing toward U.S. diplomatic policies in the region, as well as its efforts on behalf of the Texas prisoners. The *National Vindicator*, a leading Houston party news organ, flatly accused Waddy Thompson of plotting to excite anti-British feelings in Texas by his revelations to the Mier prisoners of the contents of Houston's now-famous letter to Charles Elliot. The newspaper also ridiculed Daniel Webster's unsuccessful efforts of the previous year to bring about an end to the hostilities between Texas and Mexico, thus indirectly blaming the United States for the unrest along the frontier. The new armistice, the *Vindicator* suggested, was proof that Great Britain had succeeded in forcing Mexico to cease its border harassment where Washington had failed.[34]

Such allegations did not do justice to U.S. initiatives. Thompson remained the prisoners' staunchest advocate in Mexico City and rarely missed an opportunity to discuss their plight with Mexican leaders. He had also asked British diplomats Pakenham and Doyle on a number of occasions to assist him in bringing pressure to bear on Mexico to alleviate their situation, but had found the representatives of Her Majesty's government decidedly cool toward the idea of acting jointly on the matter.[35] To be sure, Houston's stinging criticisms of U.S. efforts were due in part to the fact that Thompson's ill-advised but inadvertent remarks to some of the prisoners had provided the President's critics with some potent ammunition to use against him. But in trying to exploit the prisoners to help drive a wedge between the major powers, Houston deserved at least some of the blame for his domestic political problems. Indeed, Houston continued to subordinate the incarceration of Texans in Mexico to his own diplomatic objectives. If his sudden hostility toward American policy makers was genuine, it also had the added benefit of sending a clear message to the United States of the dangers of a British ally on its southwestern border. Such, at least, was the message received by U.S. chargé d'affaires Murphy, who that fall warned his government of the perils which such a scenario would pose to the interests of slavery. "The great blow to our Civil Institutions is to be struck here," Murphy wrote, "and it will be a fatal blow, if not timely arrested."[36]

American fears of British intrigues in Texas were fast approaching hysterical proportions. In July, newly appointed U.S. Secretary of State Abel Upshur received a report, later proved groundless, from an American agent in London that Great Britain had promised a guaranteed, interest-free loan to Texas in exchange for the abolition of slavery.[37] Even from far-off Perote, Thomas Jefferson Green had warned his friends in the southern states of British designs. Prior to his escape, he had written to John C. Calhoun, "however timid politicians may for the present dodge the question, your country and mine is one and the same, and to keep yours whole, she must promptly check the influences of that *great and mighty nation upon which the sun never sets.*"[38] Rumors such as these were enough to terrify southern slaveholders, who were by now showing symptoms of acute cultural paranoia. Faced with what they perceived to be the specter of abolitionism, their efforts to bring Texas into the Union were quickly becoming nothing less than a crusade for the very survival of their cherished institution.

The upcoming peace talks with the Mexican government no doubt heightened American anxieties about a British conspiracy and increased Tyler's resolve to push annexation forward. For its part, the Houston administration announced that it had high hopes for the negotiations. But if Hockley and Williams believed that their efforts might result in a resolution of the difficulties between Texas and Mexico, Houston's objectives were much more limited. The President appears to have seen their mission simply as a means to gain time in which to pursue his annexation gambit and, if possible, to bring the Perote prisoners home. Houston's desire to effect the release of his incarcerated countrymen, however, was never more than a secondary concern. Now that it looked as if the Tyler government might pursue annexation, he was in no hurry to engage in negotiations with Mexico which had little hope of success. In fact, Houston was perfectly satisfied with the existing armistice, and asked his secretary of state, Anson Jones, to delay sending his negotiating team to the Río Grande as long as possible.[39]

As usual, the President appears to have released information to his subordinates on a "need-to-know" basis. The Texas secretary of state himself seems to have entertained a far more optimistic—and given the President's own attitude, somewhat naïve—assessment of the situation regarding the Perote prisoners. Even before the negotiations between Texas and Mexico had begun, Jones was thanking Elliot for his "assistance in procuring the release of the Mier and other prisoners in Mexico, which we now hope to have home soon."[40] As for Williams and Hockley, they seem to have been kept completely in the dark about Houston's strategy, and indeed were to be given only, in Houston's words, "a hint of what will be wanted of them."[41] They knew nothing of the President's annexation plans, and in all likelihood would have refused to undertake their mission if they had known.

By October the peace talks could be postponed no longer, and Hockley and Williams sailed from Galveston to Matamoros, then up the Río Grande to General Adrian Woll's headquarters. Along the way they stopped at Mier, where the Texas representatives expected a hostile reception, but to their surprise the townspeople held a banquet in their honor.[42] Their final destination was Sabinas, a remote village southwest of Mier. Once there, they were dismayed to learn that one of the Mexican commissioners appointed by Woll had been taken ill, and talks could not begin until he recovered. For several weeks Hockley and Williams waited in a posada in a windswept little town on enemy soil, only occasionally receiving word from the government that had sent them there. The Texans did not actually sit down to discuss the armistice with their Mexican counterparts until December.[43]

If Williams and Hockley were frustrated by the lack of activity, they would certainly have been more upset had they known that they were wasting their time. They were not aware that in their absence, the volatile political situation in Texas had changed dramatically. In September, Houston's young friend Washington D. Miller had written a follow-up letter to the one he had sent to President Tyler in January expressing his fears of British involvement in Texan affairs. If his first letter had tried to impress upon the U.S. President the urgency of the situation, this second epistle sounded a note of frantic alarm. "Great Britain is doing or pretending to do a great deal for us," Miller explained, in return for which it expected "*territory and abolition.*" Miller continued: "Every day that the action of the U.S. is delayed the prospects of GB are brightening. Will Mr. Upshur permit another year to elapse without doing something effective? Will you not do it?"[44] Such imprecations, it turned out, were unnecessary, for Tyler had long been convinced of the need to take action on the annexation question. Shortly after Hockley and Williams sailed from Galveston, Houston received word from Isaac Van Zandt in Washington that a formal offer to reopen the issue was imminent.[45]

Despite its desire for annexation, the Houston administration would require a number of guarantees from the Tyler government before deciding to embark on a new round of talks with the United States. Any discussions with American representatives would have to be undertaken with the utmost secrecy, for once it became known that Texas was seeking annexation, Santa Anna could be expected to break off the armistice and resume hostilities. Thus, Houston insisted on assurances from Washington that the Tyler administration had enough votes in the Senate to ratify the treaty and, equally important, a pledge of U.S. protection if Mexico attacked Texas while the talks were underway. After months of preliminary negotiations, a cautious Houston finally brought the matter before the Texas Congress, with his recommendation to accept the U.S. proposal.

But the President still wished to keep the armistice with Mexico in effect as a precaution in case his annexation initiative failed.[46] While giving Van Zandt the go-ahead to open secret annexation talks in Washington, he continued to instruct his commissioners in Mexico to negotiate for the independence of Texas. Houston could not have it both ways, but it was a sound policy to work for both until one was assured. Houston was still hopeful that Mexico might release the prisoners, and for this reason he saw no need to recall his commissioners, nor even to tell them, at this late stage, what he was up to. He continued to send them instructions, expressing every confidence in their ability to negotiate a satisfactory peace. In his last dispatch to Hockley and Williams, the President reminded his two diplomats that the release of the Perote prisoners would pave the way toward an amicable resolution of the difficulties dividing the two countries. "Another subject which you are aware is of deep concern to the people of this country is that of the liberation of our prisoners," Houston wrote. "You will perceive, and the Mexican commissioners ought to perceive also, that negotiations for a general peace under an armistice would progress much more agreeably if the prisoners were restored to their homes."[47]

Unaware that their efforts had been rendered meaningless by events in the United States and Texas, Hockley and Williams continued to work doggedly toward a permanent peace. But as the negotiations continued into the new year, they began to detect a definite shift in attitude on the part of the Mexican delegates. Evidently Santa Anna had gotten wind of Tyler's new overtures to Texas from his minister in Washington and instructed his representatives on the Río Grande to take a much harder line.[48] In early February the Mexican commissioners received new orders from the capital: Texas would be readmitted as a department of Mexico with no special privileges whatsoever. Now even Hockley and Williams realized that any hope of conciliation between the two governments was impossible. Fearing General Woll would not allow them to return to Texas if they did not accept the Mexican demands, they signed the revised document without argument; since the armistice had to be ratified by both governments, it was not binding. They had made no headway with regard to the Perote prisoners. Still unaware that they had been acting out a charade to buy time for Houston's annexation plans, they packed up and went home.

In mid-March, the *Daily National Intelligencer,* an influential Whig newspaper published in Washington, broke the story that Texan and American diplomats were in the process of concluding an annexation treaty.[49] Although word of the secret negotiations had been leaking out for some time, the news touched off a firestorm of protest, as might be expected, in the northern states, Mexico, and Great Britain. The clandestine nature of the Houston-Tyler initiative only served to fuel the controversy. With the annexation question now out in the open, the Houston administration abandoned all pretense of interest in the peace treaty with Mexico. Having gained the maximum political advantage from the armistice, Houston chose to ignore the document which his representatives had signed at Sabinas. Mexico charged that Texas, by entering into secret annexation talks with the United States, had negotiated in bad faith; Houston countered that the Mexican government had failed to honor the Texans' rights as prisoners of war and had violated its initial promise to release the Perote prisoners before the talks began.[50] In the weeks that followed both Santa Anna and Sam Houston did their fair share of pos-

turing, with each blaming the other for the failed negotiations. But neither man seems to have expected much from the peace talks, and thus
neither could have been particularly surprised by the outcome.

Charles Elliot, on the other hand, could hardly believe the news that
Texas had rejected the peace treaty and was now negotiating with the
United States. In the several months since the armistice had gone into
effect, Elliot had managed to overcome his skepticism of the proceedings,
and had convinced himself, with Houston's prodding, that the negotiations on the Río Grande could well lead to a lasting peace between Texas
and Mexico. The President had repeatedly told Elliot that under no circumstances would he reopen a dialogue with the Tyler government on the
subject of annexation if Mexico's recognition of Texas' independence
could be secured. The sickly Elliot, who had fled the Gulf Coast some
months earlier for a milder climate in the United States, had found comfort in Houston's emphatic assurances that as far as annexation was concerned, "that door is closed." [51] But while Elliot was predicting the fulfillment of his hopes for an independent Republic, Houston had decided
that it was time to open the door wide. "I am longing for tidings from
your Commissioners, and for news of the release of the prisoners," Elliot
had written to Anson Jones in January. "I see good reason to hope that
those negotiations will reach a happy conclusion." [52] Even as late as mid-
February he had told the Foreign Office in London not to worry about
annexation, so confident was he that Houston and Santa Anna would
come to terms. [53]

In April, despondent over the failure of the negotiations at Sabinas and
wracked by dysentery, Elliot summoned up enough strength to return to
Texas. Houston met the British diplomat in Galveston, where he provided him with a less than accurate briefing on the recent peace talks,
blaming their failure entirely on Mexican intransigence and Santa Anna's
refusal to release the Texan prisoners. In a plaintive and somewhat pa-
thetic note to the Foreign Office following this meeting, Elliot expressed
his disappointment that the negotiations had not gone according to
plan. [54] He remained convinced, however, that with Houston's help Texas
might yet be saved from annexation. The President had urged Elliot not
to give up hope, for Texas might require the good offices of Great Britain
again if the present discussions with the United States fell through. No
doubt Houston wanted to keep all his options open, but his avowed indifference to the annexation talks did not ring true. He had not made the
trip from the Brazos River to the port city of Galveston for the purpose of
conferring with Elliot, but to receive the reports from his negotiating
team in Washington, D.C., the moment they arrived in Texas. [55]

It was not so easy to conceal the truth from Hockley and Williams. They were astounded when they learned that Houston had used them to allow the U.S. annexation proposal to mature. Their anger was certainly understandable. They had gone to Mexico for the purpose of keeping Texas independent; when they returned, negotiations were well underway in Washington, D.C., to fasten it to the Union. What was more, they had considerable difficulty explaining the fact that they had signed a treaty which surrendered the Republic to Mexican rule, for which they were loudly denounced in the Texas press. Thereafter the President's friendship with both men cooled.[56] It was easy enough for Sam Houston to make enemies. His manipulative nature made it equally difficult for him to hold on to his friends.

The real losers of the failed negotiations were the prisoners at Perote. With the armistice dead and the annexation issue now very much alive, the whole question of their release was left hanging fire. The news of the truce was one of the few consolations for the Mier prisoners, and had done much to boost their flagging spirits during the long and brutal winter as the typhus epidemic slowly reduced their numbers. The reports they had read in the American press seemed so encouraging that they could not understand why they had not already been released. "We see from the papers that an armistice has been agreed upon," wrote one prisoner to the Texas secretary of state, Anson Jones. "We see that trade has recommenced, and that Texas is at peace with all the world. Then why do we suffer the consequences of war? And as we receive no news from Texas, you will please let me know, as a friend, the true relations of the two governments; for nothing but imprisonment is so irksome as suspense."[57] He did not yet know that the armistice was a dead letter and the chances for liberation were just as slim as they had always been.

WHILE HOPES FOR the release of the prisoners were being undermined by Houston's dalliance with annexation, the legislature had convened again in Washington-on-the-Brazos. Unlike its predecessors, the Eighth Congress was more kind to the President of the Republic. By election-time, Texas was enjoying peace on its border with Mexico, significant treaties had been signed with the Indian tribes, and the national economy, if not in robust condition, at least seemed to be showing definite signs of improving health. Some men with strong Houston sympathies had won election in both the House and the Senate, and for the first time in his administration, the chief executive's veto could not be overridden at will by the opposition party.

Many anti-Houston stalwarts were back, however, and they were joined by Thomas Jefferson Green. Returning to Texas just in time for the congressional races, the former Perote inmate had been elected by the citizens of Brazoria County to a seat in the House of Representatives. His efforts in Congress were not without merit, and he was instrumental in passing legislation to aid those he had left behind in Mexico. Congress exempted the families of the men killed on the expedition from all forms of taxation and appropriated the sum of $15,000 for the relief of the survivors at Perote.[58] These were constructive measures; the wild talk of a lightning rescue raid or another strike against the lower Río Grande Valley to grab hostages of their own was no longer considered by Houston's opponents, who had once been so vociferous in their demands for retribution. Only the prisoners themselves entertained such fantasies.

Green devoted much of his energy to what had become for him nothing less than a mission: to make life miserable for Sam Houston. He had always been an enemy of the President, but the months spent at Perote had given him time to brood and sharpen his hatred to the point where it was now virtually an obsession. He was determined to prove that Houston was personally responsible for the failure of the expedition and the execution of the men at the Hacienda del Salado. Much to his annoyance, all efforts to obtain from the British government a copy of Houston's letter to Charles Elliot were unsuccessful. Green took his case to the newspapers, and a series of articles attacking the President were published in the anti-Houston journals. "No man of sane intellect," Green wrote, "whatever may be his devotion, personal or political, to President Houston . . . can for a moment doubt that he was the malicious, vindictive, and cold-blooded author of their execution."[59]

Samuel Walker, though not one to seek the headlines like Green, also tried unsuccessfully to obtain a copy of Houston's letter to Elliot from the British chargé d'affaires. Equally enraged by what he perceived to be the President's indifference to his imprisoned colleagues, Walker had written to Houston demanding an explanation, but had received no answer.[60] He had occasion to meet with Houston in Galveston shortly after his escape, and insisted that the President provide evidence to show that he had in no way brought harm to the Mier prisoners by his communications with the British government. Houston ignored this request, but some time later the President met Walker again at a public meeting in Galveston. As Walker descended a flight of stairs, Houston greeted him cordially and offered his hand, but the young ranger walked by, scowling. "I am very sorry you are indisposed, Mr. Walker," the President called out after him.[61]

Houston evidently considered the matter closed; in an address at the Huntsville Presbyterian Church back in November, he had taken the opportunity for the first time to publicly defend himself against his detractors. He continued to insist that his correspondence with Elliot was not designed to harm the prisoners in any way: "No matter under what circumstances they went, their capitulation had brought them within the pale of prisoners of war. I demanded it as a right that they be treated as such." [62] On the contrary, he argued, it was the Texas newspapers which should bear the responsibility for the trials and tribulations of the Mier men. In his defense, Houston noted that Francis Moore's *Telegraph and Texas Register* had printed the news of the mutiny against Somervell as early as January 18 (several days, in fact, before Houston's letter to Elliot), announcing to the Mexican government and the world that Fisher's men were acting without orders from their government.

But the charge that Houston had callously abandoned the Mier men was, by this time, of little concern to most Texans, if for no other reason than that it was old news. Hatred of Houston was no longer the national pastime now that annexation was the talk of the day. While Houston's enemies continued to assail him in the national press, their charges were blunted by the enormous popularity of his policies. The plight of the Perote prisoners, no matter how tragic, was not enough to sustain an effective campaign against him. Houston's enemies were placed in the embarrassing position of having to follow his lead on the issues that were of crucial importance to most Texans, although naturally they did not give him credit for his role. There was, in fact, a veritable stampede on the part of the anti-Houston press to endorse annexation once it became known that a treaty between Texan and American diplomats was in the works. "The opposition newspapers are going in favour of annexation to the United States now that they see that they will not do anything upon their own hook," observed one Galveston resident, who added that the "patriotic blood" which had been shed by Texans in recent years, "the massacre of Fannin and his four hundred—the fall of the Alamo, and lastly the decimation of the Mier prisoners," had been largely forgotten in the wake of recent events. [63]

THE EPIDEMIC AT Perote continued to claim victims throughout the winter, and by February 1844, its worst effects had been felt. All but three of the Texans had come down with the disease. As many as twenty had died. [64] Among the dead was Norman Woods, who had miraculously survived the Dawson Massacre. Of all the Perote prisoners, perhaps no

man had suffered more, nor showed more courage. While many succumbed to self-pity, Woods had remained unshakably sanguine throughout his ordeal. His letters to his wife and brother were filled with hope for
the future, rarely betraying his anxieties or his pain. He had ended his last
letter, written back in September before the outbreak of the epidemic, on
a customary note of optimism:

> *I have never despaired, [and] I hope ere long to be with you all
> and talk over the scenes past and gone. Jane you must do the best
> you can . . . try and have our little children go to school . . . All
> my trouble is the absences from you and my family. Yours until
> death*
>
> *Norman Woods*[65]

For those who recovered, convalescence was slow, and accompanied
by extreme fatigue and depression. The news of the failure of the armistice talks only added to the general mood of despair. "We have received
many fair promises of Liberty, many cheering and pleasant stories have
been whispered in our ears by the foreigners, and citizens of this place,
but all have failed, we have now no flattering prospects ahead, but everything dark and gloomy."[66] The death of close friends and Perote's unre-
mitting rains caused many to lose hope of ever seeing their homes again.
One prisoner, Campbell Davis, already little more than a skeleton after
months of chronic diarrhea prior to the outbreak of the epidemic, spent
forty days in the hospital that winter. Upon his return to the prison,
he went into the medicines of one of the doctors during the night and
drank an entire vial of laudanum. He lay in a torpor, regaining consciousness only long enough to tell his friends what he had done. He died later
that day.[67]

There would be no special treatment for the prisoners now that the
epidemic was over. Beef offal and rice were again their standard fare. A
few of the guards took advantage of their weakened state, and for the
first time physical abuse of the Texans became common. Captain Miguel
Arroyo, who had taken Guzmán's place as the daytime officer of the
guard, proved to be much less hesitant to strike a prisoner who got out of
line, and some of his subordinates appear to have followed his example.
Although many prisoners were too weak from lengthy bouts with fever to
resist this kind of treatment, a few managed to defend themselves.[68] When
the prisoners read in the New Orleans *Daily Picayune* a statement by
Waddy Thompson in which General Jarero was said to be treating the

incarcerated Texans with kindness and humanity, they felt compelled to issue a reply. The Texans charged that General Jarero had, in fact, authorized his subordinates to abuse them, and even alleged that their mistreatment was a calculated effort on the part of the prison authorities to provoke them "into some mad and desperate act which may furnish an excuse for a general massacre." As evidence of the commandant's "utter want of humanity," they offered a list of indignities which they had suffered during the course of a week. These included throwing eleven prisoners in the *calabozo;* the beating of seventeen-year-old Gilbert Brush with an oak stick; the assault on one prisoner when the rivets of his chains were found to be loose; and an assault upon William Clopton for refusing to work.[69]

Nonetheless, most of the prisoners tried to keep their spirits up, determined to pass their confinement as agreeably as possible. There were several fiddlers in the group, and the skilled craftsmen who worked in the carpentry shop set about making instruments for them. In a few weeks there were no less than five fiddles in the Texan cells, where dances were held every night.[70] The prisoners had not yet lost their sense of humor, borrowing a dozen dresses from the soldiers' wives for one evening's festivities. With a sufficient quantity of liquor they managed to have a good time of it, dancing until they were "too much corned to continue the ball any longer."[71]

But for the most part, their time when they were not engaged in their duties about the fort was spent in idle talk. One bored inmate complained: "Our very speculations grew as old and trite as our reminiscences, and the latest criticism on the governor's daughter, the castle's strength, or the officers' habits, was received with such yawns as time out of mind have strangled the thrice-told tale."[72] The Texans devised a plan to storm the magazine, but nothing came of it. There was another plan to steal enough gunpowder to blow a hole through the wall of one of the cells. This scheme, too, went nowhere. Rumors about their release, about affairs in Texas and the United States, were circulated and embellished among the inmates. For a while they were under the impression that a peace treaty with Mexico had been signed, and a Texas ship was in Veracruz harbor to take them home.[73] There was even one story that a group of Texans had been sent to assassinate Santa Anna.[74] They clung desperately to every rumor, no matter how far-fetched. At least it helped to pass the time, for there was nothing else to do but count the days and dream of home.

The Annexation Crisis

IN MEXICO CITY, Waddy Thompson had decided to resign his post and return to the United States. The American minister missed his wife and children, whom he had left behind in South Carolina two years earlier.[1] But his decision was probably prompted as much by political as by familial considerations. Though far removed from the Washington scene, Thompson was not unaware of the Tyler government's misfortunes and as a loyal Whig believed the time had come to disassociate himself from an administration that most members of his party were ready to forget. Henry Clay seemed assured of heading the Whig ticket in the upcoming fall election. As a long-time supporter and friend of Clay, the U.S. minister thought it best for his own political career if he left the Tyler government, in order to be in line for a prestigious appointment should Clay win his bid for the presidency.[2] Nor could he in good conscience continue to serve in his present capacity now that his government was bent on the annexation of Texas. This was a complete about-face for Thompson, who as a South Carolina congressman had built his political reputation as a dedicated expansionist. His new attitude may have been due in part to his allegiance to Henry Clay, who had come out strongly against the annexation of Texas. But it may also be said that in Mexico Waddy Thompson had had a chance to see Manifest Destiny from another point of view. He could no longer advocate annexation, knowing that it would irreparably damage relations with a country and a people he had grown to admire.

Thompson could leave Mexico with the satisfaction that he had acquitted himself with a reasonable amount of success. Affairs between the United States and Mexico, while perhaps no better since his arrival, were at least no worse, and that was no mean feat under the circumstances. It had not all been smooth going, but Thompson deserved a large share of the credit for keeping relations between the two countries on an even keel. The news of Thompson's imminent departure saddened the Texas prisoners. If at times they had grown exasperated with his repeated promises of liberation, they recognized that he had been unstinting in his efforts to bring them home.³

Now that the United States was ready to proceed with the annexation of Texas, the next diplomatic representative in Mexico City would face a situation far more sensitive than anything Thompson had dealt with. After some deliberation, John C. Calhoun—who had assumed the post of secretary of state following the death of Abel Upshur—offered the job to Wilson Shannon, the governor of Ohio. Shannon had not sought the post, nor had his name even been mentioned as a possible candidate. Shannon was not picked for his diplomatic experience; he had none. But as a northerner he would satisfy the antislavery forces in the Senate, and as an ardent expansionist he could be counted on to support the party line with regard to Texas.⁴ It would, however, be some time before Shannon could resign as governor of Ohio and make his way to Mexico. Thus the United States was left without a seasoned representative in the Mexican capital for five months. In the interim the job fell to Benjamin Green, the twenty-two-year-old secretary of the legation and the son of Duff Green, a politically active newspaperman and entrepreneur.

Thompson decided to pay Santa Anna one last visit before he returned to the United States. On his way to Veracruz he stopped at Encero, the Mexican President's new estate below Jalapa. Although the hacienda was not quite as large as the one at Manga de Clavo, his home near Veracruz, Santa Anna preferred Encero's healthy mountain climate, its stunning scenery, and its proximity to the capital (a four-day journey to Mexico City, as compared to six from the coast). A deep mutual respect had developed between the two men that had hardly seemed possible when Thompson first arrived in Mexico City. Santa Anna had expected to have little intercourse with an American diplomat whose pro-Texas and pro-annexation sentiments were a matter of record. Thompson, for his part, believed that Mexico was not yet ready for democracy, and at this stage in its development could do no better than to have a strong leader like Santa Anna in charge. Shortly before leaving Mexico City he had written to Andrew Jackson:

> *Santa Anna is a man of talents and many noble qualities. You must not judge him with reference to the state of things in our own happy country. He has a very different people to govern, and I think he is not only a patriot, but that he understands his coun-*

*trymen and their true interests. A government like ours would be
no government for Mexico. You may use a light reign [sic] on
your horse because he is gentle and well broke, but it is no reason
why I should use a similar one upon mine, which is wild and
untractable.*[5]

Upon Thompson's arrival at Encero, Santa Anna conducted the ex-
minister on a tour of the chicken coops where his fighting birds were
kept. Thompson followed as his host stopped at each coop with obvious
pride, occasionally giving directions to his bird handlers to give one
animal more feed, another less. There was one bird that was particularly magnificent, all white except for the tips of the feathers, which
were black. Santa Anna inquired if they had such splendid creatures in
Thompson's native country. The American diplomat, who found the
sport, like bullfighting, "barbarous and vulgar," politely replied that they
did not. Santa Anna told Thompson that if the bird won its match, he
would send it to him on the next boat to the United States.[6]

At length Santa Anna dropped his easy and informal manner and
asked Thompson about U.S. intentions toward Texas. Although the departing American minister since his resignation had not been kept up to
date by the Tyler government about its annexation plans, he had read the
Mexican news reports that talks were now underway between U.S. and
Texas representatives in Washington. While his personal views were no
longer in accord with his government's, he still had a responsibility as the
American representative in Mexico to stand by U.S. policy. Having received no orders from Washington, Thompson told the Mexican President that he was not at liberty to discuss the matter. He could neither
confirm nor deny that his government had any annexation plans. Santa
Anna did not try to press the issue. Evidently the Mexican President did
not wish to spoil their last meeting with a bitter anti-American harangue,
and saw no point in lecturing the departing minister on his government's
position, which was well known to Thompson in any case. However,
Santa Anna added that if the United States attempted the annexation of
Texas, "England would have a hand in the matter," leading Thompson to
believe that Santa Anna was counting on British military support in the
event of war between Mexico and the United States.[7]

Thompson quickly turned the conversation to the matter of the Texas
prisoners. Santa Anna replied that he had released Texas soldiers on parole before—those of the Santa Fe Expedition—and they had immediately joined the next raid against Mexico. Thompson persisted, however, knowing that this would be his last opportunity. On the question of

the Mier prisoners Santa Anna was adamant. They were robbers, he exclaimed vehemently, who had invaded Mexico with plunder as their sole purpose and did not deserve their freedom. Seeing that Santa Anna would not be dissuaded, Thompson limited his request to the liberation of the San Antonio prisoners only. These men were not robbers, but peaceful citizens who had every right to take up arms against General Woll's invasion force. "They were defending their homes," Thompson said, "and a generous enemy should respect them more." [8]

Santa Anna conceded that the circumstances of the San Antonio prisoners were altogether different from those of the Mier men, and asked if there were any that Thompson wished to have released. When Thompson told him that there were, the Mexican President asked that he send him a list of their names. Thompson replied, "How can I distinguish between men, all strangers to me personally, whose cases are in all respects the same, and why should you?" [9] In the end, Santa Anna, who recognized that Thompson was a valuable ally who might very well provide support for Mexico when he returned to the United States, relented and signed an order freeing all the San Antonio prisoners. Thompson later wrote to the U.S. secretary of state: "Nothing could have been more handsome than the manner in which this was done and I am sure I have never experienced a more heartfelt pleasure." [10]

On March 24, 1844, all the remaining thirty-five Texans captured by General Woll some eighteen months earlier were given letters of transit and escorted from Perote Castle as free men. A handful of Mier prisoners got in among them, but were stopped by a suspicious guard as they passed out the main gate. [11]

As for Thompson, he went home with an entirely different outlook on the Mexico-Texas question. Dismayed by his countrymen's "rabid craving for more territory," he believed that the United States had a duty to befriend a sister republic, not profit from its weaknesses. [12] Thompson's views were anything but popular in his home state of South Carolina— among slaveowners they were nothing less than heretical—and he may have realized that unless he changed them his political career was over. He never did. The former minister retired to his home near Greenville, and remained a vocal but ineffective critic of American foreign policy. Reflecting fondly on his experiences and impressions of Mexico, he would later write: "I was treated with so much kindness by people of all classes, from the lepero in the streets up to the President . . . I assure them in all sincerity that I take a deep interest in their continued advances in the great career of civil liberty, and their ultimate success in establishing Republican institutions on a permanent basis. God grant them success, both on their own account as well as for the great cause in which they have so long struggled, and under circumstances so discouraging." [13]

Soon after his return to the United States, Thompson was informed that a crate from Mexico had arrived in New York City. It was the bird Santa Anna had promised him.

THREE DAYS AFTER the departure of the San Antonio prisoners, the turnkeys discovered that sixteen more Texans had exited from Perote by more clandestine means. A tunnel had been cut through the floor and straight down the wall, coming out at the bottom in the reeds of the moat. It had taken the Texans six weeks to complete.

The soldiers at Perote rechained the remaining Texas prisoners and in the days that followed took special care to ensure that their leg irons were fastened securely. Every morning and evening the officers and their guards conducted thorough searches of the cells, stripping the prisoners, rummaging through their belongings, tapping at the paving stones for hollow sounds, examining every nook and cranny for new signs of an escape tunnel.[14] By May, nine of the sixteen were recaptured—the others made it safely back to Texas—and the daily cell searches were discontinued. Work on another tunnel began almost immediately.

Shortly afterward, according to the New Orleans *Daily Picayune,* Santa Anna wrote to Thompson, informing him that he had decided to release all the prisoners, but changed his mind when he learned of the recent escape. "This has very much changed the aspect of things, and I cannot now offend public opinion by another act of magnanimity, of which these men have shown themselves entirely unworthy." [15]

A letter from Thomas Jefferson Green arrived at Perote in April, informing the prisoners of the $15,000 the Texas Congress had allocated for their relief.[16] They could take little comfort from this news, for as yet they had seen no evidence of their government's largesse, nor would they for quite some time. The administration could not openly aid the prisoners; since its failure to ratify the armistice agreement it was once again on the most unfriendly terms with Mexico. The funds were therefore allocated in secret session and an agent in New Orleans, Reuben Potter, was contracted to travel to Mexico and secretly put them at the disposal of the imprisoned Texans.[17] Unfortunately, Potter had all the imagination but none of the daring needed for covert operations. Afraid that he might be exposed as a Texas agent and end up sharing the fate of the prisoners, he took the most elaborate precautions. He designed a special cipher in which he intended to send coded messages back to Texas, and assumed the unlikely alias Ebenezer Higgins. Potter did not reach Veracruz until early August. No sooner did he arrive in port, however, than he was recognized by a Mexican officer who had known him some years earlier. Losing his nerve, Potter left the money in the hands of the American consul in Veracruz rather than risk the journey to Perote, and beat a hasty retreat back to New Orleans.[18]

The Texans in Perote did, however, receive financial aid from an unexpected quarter: the San Antonio prisoners. Upon their arrival in New Orleans, the men captured in the Woll invasion received $500 as well as other items donated to them by the people of the city. A portion of this money—about $150—was set aside for the men they had left behind in Mexico.[19] Efforts on the part of other private citizens' groups in Texas were not as successful. One committee in Montgomery County was established to raise money, and according to a resident managed to collect "between fifty and sixty dollars." But as a result of "the difficulty in forwarding and . . . the inactivity of the committee," the funds never reached their destination.[20]

WHILE SANTA ANNA spent the spring in semi-retirement on his estate, events in the capital were taking a decided turn for the worse. Mexico hovered near bankruptcy, unable to meet its financial obligations with any regularity, and in April the government was compelled to suspend its quarterly claims payments to the United States. Nor had the newly elected Congress proven to be the pliant tool Santa Anna had hoped for. Notwithstanding his efforts of the previous year to rewrite the constitution and secure a pro-centralist Congress, the new members assumed an openly defiant stance against the regime as soon as they took their seats, angrily protesting the country's wretched financial state of affairs. In spite of—or perhaps because of—these troubling developments, Santa Anna chose to postpone his return to Mexico City.

Annexation was one problem Santa Anna did not shy away from, evidently because he saw in it a perfect opportunity to regain his dwindling popular support. In April, Calhoun concluded annexation negotiations with the Texas representatives in Washington and sent the treaty on to the Senate for appropriate action. The response of the Mexican government was predictable. There could be no turning back from the course Santa Anna had charted at the outset of his presidency when he promised to plant Mexico's "Eagle standards on the banks of the Sabine." *El Diario del Gobierno* urged the nation "to repel force with force; to fight to win, or to succumb with glory."[21] Foreign Minister Bocanegra issued a series of scathing denunciations of the Tyler policy, reiterating the Mexican position that annexation meant war. Texas was still a province of Mexico, Bocanegra maintained, which "by ownership and by possession belongs to her, and always has belonged to her." [22]

The annexation issue suddenly thrust into the spotlight Benjamin Green, who had to handle things as best he could until Wilson Shannon arrived. The young secretary of the legation had only recently graduated from law school and owed his appointment to his father's close friendship with Tyler and Calhoun. Nonetheless, Green proved to be an intelligent and capable representative, although he did not share Waddy Thompson's solicitous attitude toward the Mexican people or their government. Within days after Green assumed his duties as acting chargé d'affaires, Mexico fired its opening broadsides at the Tyler government for its annexation policy. Green succeeded in matching Bocanegra's diplomatic notes bluster for bluster, observing that after eight years of independence, Texas was no longer Mexico's to claim. The Republic had, after all, been recognized by most of the world's major powers, just as Mexico had been recognized by them (the United States included) after winning its own independence from Spain in 1821. That the Mexican government should continue to assert its sovereignty over Texas, Green noted, when it "has been unable to reconquer her, and has of late ceased all efforts to do so, is truly novel and extraordinary. As well might Mexico, by similar protests, declare that the world is her empire, and the various nations who people it, her subjects; and expect her claim to be recognized." [23]

Throughout the spring and early summer of 1844, Mexico continued to fight its war of words with the United States. This was almost certainly the only kind of war Santa Anna had in mind. While a direct military confrontation between the two nations was to be avoided at all costs, the government's tough talk, intended for domestic consumption only, would divert attention from its many other problems. No doubt Santa Anna expected Congress and the Mexican people to follow his lead in pointing an accusing finger at the United States. In times of crisis they had rallied to his standard; there was no reason to believe they would not do so again.

There were a number of factors in Santa Anna's favor. For one thing, the United States was presently involved in a bitter dispute with Great Britain over the Oregon territory, which might well lead to war and distract Tyler's attention from Texas. As for the annexation treaty, it was encountering stiffer resistance from northern senators than the Tyler administration had expected. If the measure was defeated, the Mexican government could claim that its warnings of grave consequences had forced the United States to back down. But for Santa Anna the serious deterioration of relations with the United States was a high price to pay for popularity at home. Instead of deterring American expansionists, the Mexican government's threats only heightened tensions between the two countries. And, of course, if the United States *did* annex Texas, Santa Anna was committed to a war from which there would be no honorable means of escape.

Now that the annexation treaty was in the hands of the Senate, Secretary of State Calhoun may have been having second thoughts about leaving the young and inexperienced Benjamin Green in Mexico City to deal with the crisis alone. Since Wilson Shannon was still getting his affairs in order before sailing for Mexico and would not be able to assume his post as the new American minister for some months, a special envoy named Gilbert Thompson (no relation to Waddy Thompson) was sent to personally deliver new instructions for Green and to otherwise take stock of the situation. Upon his arrival in Veracruz in mid-May, Thompson asked for an audience with Santa Anna, and a meeting was arranged at the National Bridge, which spanned a deep gorge on the road to the capital. Thompson assured the President that his government had no wish to offend Mexico, and reportedly offered a $10 million cash sum to smooth any ruffled feathers which annexation might cause.[24] Santa Anna, who by this time was feeling reasonably confident that the Senate would reject Tyler's treaty, wasted little time in rejecting this suggestion.

This was not the first time the United States had tried to buy Texas. Washington was growing quite exasperated with Mexico's claim to land it had never been able to populate or control, and which had been irretrievably lost eight years earlier at San Jacinto. But there were many reasons for Mexico's repeated rejection of U.S. offers for Texas. Suspicious of a country that appeared all too willing to capitalize on their misfortunes, Mexicans had not forgotten that the United States had smiled upon—and many believed covertly sanctioned—the revolution in Texas in 1836. And they were convinced, not unreasonably, that the surrender of Texas would only whet the appetite of American expansionists for more land in the west. If there were those in Mexico who reluctantly conceded the loss of territory above the Río Grande, they did not want the United States to have it. Perhaps most important, Mexico could not be expected to seriously consider the sale of Texas when the principal objective of the present regime was to perpetuate the myth of its reconquest. As long as Santa Anna remained in power, the Mexican government's reply to any offer to buy Texas would be the same.

On the first of June Santa Anna returned to Mexico City, where he was greeted by the customary parade and salvos of artillery. But this martial display could not mask ominous signs of discontent. The Mexican President was to find that his nine-month absence had cost him dearly; the problems he had ignored for so long now threatened to engulf him. Ironically, it was the annexation of Texas, the very issue which Santa Anna hoped to exploit, which seems to have triggered the outcry against his regime. While *El Diario del Gobierno* continued to heap scorn upon the United States with the clear intention of whipping up popular enthusiasm for the government's cause, such tirades were having exactly the opposite effect. For three years the Mexican President had kept the Texas question squarely in the foreground, promoting himself as the only man capable of restoring the nation's lost honor. The government's bombast, however, actually served to publicize the fact that it had done nothing to accomplish this goal, and that for all the rhetoric, Texas was as free of Mexican control as it had been when Santa Anna first came to power.

Upon his arrival in the capital Santa Anna took immediate steps to head off the impending crisis. Compelled to embark upon the course he had tried for so long to avoid, the Mexican President on June 17 ordered General Adrian Woll, now in command of the Army of the North, to send Houston a formal declaration of war. Troops were mobilized in Veracruz, Jalapa, and San Luis Potosí, perhaps as many as thirty thousand in all. The government planned a two-pronged attack against Texas: Woll would bring his much-strengthened Army of the North across the Río Grande, while another force sailed to Galveston. It now appeared that Santa Anna's regime would survive or fall on his promise to resubjugate Texas. Half-measures, inconclusive raids upon the Texas frontier, this time were no longer sufficient. Santa Anna had rattled his saber long enough; however reluctantly, he would now have to unsheath it.

For three years Santa Anna had refused to undertake a full-scale war against Texas, and yet now Mexico was gearing up for a conflict that might well involve both Texas *and* the United States. Waddy Thompson had correctly guessed that the Mexican President did not plan to go it alone; he was counting on the British to join him if an invasion of Texas brought the United States into the war. Great Britain's dispute with the United States over the Oregon territory might result in war in any case, and Santa Anna was clearly hoping that these combined circumstances would force his ally to take this drastic step.

But the position of Her Majesty's government with regard to Texas was at this time ambiguous. Caught off guard by the news of the annexation treaty, Whitehall was scrambling to formulate a new policy of its own to thwart President Tyler's plans. Britain was strongly committed to an independent Texas free of U.S. involvement, but nothing the Aberdeen government had said or done could give Santa Anna any assurance that it would go so far as to take military action if annexation appeared inevitable. Certainly the British newspapers, which were closely scrutinized by the Mexican government, were taking an aggressive stand against the annexation treaty.[25] Santa Anna assumed that Whitehall was of a similar frame of mind. Previously, the British government had stated quite explicitly that it would not resort to military means to prevent the annexation of Texas, but this warning had been issued prior to the news of annexation, and Santa Anna appears to have believed that present circumstances would force Great Britain to reevaluate its policy of neutrality.[26] Charles Bankhead, the new British minister in Mexico City, was sounded out, but since communications with London took several weeks, he was just as much in the dark about his government's policy as Santa Anna. While urging caution, Bankhead was unable to state with any authority what his government would do in the event of a Mexican invasion of Texas.[27] Bankhead's equivocal reply was a mistake, for it left Santa Anna free to draw his own conclusions, and he was now so frantically looking for a way out of his predicament that he seems to have convinced himself that there was indeed a very real possibility that Great Britain would step in with military aid.

Only with Great Britain on its side could Mexico afford to risk its rusty and antiquated military machine, although even now, in spite of the troop mobilization, Santa Anna was hopeful that war could be avoided. A pledge of support from Her Majesty's government might be all that was necessary to make the United States think twice about annexation. But as usual, the Mexican policy left no room for compromise or retreat. Everything hinged on British support. Santa Anna had committed his government to a war that he knew would have disastrous consequences for his nation without any explicit assurance that Britain would come to his rescue.

Few people, however, seem to have taken Santa Anna's threats of war very seriously. The New Orleans *Daily Picayune* believed Mexico's war preparations to be a sham, a sentiment shared by foreign observers in the Mexican capital.[28] The Mexican Congress was equally skeptical, and balked at his request for more money to carry out the proposed invasion of Texas, insisting that he make do with the funds that had already been appropriated. Many legislators were convinced that Santa Anna had no intention of invading Texas, but planned either to embezzle the funds or use them to shore up his support among Mexico's military chieftains. Only after much wrangling and heated debate did Congress pass an appropriations bill, and it was considerably less than the President had requested. Even the Mexican officers at Perote, who "say they are all federals but they dare not express themselves openly," were doubtful that the President was actually contemplating an invasion of Texas.[29]

In mid-July Santa Anna learned that the annexation treaty had been defeated in the U.S. Senate by a vote of 35 to 16. For the second time in eight years, the slavery controversy had blocked Texas' entrance into the Union. Far from quieting the clamor for annexation in the United States, however, the Senate vote only served to sharpen the debate. President Tyler was still determined to redeem his much-maligned administration with the acquisition of Texas. Only three days after the Senate vote, the chief executive announced that he would try to annex Texas again in the next session of Congress by a joint resolution, which would stand a much better chance of passage than a treaty, requiring only a simple majority of both houses. It soon became apparent that Manifest Destiny would be the decisive issue of the upcoming presidential campaign. American expansionism, once veiled, however thinly, by respect for the sovereignty of neighboring peoples, now emerged in naked and triumphant form. The appetite for more land had become a national obsession. Santa Anna could therefore take little satisfaction in the defeat of Tyler's treaty, for if Democratic candidate James K. Polk was elected President, annexation would surely follow. In a report to the Mexican Congress, Secretary of War Tornel predicted that the recent defeat of the treaty would only postpone American efforts to bring Texas into the Union.[30] Thus, Santa Anna was left with no choice but to continue to prepare for war, or at least pretend to do so.

IMMEDIATELY FOLLOWING THE Senate vote, Houston threatened to have nothing more to do with the United States, but as this appeared to be only a temporary setback and not the death-knell for annexation, he was soon indicating that the matter was not yet closed. Meanwhile, Texas was entering a hot political summer of its own. Houston, whose presidential term expired at the end of the year, picked Secretary of State Anson Jones as the administration candidate. Running against Jones was Edward Burleson, Houston's former Vice-President, who had long since parted company with his old chief and was now a staunch enemy. Thomas Jefferson Green's name surfaced as a possible running mate for Burleson, but he had other plans; he was busy putting the finishing touches on a book about the Mier Expedition, which he hoped would expose to the world the perfidious character of Sam Houston.[31]

Green would never forgive or forget, but it was clear that the vast majority of the Texas electorate had already done so. Houston's popularity had never been higher. With both parties favoring annexation, there were few issues which the opposition could use against Houston's candidate with any success. Burleson promised if elected to move the seat of government back to Austin, but Jones countered that he would also endorse the move if Congress gave its approval. Francis Moore's *Telegraph and Texas Register* continued to assail Houston for his weak-kneed posture against Mexico, as well as his inability to bring home the Perote prisoners.[32] Houston opponents cried futilely that Jones was merely the President's stooge, a charge that, given Houston's popularity, may have actually helped the nominee's election chances. The *LaGrange Intelligencer* tried to call attention to the fact that Jones, unlike its own candidate, had never fought for his country, dubbing the urbane physician the "Apothecary General."[33] But while Jones had no following of his own and elicited little excitement among the voters, the shadow of the incumbent President loomed large on election day. With Houston's endorsement, the secretary of state won handily.

THE MIER PRISONERS heard bits and pieces of news about Texas, and they were upset by them. Many were baffled by the enthusiasm which their countrymen expressed for annexation. When they had joined the Somervell campaign of 1842 they had left behind a proud, if beleaguered nation; now they saw a people crying out to join the Union, and a government that appeared ready to expire at any moment. In their own way, the Mier men had done much to bring about this shift in attitude. Their misadventures had demonstrated to Texans the folly of independence and driven them into the arms of the United States. But for the Perote prisoners, who were inclined to see the Mier Expedition as a gallant enterprise instead of a humiliating defeat, this was something they would never understand. From his dark cell Joseph McCutchan wrote in his diary:

> We hear that [the] annexation of Texas to the United States will take place. . . . If I could for myself exercise influence it would be to say to Texas and the Texians hold dear those rights so dearly bought and promptly payed for in the blood and misery of your countrymen. Part not so freely with that which has cost you your best citizens at the Alimo, Goliad, and San Jacinto. Remain a nation yourselves, or Nobly Perish![34]

A few days later McCutchan again expressed his thoughts on annexation in his diary: "We are not much elated with the idea of Texas salling [*sic*] under another nation for protection. . . . as for my self (and it is, I believe, the opinion of the majority)—let me die—let me perish, neglected, and obscure in prison—let my frame sink under cruelties such as man never endured,—let me go among the unnumbered dead—and, in short let my body decay in obscurity and my name sink into oblivion! but annex not Texas to *any* government." [35]

McCutchan may have been exaggerating his colleagues' sentiments on behalf of independence, since it is clear that bitterness, for many, was slowly displacing the patriotism they felt for their adopted land. "I never will rase a gun in her defence agane," exclaimed one; "when I fight for her agane it will be for reveng and not for Texas." [36] Wrote another disillusioned prisoner, "I have seen our companions led out and shot . . . I now see them in daily starvation, and beat with sticks and swords, leaving marks which they will carry to their graves, and I have seen them dying, more from neglect than disease, and all this for a heartless and ungrateful country." [37] Captain Ryon wrote, "our situation is truly miserable and deplorable—and little do the Government of texas care or even think of us—I am Rather inclined to believed [*sic*] that the Greater mass of the people equally neglectfull of our condition—we could bear our imprisonment with much better fortitude if we could only believed [*sic*] that we ever had the sympathy of the texian people." [38]

With Texas preoccupied with its impending marriage with the United States, the prisoners felt their government had forsaken them. And they were not far wrong. Since the failure of the armistice talks, the Houston administration for all intents and purposes had abandoned its efforts to gain their freedom. Now that Mexico was mobilizing for war, their chances of release seemed all the more remote. A few prisoners thought that annexation might be a good thing, enabling the stronger United States to bring its full weight to bear upon Mexico and force Santa Anna to release them. [39] But this seemed unlikely, for relations between the two countries were at their lowest point ever. If it came to war, they could expect to be in Perote for the duration. One prisoner speculated that the effects of the annexation controversy "will be sorely felt by us. It will certainly prolong our terms of imprisonment, and perhaps, compel us to pay the debt of all nature as many of our friends have done." [40] Giving up on any help from either their own government or the United States, they appealed directly to the British minister, but he too could do nothing. [41] All they had to look forward to was June 13, Santa Anna's saint's day, although this year there had been no indication that he might use the occasion to release them. The day opened with the firing of cannons and the ringing of bells, and both prisoners and guards were excused from their regular work details to celebrate. Dinner was better than average, and their enjoyment of it was not greatly diminished by a rat found dead at the bottom of a pot of rice.[42] But there was no order for their liberation.

With this last hope extinguished, they gave themselves up completely to despair. Alfred Thurmond, the interpreter who had witnessed the executions of the Salado victims and Ewen Cameron, simply threw down his shovel while working outside the fort one morning and ran off in full view of the guards. They soon caught up with him, and brought him back to Perote bleeding and in double irons.[43] Even the diaries which some of the men had diligently maintained during their captivity seemed too much effort, as a series of July entries of one chronicler testified:

6th. Hard times.
Sunday, 7th. Nothing scarcely to eat.
8th. Nothing to eat with it.
9th. Badly cooked.
10th. Worse than ever.
11th. Too much to stand. . . .[44]

In early August, having made all the necessary preparations, Wilson Shannon was at last ready to begin his trip to Mexico and assume his duties as American minister. Although most of Shannon's career had been spent in public life, his basic inclinations were those of a narrow-minded, backwoods lawyer. Like Thompson, he knew little about Mexico upon his arrival; unlike him, he showed a stubborn unwillingness to learn. Speaking no Spanish, he relied entirely on translators during his stay.[45] It is hardly surprising, then, that the new American minister's immediate impressions of Mexico were unfavorable, or that he would see no need to change them.

In 1844 travel in Mexico was always an uncomfortable, sometimes a hazardous undertaking, and a great deal of fortitude and forbearance were required on the part of the foreign visitor, particularly the uninitiated. It was Shannon's misfortune to arrive in Veracruz at the worst time of the year, and he quickly left for the capital to escape the oppressive heat and the yellow fever that was sweeping the city. Like all foreign dignitaries, he was provided with an armed escort, a necessary precaution on the bandit-infested road.

Three days later Shannon reached Perote, the midway point of his journey, late on the night of August 21. Obtaining a room at the posada in the village, he borrowed a mule and rode down to the castle. Although it was late and the prisoners had been locked up for the night, General

Jarero allowed him to see the men. Shannon was clearly shocked by what he saw. "They were in a wretched condition, being almost naked," he later wrote to Secretary of State Calhoun.[46] He pledged that he would help them in any way he could. The prisoners in cell no. 7 told him that would be unnecessary as far as they were concerned. A third tunnel had just been completed, and they planned to make use of it in a few days. Shannon urged them to wait. He would petition for their release as soon as he arrived in Mexico City. This was not the first time the prisoners had heard such promises. Nevertheless they agreed to postpone the escape until they received word from him. The prisoners knew that pressure to release them had been brought to bear upon the Mexican government from a number of quarters. A petition from members of the U.S. Congress, signed by Henry Clay, Thomas Hart Benton, and many others, had recently gained the release of five Mier men, among them Big Foot Wallace.[47] Andrew Jackson had urged the Mexican President that spring to free the balance of the Texas prisoners, while Charles Bankhead had promised to ask for the release of fourteen who could claim British citizenship.[48] There was, therefore, some reason to think that a new minister in Mexico City might be able to accomplish something on their behalf.

Shannon resumed his journey the next morning. He arrived two days later in Puebla, where he learned that Doña Inés de Santa Anna, the Mexican President's wife, had died in that city only hours before. Unable to obtain an escort, Shannon was obliged to start the final leg of the journey alone. He did not get far. Two miles outside Puebla, in broad daylight, his coach was stopped and surrounded by bandits, who robbed him of everything he had.[49]

When Wilson Shannon arrived in the capital he found the city in mourning. Archbishop Posada conducted an elaborate funeral service in the cathedral, where one thousand masses were said for the first lady of Mexico. At Perote, as at all garrisons across Mexico, the fortress flew its flag at half-mast and cannons were fired every fifteen minutes throughout the day. Santa Anna played the part of the bereaved husband well, but he was not surprised by the death of his thirty-three-year-old wife, who had been in failing health for some time. The Mexican President, who seems to have had a much better sense of contingency-planning in his private life than in his politics, had already picked out another matrimonial partner.[50]

Santa Anna seemed less concerned with his domestic tragedy than with his political situation, which was growing increasingly desperate. In late August he received news that dealt his crumbling regime a severe blow, when a letter arrived from the Mexican representative in London, outlining in detail his discussions with Prime Minister Aberdeen on the threat of the U.S. annexation of Texas. The British government would go "to the last extremity" to prevent annexation, but with one important and, for Santa Anna, impossible condition: Mexico must recognize Texas' independence. Santa Anna shortly held a meeting with British minister Bankhead, who had received a similar dispatch from London. Her Majesty's government would not, under any circumstances whatsoever, Bankhead emphasized, participate in an invasion of Texas with the object of bringing the Republic back under Mexican rule.[51]

This ended all thought of reconquest. Without British military aid, an invasion of Texas was out of the question. Indeed, there was considerable doubt as to whether Mexico could field an army at all. In spite of the government's conspicuous efforts, the invasion plans were quickly going awry for lack of funds. Of the money Congress had grudgingly appropriated for the war effort, almost one-third had been secretly earmarked for general operating expenses. Reports from the army were filtering into the capital that the regulars were inadequately equipped for the campaign, while the new recruits had no supplies whatever. The desertion rate among the conscripts was so high that many had to be chained together to keep them from returning to their villages.[52]

The Mexican President now asked Congress for a leave of absence to return to his estates during his period of grief. Congress was skeptical; he had used ill health as grounds to excuse himself from office before, and then promptly acted to dissolve that body. His request was granted, but there were rumors in the capital that Santa Anna planned to break up Congress, rewrite the constitution, and establish himself as an absolute dictator with the support of the army.[53] Significantly, he took most of the Mexico City garrison with him to Jalapa, leaving Valentín Canalizo in charge as interim President. If order could not be restored, Santa Anna would be ready to march on the capital with his army.

Owing to the death of Doña Inés, it was not until September 5 that the American minister, accompanied by Benjamin Green, met with Santa Anna at Tacubaya to formally present his credentials. The reception went as well as could be expected, given the hostility between the two governments and the fact that both American representatives seem to have been in no mood for the pleasantries of protocol. Shannon was still annoyed about the incident on the Puebla road, but he chose not to make an issue of the government's failure to provide him with adequate protection. Instead he used the occasion to hand Santa Anna a letter he had drafted on behalf of the Mier prisoners. As for Green, his six-month tenure as the senior American diplomatic representative in Mexico was over. The job had been full of frustration for him, and he left it without regret, glad to be rid of the seemingly endless bickering with Mexican diplomats over the annexation issue. Green could not help noting rather peevishly that conversation during the reception was limited to "a thousand civil things with all the fine phrases with which a Mexican says so much and means so little." [54]

The next day Shannon received a cryptic reply to his letter. While not cutting off all hope, the note from Santa Anna did nothing to indicate that the Mier men could expect their freedom in the near future:

> *I have liberated many of the Texian Prisoners . . . and now only those are retained in prison, who . . . have attempted to escape, assassinating the Mexican soldiers who guarded them. These criminales deserve death, and nothing but the mildness and benignty natural to the Mexican character has prevented its application.* [55]

Unsatisfied, Shannon wrote back to request another interview with the President. The U.S. minister told Benjamin Green to write to Perote and urge the prisoners to postpone the escape a little while longer, at least until a second meeting could be held to precisely determine Santa Anna's feelings on the matter. The Texans received the American diplomat's message, which included the text of Santa Anna's letter, on September 9. "From this we have lost all hopes although Santa Anna does not deny Shannon's request, but from the light he views us it [does] not much look like we would get off." [56] Early the following week the prisoners received another letter from Benjamin Green. Although the situation remained unchanged, Green sounded optimistic, perhaps with the intention of boosting their flagging spirits or to prevent the prisoners in cell no. 7 from making their intended escape. The young American diplomat indicated that there was "a pretty fair chance" that Shannon's second meeting with the Mexican President would be more successful, and that some, if not all, of the prisoners would be released. [57] The prisoners in cell no. 7 agreed to wait for news of Shannon's second interview with Santa Anna before putting their escape plans into effect.

On September 12 a carriage took Wilson Shannon and Benjamin Green the four miles to Tacubaya, traveling the last part of the journey on the road that the Texans had taken so long to build. At noon they were ushered into a drawing room where they met with Santa Anna and Foreign Minister Manuel C. Rejón (Bocanegra having recently resigned).

Shannon quickly got down to the purpose of his visit and asked Santa

Anna to reconsider the release of the Mier men. The U.S. minister wisely made no attempt to condone their actions, arguing only that the plight of these men was a matter of great concern to many Americans and their release would have a highly favorable impact on relations between the two countries. He may also have suggested that clemency for the prisoners would do much to smooth the way toward a satisfactory resolution of the issue of Mexico's unpaid claims.[58] But before a new repayment schedule could be arranged, indeed before there could be substantive discussions on any matters of importance, it would be a promising sign of goodwill if the Mexican President would set the Mier prisoners free.

Santa Anna agreed to Shannon's request without further discussion. He would liberate the Mier men as "a personal favor" to the American minister. He reiterated that he had no desire to see the worsening of U.S.-Mexican relations, and hoped that the release of the prisoners would be seen as evidence of his "liberality and friendly disposition."[59] The President added that his blanket pardon included all the Texans held in Mexico save one: José Antonio Navarro, the last of the Santa Fe Expedition prisoners. A native of San Antonio and a prominent landowner, Navarro was one of three Mexicans to sign the Texas Declaration of Independence in 1836, an act of treason for which he was separated from the others on the expedition and confined in the dungeons of the Veracruz fortress San Juan de Ulloa. The Texas patriot had spent the past three years chained to an iron ring in the floor of his cell, his sentence commuted from death to life imprisonment by Santa Anna in the hope that he might recant his allegiance to the Republic.

Shannon was in no position to quibble with this exception. Foreign Minister Rejón sat down before Santa Anna and the two American dignitaries and drafted the orders for the prisoners' release, to be effective on September 16, the anniversary of Mexican independence. It read:

> [T]he constitutional President of Mexico, on such a memorable day as the sixteenth of September, wishes to give all friendly powers unequivocal proof of the magnanimity of the Mexican Republic, and of his commitment to encourage better relations with them; and to that end, orders that all the Texans who have been made prisoners in acts of war or invasions of territories . . . and who find themselves stationed in some part of the Republic, be immediately set free . . .[60]

With Mexico at the brink of war with Texas, Santa Anna's decision to free the prisoners seemed as inexplicable as it was unexpected. One

American newspaper invented the rumor that Doña Inés had implored her husband on her deathbed to let the Texans go.[61] This made a good story, and for want of a better explanation it was widely circulated as fact. But a much more convincing explanation was that Santa Anna meant what he said, and felt the need to start off on a cordial footing with his new American diplomat. Santa Anna frequently made it a point to grant favors to departing and arriving ministers, a policy that had paid dividends in the past. It had probably not escaped his notice that Waddy Thompson, for whom he had released the San Antonio prisoners, was turning out to be a true friend to the Mexican cause back in the United States. The former minister had spoken out publicly against annexation since his return to South Carolina, and although as a supporter of Henry Clay he could hardly have done otherwise, his feelings on this issue appear to have been due to "a grateful sense of the many kindnesses which I received during my residence in Mexico." As he explained in a letter to the *Daily National Intelligencer* in July, "President Santa Anna has so often made me happy by making me the instrument of making others happy, that I take special pleasure on all proper occasions in bearing testimony to his many noble and generous qualities."[62]

Santa Anna had every reason to hope that his policy of selective release of the Texas prisoners would enable him to forge a similarly close personal relationship with Wilson Shannon, and in so doing minimize the state of tension between the two countries over the issue of annexation and Mexico's unpaid claims. Santa Anna had painted himself into a difficult corner, with nothing to show for six months of bitter anti-American tirades. He had been unable to win the confidence of the Mexican Congress or the people, and the recent news that Great Britain would not stand by him had left his regime dangerously isolated on the diplomatic front. All formalities aside, when Santa Anna told Shannon that he wished to cultivate the most amicable relations with the United States, the remark probably contained more truth than the American minister realized. If Santa Anna's fiery rhetoric had not inflamed the Mexican desire for war, it was certainly having this effect on American public opinion. Now that his efforts to launch a full-scale, hemispheric conflict between the United States and Great Britain had failed, he shrank from a war which he had never really wanted in the first place. Releasing the Texas prisoners was a first step toward placating the United States and, in so doing, defusing a powder keg which the Mexican President was reluctant to light.

Ironically, the very man responsible for the imprisonment of the Mier men, General Pedro de Ampudia, may also have played an indirect role in

bringing about their release. Since his victory at Mier, Ampudia had successfully commanded Mexican forces in the Yucatán, but his recent mis-
handling of a revolt in Tabasco had become a serious embarrassment for
Santa Anna. In early June, General Francisco Sentmanat, a former governor of the state who had been forced into exile by the centralist regime in
1843, had returned with fifty recruits, apparently with the intention of
inciting a rebellion there. Captured shortly after their arrival, thirty-eight
of Sentmanat's men, most of whom were foreigners, were summarily executed, although they had laid down their arms on the promise of clemency. The victims included three Americans and a number of French and
Spanish citizens. Sentmanat, too, was shot, then decapitated; his head
was fried in oil and displayed in an iron cage for several days. The diplomatic corps in Mexico City lodged furious protests, while the news caused
a sensation in the international press. The New Orleans *Daily Picayune*
raged: "There's humanity for you! there's nineteenth century civilization!
there's Mexican magnanimity!"[63] Ampudia was promptly relieved of his
command, but the damage could not be undone. This regrettable affair
could not have come at a worse time for Santa Anna, and the need to
deflect worldwide condemnation of his regime may well have been a factor
in his sudden decision to release the Perote prisoners.

On September 14, the news of Shannon's Tacubaya meeting with Santa
Anna reached Perote Castle. The men sang and danced into the night,
with only exhaustion putting an end to the festivities shortly before dawn.
The guards knew nothing of the order, however, and in the morning the
Texans were told to report to work as usual, leaving them to wonder if
this was just another rumor to torment them. But that evening the official
directive from the capital arrived. Only then were the chains of all the
men taken off—for the first time since the last escape in March—and
they could feel confident that the order would actually be carried out.
The running sores on their ankles would leave deep, permanent scars, to
remind them always of the one year and seven months spent in captivity
in Mexico.

The next day, at 3:00 P.M., the 104 Texans were formed in double file
in the plaza as a light rain fell.[64] Some of the men carried handkerchiefs
and blankets in which were bound up all their worldly possessions. Some
still wore their prison stripes, but those who had them had changed into
civilian clothes.

General Jarero and the garrison turned out in full dress uniform to bid
the prisoners farewell. He embraced those he knew personally, as did
other soldiers with whom the men had formed friendships. The Mexican
women who operated the prison stores, who had frequently bent the rules

and shown so much kindness to the Texans, were also there to say good-bye.[65] But for the prisoners any fondness was lost in the extreme emotions of the moment. One prisoner was overcome by "a sickly sensation at heart, and a feeling like something sweling in the throat and breast, at times almost to chokeing."[66] After half an hour the commandant called them up to his office, where they took an oath and signed a document swearing never to take up arms against Mexico.[67] This ceremony appears to have been identical to the one performed for the benefit of the San Antonio prisoners in March. In this solemn and perhaps overly dramatic affair, the room was lit only by two small candles on a table at the far end of the room, on which were also placed an open Bible and a crucifix, General Jarero evidently wishing to impress upon the prisoners the gravity of an oath before God. Standing behind the table with his officers, Jarero first read the official order for their release, then the oath, admonishing the Texans that they would be shot if captured again.[68] The purpose of the ceremony seems to have been lost on them. Some raised their left hands to take the oath, some their right, some did neither, some mumbled in the affirmative, some remained silent. But according to one Texan "*all*, or nearly so, were scinscere in vowing *revenge* (even while the oathe was being administered to them) for the fall of our companions in arms and countrymen, and for the ha[r]sh treatment which we as a body had received while in the power of the brutal foe."[69] Each signed his name to the paper, and was given one dollar to see him to Veracruz. After that he was on his own.

It was raining heavily when they left the commandant's office. The garrison was paraded in the courtyard, as the prisoners received their letters of safe-conduct, after which Jarero gave a short speech in Spanish. When he was finished, he turned to his troops who let loose with three cheers: "Viva la Republica Mexicana!"[70] The Texans filed out the main gates. Standing outside the walls of the castle, no longer prisoners but free men, they erupted with heartfelt cheers as a cannon boomed and echoed up the mountainside.

Epilogue

AT DAWN ON November 10, 1844, the steamship *New York* approached Galveston Island, with seventy-six of the former inmates of Perote aboard. Standing on the deck in a stiff wind, the Texans were numb with cold. Having spent the last of their money on the trip from Veracruz to New Orleans, they had been obliged to sleep the past two nights in the open air, unable to pay for rooms below deck. When the steamer was moored, the Texans moved down the gangway, and word spread among the crowd that these were the Perote prisoners. A few curious onlookers stepped up to inquire about their ordeal, but the rest passed by to greet others on the boat, leaving them alone, disconsolate and forlorn, save for a lucky few whose families and friends had learned of their arrival and come down to greet them. The Texans milled about at the wharf for a few minutes and then moved on, there being nothing else for them to do, their thoughts turning to how they might find food and shelter for the night. No longer were they soldiers in a noble cause, but ordinary civilians, and flea-bitten, mangy ones at that.[1]

With Texas and the United States preoccupied with annexation, the Mier men returned to obscurity. There was even one hapless adventurer who, having been reported dead after an unsuccessful escape attempt from Molino del Rey, returned to find a wife who had remarried and a gravestone in a cemetery bearing his name.[2] It was a bitter homecoming for all of them. Expecting a tumultuous welcome, they were sorely disappointed to find no laurels, nor any thanks from a government that still regarded them as freebooters for their mutiny on the Río Grande. On this point they steadfastly proclaimed their innocence; as far as they were concerned, there was nothing blameworthy about their decision to press on into Mexico after Somervell had ordered the army to turn back. Far from participating in a calculated act of mutiny, they believed they had simply taken the initiative when the courage of their commander had faltered. What made it all the more difficult to bear was to see Sam Houston, whom they had cursed a thousand times, now hailed for his annexation strategy.

If the Mier prisoners received no welcome mat from the government of Texas, they certainly expected more from its people. But the turbulent events of 1842—the Vásquez and Woll invasions, the Dawson Massacre—that had led to Somervell's ill-fated expedition into the Río Grande Valley were for many Texans events of the distant past. Moreover, the population of the Republic during their absence was a transient one; many who had once hailed the Mier men as suffering heroes were no longer in Texas to welcome them home, while newcomers were unfamiliar with their story. At the same time, the Texas they had known was changing. The line of settlements bulged inexorably westward as yeoman farmers from the southern states and Europe staked their claim to the fertile soils of the Red River Valley and hill country, lands once exclusively the preserve of nomadic Indian tribes. As the economy improved, a new propertied class of men emerged: men esteemed not for their prowess in battle—many had never fought an Indian or a Mexican—but for their good business sense. The Mier prisoners were the forgotten men of a forgotten war. This, certainly, was the most painful ordeal of all. Shortly before his return, one frustrated soldier had written in his diary:

Oh Texians—*can we ever forgive you for what you have done? Nay but you ask not our forgiveness, but boast of your generous acts!* Generous, indeed! . . . *Base ingratitude! But this will not do. I cannot morralize—my blood boils within me as if* heated by the demons *from the* infernal pitt of Hell![3]

In December, when Sam Houston stepped down as the President of Texas, the annexation of his country to the United States seemed close at hand. The day after handing the reins of government to Anson Jones, Sam Houston took a moment to pen a letter to Santa Anna. Adversaries for the better part of a decade, the two men had maintained a correspondence that was at times stiffly formal, at times fiercely hostile. Writing now as a private citizen, Houston could afford to assume a more congenial tone:

The satisfaction with which on yesterday I laid down the cares and responsibilities of Government, was greatly heightened by the

*recollection that your Excellency had recently released from con-
finement all, save one, of the Texans who had been retained in
prison. This act . . . did not disappoint me; and the only regret
arises from the knowledge that your Excellency has thought
proper to withhold the same kindness from the unhappy Jose
Antonio Navarro.*[4]

If the Mexican President had expected that his release of the Mier prisoners would flatter Wilson Shannon and signal the beginning of a more
favorable dialogue with the United States, he could not have been more
wrong. The ex-governor of Ohio proved himself to be no diplomat and
was quite incapable of dealing with the highly charged atmosphere he
found upon his arrival. An experienced minister might have understood
that Mexico was making an effort to ease tensions, but Shannon saw the
situation in a different light. Shortly after the release of the prisoners,
Shannon sent Foreign Minister Rejón a letter protesting Mexico's threatened invasion of Texas.[5] Though no friend of the United States, Rejón
responded on October 31 with a reply that was largely free of the belli-
cosity which had characterized Mexico's attitude since the Tyler government first tendered its offer of annexation to Texas. In a sharp but reasonable tone, Rejón restated the Mexican position, conspicuously refraining
from any overt threat of war against the United States. Surprisingly, this
only had the effect of a red flag on the bull-tempered Shannon. He professed to be shocked by the "grossly offensive" tone of Rejón's correspondence. Shannon demanded an apology.[6] When the Mexican foreign minister refused, Shannon suspended his diplomatic functions in a huff.[7]
"The insolence of this Government is beyond endurance," he wrote to
Secretary of State Calhoun, and although he remained at his post for another six months, he would have nothing more to do with the Mexican
government.[8] The release of the Mier prisoners was to be his single accomplishment as American minister.

As it turned out, Shannon's rash behavior made little difference, at
least so far as Santa Anna was concerned. Six weeks after the release of
the Mier prisoners, General Mariano Paredes led the Guadalajara garrison
in a revolt against the government. This in turn sparked angry riots in
Mexico City, where Congress ousted Santa Anna's loyal subordinate, Canalizo. As the news spread, demonstrations against the dictator flared up
in every city. Santa Anna was captured as he tried to make his escape
from the country, and the former President of the Republic of Mexico
found himself incarcerated in the same prison to which he had dispatched

so many Texans. He remained a prisoner at Perote for four months before being exiled to Cuba.

The controversy generated by the Mier Expedition continued to dog Sam Houston long after he had stepped down from office as President. By the time the Mier prisoners reached Texas, Thomas Jefferson Green had already finished his manuscript and gone to New York to find a publisher. The book was released by Harper & Brothers a year later. To no one's surprise, Green's *Journal of the Texian Expedition against Mier* revealed the author's searing hatred of Sam Houston and a high regard for his own accomplishments. William Fisher read a copy, and though he found it to be accurate in most respects, he was irritated by the overbearing conceit that came through on every page.[9] One eastern reviewer complained that the book's principal fault was "the constant intrusion, on the part of the author, of a determination not only to prove himself a fine writer and elegant scholar, but as well a Texan Hero in his own person. He does not pause at the last climax even, but insists on being recognized in his own narrative as the very Bayard of Texan heroes. These two wretched dandyisms greatly mar the spirit and effect of the book."[10]

The publication of Green's book compelled the ex-President to once again defend himself against the charges that he had turned his back on the Mier prisoners. In a speech at the Houston Methodist Church in December 1845, Houston agreed that they "were a gallant band of men," but suggested that they had either been "seduced by the reckless or misled by the imprudent."[11] In a letter to Hamilton Stuart, a close friend and the editor of the Galveston *Civilian*, Houston compared himself to the beleaguered King Lear, and continued to insist that the allegations against him were groundless. He wrote: "I did all that was in my power to save and to serve, and nothing to injure the prisoners."[12]

Certainly the ex-President bore no responsibility for their harsh treatment or for the decimation at the Hacienda del Salado, as Green and others continued to maintain. Still, he might have done more. While Houston called mainly upon British diplomats to win the liberation of these men, it was the efforts of Waddy Thompson and Wilson Shannon—undertaken largely on their own initiative—which had brought most of them home. Perhaps Houston felt that U.S. ministers would have less success than their British counterparts, given the generally tense relations between the United States and Mexico, and if so he was clearly mistaken. But it is more in keeping with Houston's character that he found it convenient to engage Her Majesty's government in this task at a time when he was deliberately playing coy to the United States. Determined to make the best of a bad situation, Houston was less concerned with the prisoners' welfare than with his broader diplomatic strategy. In view of their intense dislike of the President when they started out on their adventure, and their disobedience that ended in the calamity he feared, Houston can perhaps be forgiven for failing to put the Mier prisoners at the top of his list of priorities. From start to finish, the expedition he never wanted had given him nothing but trouble.

Houston had his own priorities, and he never lost sight of them, even in the face of widespread public censure. The frontier politician was no lover of frontier democracy; affairs of state, he believed, were too important to be left to men less capable than himself. More often than not, his function as President was to circumvent the will of the people rather than implement it. When Texans clamored for a war against Mexico in 1842, he threw every conceivable obstacle in their way. Once he had sanctioned such a campaign, he made every effort to discourage his commander from fulfilling the mission assigned to him. After the battle of Mier, when the citizens of the Republic were chastened by the disastrous results of their military adventures and looked to the United States for succor, he sought to hold them back until the time was right. Overall, his primary concern was to keep in check the impulsive, reckless nature of his rambunctious citizenry.

In the long run he succeeded. But if Houston had reason to be proud of his political sleight-of-hand, the tight-lipped, enigmatic leader at times carried his penchant for secrecy too far. Houston's decision to rely solely on British interposition to win the release of the prisoners left Waddy Thompson and the people of Texas guessing as to his real intentions, thereby contributing to the debate that surrounded his handling of the issue. Moreover, his reluctance to reveal his plans often alienated and embittered some of his most loyal supporters. Houston seems to have accepted the censure often heaped upon him as an unfortunate though inevitable price of high office. Candor, however, was never his strong suit. Intrigue held a much greater fascination for him than the forging of a consensus. Artifice and cunning came naturally to Houston, and though he employed them always with the best of intentions, it is also true that these were tactics of preference as much as expediency. It was not by chance that his public career was from beginning to end a lightning rod for controversy. There is every indication that Houston delighted in the role.

Houston's long-standing quarrel with Thomas Jefferson Green would simmer for several more years. While in New York to publish his book, Green had the good fortune to meet a rich widow whom he quickly married, and the aging adventurer settled into a life of leisure. But with the news that gold had been discovered in California in 1849, Green was off again to make his fame and fortune. He made neither, although he continued to dabble in politics, winning election to the California legislature.[13] Ever the entrepreneur, Green visited Texas again in the 1850s to lobby for the construction of the Southern Pacific Railroad. His very presence in Texas reopened the old feud with Houston, now a U.S. senator in Washington, who was still smarting from the lambasting he had received in Green's book. Hoping to discredit his old nemesis, Houston rose on the floor of the Senate and denounced him as a scoundrel. Recalling Green's treatment of Santa Anna at Velasco Beach in 1836, Houston suggested that the Mexican President had shown remarkable restraint in not executing Green when he had the chance, and indeed should have done so to "relieve the world of this putrescent piece of mortality."[14] Houston offered his own version of the Mier Expedition, attacking Green's account point by point. As for the book itself, which Houston noted had disparaged him no less than 117 times, it was an "unclean thing, which should never defile a library."[15]

Green got wind of this speech, and six months later there appeared on the desk of every senator a lengthy pamphlet in which Green provided a detailed reply to each of Houston's charges, and took the opportunity to launch another scathing attack on his rival's character. Green regretted having failed to use Houston's name more often, and proceeded to give a more complete list of his crimes, which included "his vulgar blackguardism—his vile debaucheries—his universal mendacity—his numerous perjuries—his personal swindles—his official peculations," and so on.[16] With neither man willing to give the other the last word, this undignified exchange might have continued indefinitely, had not the Civil War intervened, diverting their attention to more important matters.

EIGHTEEN MONTHS AFTER the release of the last Perote prisoners, U.S. and Mexican troops clashed in the Nueces Strip, prompting President Polk to declare war on Mexico. Not surprisingly, the survivors of Mier greeted the news with jubilation. If there were some too broken in health and spirit to take up arms, many were eager for a chance to win the glory earlier denied them. Like many Texans, they rejoiced at the opportunity to exact a bloody retribution for indignities which they believed they had suffered at the hands of Mexico. One American recruit observed that some of the former inmates of Mexican prisons "did not enter the service altogether through motives of pure patriotism, but for the sake of the spoils, and to glut their vengeance." [17] After one early skirmish, Bate Berry, whose brother Joseph had broken his leg before the battle of Mier and was later killed by Ampudia's men, had to be reprimanded by General Zachary Taylor himself for scalping his Mexican victims. [18] "Most of these [Texas] rangers," wrote one American soldier, "are men who have either been prisoners in Mexico, or, in some way, injured by Mexicans, and they, therefore, spare none, but shoot down every one they meet. It is said that the bushes skirting the road from Monterrey southward, are strewed with skeletons of Mexicans sacrificed by these desperadoes." [19]

A few Mier men were destined to become widely celebrated for their exploits in the Mexican War. Daniel Drake Henrie, who had tunneled out of Perote with Green, gained national attention when, after being captured again by Mexican soldiers, he succeeded in making yet another daring escape. [20] Samuel Walker emerged as perhaps the best-known hero of the war, serving with distinction in both the Taylor and the Scott campaigns. Although Walker seems to have discouraged his men from engaging in pillage, he had nothing but hatred for the Mexican guerrillas who harassed Winfield Scott's army, and he rarely brought in prisoners. [21] For the thirty-two-year-old Walker, the path of vengeance came to an end at the little town of Huamantla, not far from Perote. Walker had seized the town and was regrouping his men in the plaza when he was fatally wounded by a sniper's bullet. Enraged by the sight of their fallen leader, his men went on a mad rampage, plundering the village and murdering its inhabitants in one of the worst atrocities of the war. [22]

The men who perished in the Salado execution were never forgotten by their comrades. As the Texas Rangers pushed into Mexico, they recognized the terrain of their ill-fated escape into the mountains. Captain John Dusenberry, a member of the expedition, was with a reconnaissance party on its way toward San Luis Potosí when he persuaded his commander to make a detour to the Hacienda del Salado. Riding all night, they arrived at dawn and made the village alcalde show them where the bodies were buried. The bones of the sixteen men were exhumed, crated in boxes, and taken back to camp at Buena Vista; they remained with Taylor's army throughout the campaign. [23] At the end of the war Dusenberry was detailed to take the remains to LaGrange, selected as the final resting place because it was the home of Captain Eastland, the highest-ranking officer among the victims. On September 18, 1848, the bodies of the Salado men and those killed in the Dawson fight were interred with full military honors in a vault on a high bluff overlooking the Colorado River (the obelisk monument that stands today was added almost a century later).[24]

The Mier Expedition was a failure. Frustrated by insubordination and disorder, its soldiers had won no great victory, served no high purpose. But the Mier men judged themselves by entirely different standards. In order of importance, military objectives ranked far below the pursuit of the heroic ideal and the exaltation of personal acts of courage. They were common men seeking an uncommon destiny, defining the experience in individual rather than collective terms, determined to distinguish themselves, to rise above the rank and file. Valor was not simply an ennobling trait—it was also a means to an end, offering a field of opportunity for men to test themselves and make their mark. Possessed by a reckless vainglory so peculiar to a modern and more cynical age, the men who crossed the Río Grande in December 1842 shared Thomas Carlyle's belief that history is but the biography of great men; the heroic mantle was bestowed not upon those who followed, but upon those who took the lead. Their unwillingness to act in concert owed as much to the romanticism of the age in which they lived as it did to the celebrated individualistic ethos of the American frontier. Renowned for their tenacity and self-reliance, the citizen-soldiers of Texas possessed, in equal measure, an obduracy and a disrespect for authority that bordered on the anarchic. It was no wonder, then, that the history of the Texas Republic was destined to be as brief as it was colorful.

For the Black Bean victims, their tragedy became their triumph. They had at last achieved some measure of celebrity. "Take away the appreciation of heroic actions," one eulogist declared, "and you deprive the warrior of his sharpest weapon. . . . Death to him is but the vestibule of fame."[25] And with respect for the dead came respect for the living. The enshrinement of the Black Bean victims paid tribute to all those who carried with them the memories of Mier, the Hacienda del Salado, and Perote. It had been a misbegotten affair, but martyrdom, the ultimate sacrifice, was capable of redeeming even the wildest human folly. The state legislature in its next session provided the Mier men with back pay for their time spent as prisoners of Mexico, thereby recognizing them as legitimate soldiers in the service of Texas.[26] They were honored not for what they had achieved but for what they had endured. Whether or not they deserved to be regarded as heroes, it was a distinction they had dearly paid for in blood, misery, and toil.

Notes

ABBREVIATIONS

BDC: Ephraim Douglass Adams, ed., *British Diplomatic Correspondence Concerning the Republic of Texas, 1836–1846*.

DCRT: George P. Garrison, ed., *Diplomatic Correspondence of the Republic of Texas*.

DCUS-IAA: William R. Manning, ed., *Diplomatic Correspondence of the United States: Inter-American Affairs, 1831–1860*.

PRO: Public Record Office (Great Britain).

El Siglo XIX: El Siglo Diez y Nueve.

SHQ: Southwestern Historical Quarterly.

TSHAQ: Texas State Historical Association Quarterly.

TMH: Texas Military History.

1. "CARTHAGE MUST BE DESTROYED"

1. Austin *Daily Bulletin*, December 14, 1841.

2. Francis Richard Lubbock, *Six Decades in Texas*, ed. C. W. Raines, pp. 141–142.

3. Josiah Gregg, *Diary and Letters of Josiah Gregg*, ed. Maurice Garland Fulton, 1:109.

4. Herbert Pickens Gambrell, *Mirabeau Buonaparte Lamar, Troubadour and Crusader*, p. 245.

5. Gregg, *Diary and Letters* 1:106–107; Lubbock, *Six Decades in Texas*, p. 143.

6. *Texas Sentinel*, September 2, 1841.

7. *Daily Bulletin*, December 14, 1841; Lubbock, *Six Decades in Texas*, p. 142.

8. Gregg, *Diary and Letters* 1:110; James Webb to James Starr, Decem-

ber 13, 1841, James Bryan Papers, Part VII. Houston's inaugural address, which according to Josiah Gregg was delivered extemporaneously, appears to have been similar to the speech he gave at Houston City before traveling to Austin. In this address, Houston stated: "When we look about us and within us, we cannot avoid the melancholy consciousness that our happiness is impaired by the misfortunes of our country. We perceive our money depreciated, our credit sunk, political institutions and laws disregarded and suspended; the highest functionaries forgetting their high destiny—the whole country languishing under oppression." "Address of General Sam Houston, President-Elect, at Houston," *The Writings of Sam Houston,* ed. Amelia Williams and Eugene C. Barker, 2:391–397; hereafter cited as *Houston Writings.* For a summary of Houston's address, see "The Inauguration," *The Weekly Texian,* December 15, 1841.

9. William M. Gouge, *The Fiscal History of Texas,* p. 115. Sam Houston estimated the public debt at ten to fifteen million dollars. First Message to Congress, Second Administration, *Houston Writings* 2:402.

10. The trials of the Santa Fe prisoners are ably chronicled by George Wilkins Kendall in *Narrative of the Texan Santa Fe Expedition.* See also Noel M. Loomis, *The Texan–Santa Fe Pioneers.*

11. Gregg, *Diary and Letters* 1:110.

12. *Daily Bulletin,* January 7, 1842.

13. Stanley Siegel, *A Political History of the Texas Republic,* p. 188.

14. *The Weekly Texian,* December 18, 1841. Rumors of the capture of the expedition persisted for several days but were not confirmed until the new year. *Daily Bulletin,* January 3, 1842.

15. *A Voice from the West!!!* Broadside, Austin *City Gazette* [1842].

16. Henderson Yoakum, *History of Texas* 2:343.

17. Houston to House of Representatives, February 1, 1843, *Houston Writings* 2:463.

18. Washington D. Miller to Houston, March 5, 1842, Washington Daniel Miller Papers.

19. Houston to George William Brown and others, March 3, 1842, *Houston Writings* 4:76.

20. "Report of the Secretary of War and Marine," *Telegraph and Texas Register,* July 6, 1842.

21. Yoakum, *History of Texas* 2:329n.

22. For more on American racial attitudes during this period, see Reginald Horsman, *Race and Manifest Destiny: The Origins of American Racial Anglo-Saxonism.*

23. Joseph Eve to John Tyler, October 11, 1842, "A Letterbook of Joseph Eve," ed. Joseph Milton Nance, *SHQ* 44:98.

24. Austin *City Gazette,* March 30, 1843, quoted in Siegel, *A Political History of the Texas Republic,* p. 194.

25. *Telegraph and Texas Register,* October 5, 1842.

26. "Colonel Swett's Speech upon the American Prisoners in Mexico," *Telegraph and Texas Register,* March 2, 1842.

27. *Telegraph and Texas Register,* March 16, 1842.

28. Ibid., March 23, 1842.

29. Washington D. Miller to Houston, February 23, 1842, Miller Papers.

2. THE VÁSQUEZ AND WOLL INCURSIONS

1. "Mariano Arista, General of Division, Commander-in-Chief of the Northern Army of the Republic of Mexico, to the Inhabitants of the Department of Texas," *The Weekly Texian*, March 9, 1842.

2. Miguel A. Sánchez Lamego, *The Second Mexican-Texan War, 1841–1843*, Appendix 3, p. 75.

3. Santa Anna to J[ames] Hamilton, February 18, 1842, *Telegraph and Texas Register*, March 23, 1842.

4. For a much more detailed study of this and other border clashes between Texas and Mexico during this period, see Joseph Milton Nance's exhaustively researched *Attack and Counterattack: The Texan-Mexican Frontier, 1842*.

5. New Orleans *Daily Picayune*, March 15, 1842.

6. Eve to John J. Crittenden, April 3, 1842, "A Letterbook of Joseph Eve," *SHQ* 43:372.

7. William Bollaert, *William Bollaert's Texas*, ed. Eugene W. Hollon and Ruth Lapham Butler, p. 34.

8. Houston to General Alexander Somervell, March 18, 1842, *Houston Writings* 2:509.

9. Houston to William Henry Daingerfield, April 1, 1842, *Houston Writings* 3:15.

10. Somervell to Anson Jones, March 25, 1842, Anson Jones, *Memoranda and Official Correspondence Relating to the Republic of Texas*, p. 173.

11. *Telegraph and Texas Register*, April 20, 1843.

12. Houston to James Davis, June 6, 1842, quoted in Marquis James, *The Raven*, p. 325.

13. Eve to Richard Southgate, May 10, 1842, "A Letterbook of Joseph Eve," *SHQ* 43:493–494.

14. Houston to George William Brown and others, March 3, 1842, *Houston Writings* 4:76.

15. "To the Citizens of Texas," March 14, 1842, *Houston Writings* 2:503; Houston to General Leslie Combs, March 16, 1842, ibid. 2:504–505; "The Proclamation of the Blockade of Mexican Ports," March 26, 1842, ibid. 2:537–538.

16. Houston to Editor of the *Galveston Advertiser*[?], March 17, 1842, *Houston Writings* 2:509.

17. Houston to Santa Anna, March 21, 1842, *Houston Writings* 2:526–527.

18. Houston *Morning Star*, October 2, 1842.

19. Houston to Davis, June 6, 1842, quoted in James, *The Raven*, p. 325.

20. David McComb, *Houston: The Bayou City*, p. 12.

21. Ibid., p. 64. See also Kenneth W. Wheeler, *To Wear a City's Crown*, pp. 60–64.

22. Houston to Texas Congress, June 27, 1842, *Houston Writings* 3:77.

23. *Telegraph and Texas Register*, August 3, 1842.

24. James, *The Raven*, p. 326.

25. Bollaert, *Bollaert's Texas*, pp. 104–105n; William Carey Crane, *Life and Select Literary Remains of Sam Houston*, p. 142.

26. Houston to House of Representatives, July 22, 1842, *Houston Writings* 3:116–124.

27. Tom Henderson Wells, *Commodore Moore and the Texas Navy*, pp. 108–109.

28. "President Houston's War Measures," Austin *City Gazette*, August 17, 1842.

29. James Morgan to Ashbel Smith, August 20, 1842, Ashbel Smith Papers.

30. Sánchez Lamego, *The Second Mexican-Texan War*, Appendix 8, p. 89.

31. John Salmon Ford, *Rip Ford's Texas*, ed. Stephen B. Oates, pp. 68–69.

32. For more on Samuel Walker before his arrival in Texas, see, for example, Walker to Brother, March 7, 1841, and April 3, 1841, Samuel Hamilton Walker Papers.

33. Jonathan Hampton Kuykendall, "Sketches of Early Texians" (Barker Texas History Center), p. 14.

34. Samuel Walker, *Samuel Walker's Account of the Mier Expedition*, ed. Marilyn McAdams Sibley, p. 5.

35. Although Big Foot Wallace gained lasting fame as a result of two biographies published during his lifetime—John C. Duval's *Adventures of Big Foot Wallace* and A. J. Sowell's *The Life of "Big Foot" Wallace*—both accounts were based almost entirely upon Wallace's own recollections. Wallace was undoubtedly a colorful character, but he does not appear to have been as prominent a figure in the Somervell and Mier Expeditions as is commonly believed. Of the many participants in these campaigns who wrote of their exploits, none considered Wallace worthy of particular notice.

36. Adrian Woll, "Brigadier General Adrian Woll's Report of His Expedition into Texas in 1842," trans. and ed. Joseph Milton Nance, *SHQ* 58:542–543.

37. Nance, *Attack and Counterattack*, pp. 358–359.

38. Memucan Hunt to Francis Moore, October 17, 1842, *Telegraph and Texas Register*, October 26, 1842. As was often the case when Texans and Mexicans met on the battlefield, casualty figures given by the two sides varied widely. General Woll reported 29 Mexican soldiers dead and 58 wounded in the fighting on September 18 (at both the Salado and the so-called "Dawson Massacre") and estimated that 180 Texans had been killed. Numerous Texan accounts estimate the total Mexican fatalities to be much higher than Hunt's account. James Nichols, for example, believed that Woll had lost 123 men at the Salado. James Wilson Nichols, *Now You Hear My Horn: The Journal of James Wilson Nichols, 1820–1887*, ed. Catherine W. McDowell, p. 108.

39. Houston Wade, *The Dawson Men of Fayette County*, p. 17; Joseph C. Robinson, "Dawson's Defeat—The Massacre," *The Texas Almanac for 1868*, p. 46.

40. *The Texas Almanac for 1868*, pp. 47–48.

41. Norman Woods to Brother, July 5, 1843, "Letters of the 'Dawson Men' from Perote Prison, Mexico, 1842–1843," ed. L. U. Spellman, *SHQ* 38:258.

42. *Telegraph and Texas Register*, October 12, 1842; October 26, 1842.

43. Bollaert, *Bollaert's Texas*, pp. 145, 148.

44. Eve to President Tyler, October 11, 1842, "A Letterbook of Joseph Eve," *SHQ* 44:97.

45. Houston to Davis, June 6, 1842, *Houston Writings* 4:116.

3. THE SOUTHWESTERN ARMY OF OPERATIONS

1. Houston to M. C. Hamilton, September 16, 1842, *Houston Writings* 3:159–160.

2. John Washington Lockhart, *Sixty Years on the Brazos: The Life and Letters of Dr. John Washington Lockhart*, ed. Jonnie Lockhart Wallis and Laurence Hill, pp. 95–96, 156–157.

3. *Telegraph and Texas Register*, October 12, 1842.

4. Nelson Lee, *Three Years among the Camanches*, p. 57.

5. Ibid. U.S. chargé d'affaires Joseph Eve reported to Secretary of State Daniel Webster that Houston had ordered troops "about to march for the army to disband." Eve to Webster, October 5, 1842, No. 28, National Archives, Despatches from United States Ministers to Texas, vol. 2.

6. Houston to Somervell, October 3, 1842, *Houston Writings* 3:170–171.

7. M. C. Hamilton to Somervell, October 13, 1842, *Houston Writings* 3:177–178. According to Barker and Williams, this letter and others received by Somervell from Washington-on-the-Brazos in the months of October and November 1843 were dictated by Houston and signed by Hamilton.

8. Ibid., p. 178.

9. William Physick Zuber, *My Eighty Years in Texas*, ed. Janis Boyle Mayfield, pp. 113–114.

10. Houston to Thomas M. Bagby, October 6, 1842, *Houston Writings* 3:172.

11. "Sketches of Travels in Texas," *Telegraph and Texas Register*, August 17, 1843; Harvey Alexander Adams, "Diary of Harvey Alexander Adams, in Two Parts: Rhode Island to Texas and Expedition against the Southwest in 1842 and 1843" (Barker Texas History Center), pp. 7–12; hereafter cited as "Expedition against the Southwest."

12. H. A. Adams, "Expedition against the Southwest," p. 11.

13. Ibid., p. 19.

14. Ibid., p. 14.

15. Joseph D. McCutchan, *Mier Expedition Diary*, ed. Joseph Milton Nance, p. 35.

16. James, *The Raven*, p. 409.

17. "Remarks Concerning the Pamphlet of Thomas Jefferson Green," February 15, 1855, *Houston Writings* 6:165–166.

18. Ina Kate Reinhardt, "The Public Career of Thomas Jefferson Green in Texas" (Master's thesis, University of Texas, 1939), p. 12.

19. Mary Whatley Clark, *David G. Burnet*, p. 124.

20. Thomas Jefferson Green, *Journal of the Texian Expedition against Mier,* pp. 486–487.

21. Reinhardt, "The Public Career of Thomas Jefferson Green in Texas," p. 74.

22. William Ransom Hogan, *The Texas Republic: A Social and Economic History*, p. 31.

23. McCutchan, *Mier Expedition Diary*, p. 14.

24. H. A. Adams, "Expedition against the Southwest," p. 64.

25. Green, *Journal*, p. 41.

26. M. C. Hamilton to William Cooke, November 7, 1842, Army Papers: Quartermaster Correspondence.

27. M. C. Hamilton to Somervell, November 9, 1842, *Houston Writings* 3:193–194.

28. Siegel, *A Political History of the Texas Republic*, pp. 212–214.

29. "Annual Message to the Texas Congress," December 1, 1842, *Houston Writings* 3:204.

30. Houston *Morning Star,* December 22, 1842.

31. Matilda C. Houstoun, *Texas and the Gulf of Mexico*, p. 217.

32. Adolphus Sterne, "Diary of Adolphus Sterne," ed. Harriet Smither, *SHQ* 35:153; Charles Raymond to Isaac Van Zandt, January 20, 1843, Isaac Van Zandt Papers.

33. Bollaert, *Bollaert's Texas,* pp. 195–196.

34. Herbert Gambrell, *Anson Jones: The Last President of Texas*, p. 247.

35. *Telegraph and Texas Register,* October 19, 1842.

36. Ephraim D. Adams, *British Interests and Activities in Texas, 1836–1846,* p. 118.

37. Kenneth Shewmaker et al., eds., *The Papers of Daniel Webster: Diplomatic Papers, Vol. 1, 1841–43,* p. 374.

38. Anson Jones to Major James Reily, January 26, 1842, quoted in Gambrell, *Anson Jones,* p. 232.

39. Reily to Jones, June 11, 1842, George P. Garrison, ed., *Diplomatic Correspondence of the Republic of Texas* (Part I) 2:567; hereafter cited as *DCRT.*

40. Eve to Joseph Waples, August 12, 1842, ibid. 2:581.

41. E. D. Adams, *British Interests and Activities in Texas,* pp. 97–122 passim.

42. Houston to Charles Elliot, November 5, 1842, Ephraim D. Adams, ed., *British Diplomatic Correspondence Concerning the Republic of Texas, 1836–1846,* p. 132; hereafter cited as *BDC.*

43. Elliot to Henry Unwin Addington, November 15, 1842, *BDC*, p. 126.

44. Eve to R. P. Letcher, December 22, 1842, "A Letterbook of Joseph Eve," *SHQ* 44:102, 103–104.

45. Ibid., p. 103.

46. Elliot to Lord Aberdeen, November 2, 1842, *BDC*, p. 123.

47. Eve to Letcher, December 22, 1842, "A Letterbook of Joseph Eve," *SHQ* 44:102.

48. Elliot to Addington, November 15, 1842, No. 13, *BDC*, p. 127.

49. Green, *Journal*, pp. 45–46.

50. H. A. Adams, "Expedition against the Southwest," p. 32.

51. Sterling Brown Hendricks, "The Somervell Expedition to the Rio Grande, 1842," *SHQ* 23:117.

52. H. A. Adams, "Expedition against the Southwest," p. 26.

53. Hamilton to Somervell, November 9, 1842, *Houston Writings* 3:194.

54. Hamilton to Somervell, November 19, 1842, *Houston Writings* 3:198–199.

55. Ibid., p. 198.

56. H. A. Adams, "Expedition against the Southwest," p. 24.

57. Ibid., p. 26.

58. Ibid.

59. Hendricks, "The Somervell Expedition," *SHQ* 23:116.

60. Somervell to Cooke, November 18, 1842, Army Papers: Army Correspondence.

61. Zuber, *My Eighty Years in Texas*, pp. 112–115.

62. Houston Wade, *Notes and Fragments of the Mier Expedition* 1:96.

63. Loomis, *The Texan–Santa Fe Pioneers*, p. 187. According to Loomis, twenty-two former Santa Fe prisoners took up arms against Mexico in the fall of 1842. Of these, thirteen men joined Somervell's Southwestern Army of Operations.

64. Llerena B. Friend, ed., "Sidelights and Supplements on the Perote Prisoners," *SHQ* 68:369.

65. H. A. Adams, "Expedition against the Southwest," p. 47.

66. McCutchan, *Mier Expedition Diary*, p. 40n.

67. Albert D. Kirwan, *John J. Crittenden*, p. 159.

68. William Preston Stapp, *The Prisoners of Perote*, p. 13.

69. Samuel Walker to Mrs. A. M. Walker, January 22, 1842; Calendar to the Samuel Hamilton Walker Papers.

70. *Telegraph and Texas Register*, September 14, 1842.

71. Hobart Huson, *Refugio: A Comprehensive History of Refugio County from Aboriginal Times to 1953* 1:430, 436.

72. Ibid., p. 447.

73. Ibid., p. 449. See also Joseph Milton Nance, *After San Jacinto*, pp. 316–377 passim.

74. John Henry Brown, *Indian Wars and Pioneers of Texas*, pp. 140–141.

75. William S. Fisher to Felix Huston, January 30, 1842, Houston Wade Papers.

76. Duval, *Big Foot Wallace*, p. 167.

77. M. C. Hamilton to Somervell, November 21, 1842, Texas Congress, *Journals of the House of Representatives of the Seventh Congress of the Republic of Texas*, Appendix, pp. 9–10.

78. M. C. Hamilton to Wm. G. Cooke, November 7, 1842, and November 22, 1842, Army Papers: Quartermaster Correspondence.

79. John Hemphill [by order of Brig. Gen. Somervell] to Quarter Master General [Wm. G. Cooke], November 21, 1842, Order No. 28, Army Papers: Quartermaster Correspondence.

80. Hamilton to Jones, June 27, 1843, *DCRT* (Part III) 2:1453–1455.

81. Houston *Morning Star,* January 17, 1843.

82. McCutchan, *Mier Expedition Diary,* p. 17.

4. THE MARCH TO LAREDO

1. George B. Erath, "Memoirs of George B. Erath," ed. Lucy Erath, *SHQ* 27:39.

2. Sánchez Lamego, *The Second Mexican-Texan War,* p. 44.

3. H. A. Adams, "Expedition against the Southwest," p. 33.

4. Ibid., p. 34.

5. Ibid.; Hendricks, "The Somervell Expedition," *SHQ* 23:118.

6. Green, *Journal,* p. 53.

7. Hendricks, "The Somervell Expedition," *SHQ* 23:118.

8. H. A. Adams, "Expedition against the Southwest," pp. 34–35.

9. Green, *Journal,* p. 53.

10. Hendricks, "The Somervell Expedition," *SHQ* 23:119.

11. Ibid.

12. Ibid., p. 120.

13. Ibid.

14. Ibid.

15. Ibid., p. 122.

16. McCutchan, *Mier Expedition Diary,* p. 19.

17. Ibid., p. 20.

18. John Henry Brown, *History of Texas from 1685 to 1892* 2:236–237.

19. H. A. Adams, "Expedition against the Southwest," p. 42; Brown, *History of Texas* 2:237.

20. George Lord, "George Lord: Mier Prisoner," ed. C. T. Traylor, *Frontier Times,* 15:535.

21. *Telegraph and Texas Register,* December 7, 1842.

22. "Speech on Thomas Jefferson Green," August 1, 1854, *Houston Writings* 6:79.

23. Lockhart, *Sixty Years on the Brazos,* p. 186.

24. Nance, *Attack and Counterattack,* p. 504.

25. Hendricks, "The Somervell Expedition," *SHQ* 23:125.

26. H. A. Adams, "Expedition against the Southwest," p. 45.

27. Ibid.

28. Green, *Journal,* p. 54.

29. Seb Wilcox, "Laredo during the Texas Republic," *SHQ* 42:101.

30. H. A. Adams, "Expedition against the Southwest," p. 44.

31. Green, *Journal,* p. 55.

32. H. A. Adams, "Expedition against the Southwest," p. 45.

33. Green, *Journal,* pp. 55–56.

34. Stapp, *Prisoners,* p. 18.

35. H. A. Adams, "Expedition against the Southwest," p. 46.

36. Ibid., pp. 48–49.

37. *Telegraph and Texas Register,* January 4, 1843.

38. H. A. Adams, "Expedition against the Southwest," p. 53.

39. Ibid., p. 46.

40. Ibid.

41. Stapp, *Prisoners,* p. 19.

42. Ibid., p. 18.

43. Hendricks, "The Somervell Expedition," *SHQ* 23:128.

44. H. A. Adams, "Expedition against the Southwest," p. 47.

45. Green, *Journal,* p. 57.

46. According to Houston, Green "was the first individual to encourage the insubordinate and irregular followers of the army to break down the doors and violate the sanctity of habitations; to strip women; to commit every outrage appalling to humanity, and infamous to a soldier. His cry was, 'Rake them down, boys; rake them down.'" "Speech on Thomas Jefferson Green," August 1, 1854, *Houston Writings* 6:77–78. For Green's rebuttal to this accusation, see *Reply [of] Gen. Thomas J. Green, to the Speech of General Sam Houston in the Senate of the United States, August 1, 1854,* p. 48.

47. McCutchan, *Mier Expedition Diary,* p. 25.

48. Houstoun, *Texas and the Gulf of Mexico,* p. 214.

49. Somervell to the Alcalde of the town of Laredo [Florencio Villareal], December 9, 1842, Army Papers: Army Correspondence.

50. Hendricks, "The Somervell Expedition," *SHQ* 23:128.

51. Green, *Journal,* p. 59.

52. H. A. Adams, "Expedition against the Southwest," p. 63.

53. Green, *Journal,* p. 60.

54. Ibid.

55. H. A. Adams, "Expedition against the Southwest," p. 55.

56. Ibid., p. 47.

57. Green, *Journal,* pp. 61–62.

58. Hendricks, "The Somervell Expedition," *SHQ* 23:130.

59. Green, *Journal,* p. 63.

60. Ibid., pp. 64–65.

61. McCutchan, *Mier Expedition Diary,* p. 31.

62. Green, *Journal,* p. 64.

63. H. A. Adams, "Expedition against the Southwest," pp. 61–62.

64. Hendricks, "The Somervell Expedition," *SHQ* 23:135.

65. H. A. Adams, "Expedition against the Southwest," p. 62.

66. Pedro de Ampudia to Ministro de guerra y marina D. José María Tornel, December 29, 1842, *El Siglo XIX,* March 1, 1843.

67. H. A. Adams, "Expedition against the Southwest," p. 63.

68. *Telegraph and Texas Register,* February 22, 1843.

69. H. A. Adams, "Expedition against the Southwest," p. 63.

70. *Telegraph and Texas Register,* January 18, 1843.

71. New Orleans *Commercial Bulletin,* January 12, 1843.

72. McCutchan, *Mier Expedition Diary,* p. 32.

73. Erath, "Memoirs," *SHQ* 27:43.

74. *Telegraph and Texas Register,* January 14, 1846.

75. Nichols, *Now You Hear My Horn,* p. 114.

76. Guy Bryan to Rutherford B. Hayes, January 21, 1843, "The Bryan-Hayes Correspondence," ed. E. W. Winkler, *SHQ* 25:106.

77. Siegel, *A Political History of the Texas Republic,* p. 209.

78. Erath, "Memoirs," *SHQ* 27:44.

79. Wade, *Notes and Fragments* 2:70.

80. Houston *Morning Star,* January 17, 1843.

81. Erath, "Memoirs," *SHQ* 27:44.

82. Hendricks, "The Somervell Expedition," *SHQ* 23:138.

83. Ibid.

84. *Telegraph and Texas Register,* January 4, 1843.

85. Ibid., January 18, 1843.

86. Ibid.

5. THE BATTLE OF MIER

1. Stapp, *Prisoners,* p. 27.

2. McCutchan, *Mier Expedition Diary,* p. 36.

3. Green, *Journal,* p. 76.

4. José Antonio de la Garza to Dr. José Luis Gonzaga García, December 15, 1842 (Texas State Library).

5. Green, *Journal,* p. 76.

6. McCutchan, *Mier Expedition Diary,* p. 38.

7. Pedro de Ampudia to Ministro de guerra y marina D. José María Tornel, December 29, 1842, *El Siglo XIX,* March 1, 1843.

8. Ibid.

9. Green, *Journal,* p. 79.

10. William Preston Stapp insisted that Ampudia's force alone, not including the men under Colonel Canales' command, was "ten times as great" as the Texan force, which in all numbered 305 men. Stapp, *Prisoners,* p. 28. Joseph McCutchan wrote that the combined Mexican forces numbered no less than 3,000 men. McCutchan, *Mier Expedition Diary,* pp. 52–53. William Fisher believed the Mexican forces numbered 2,500. *Telegraph and Texas Register,* August 2, 1843.

11. "Triunfo sobre los Tejanos," *Político Semanario,* December 29, 1842.

12. Wilcox, "Laredo during the Texas Republic," *SHQ* 42:101.

13. Green, *Journal,* p. 81.

14. Walker, *Samuel Walker's Account,* pp. 35–36.

15. Ampudia to Tornel, December 29, 1842, *El Siglo XIX*, March 1, 1843.

16. Green, *Journal*, pp. 83–84.

17. Stapp, *Prisoners*, p. 32.

18. Duval, *Big Foot Wallace*, pp. 178–179; Stapp, *Prisoners*, p. 33.

19. McCutchan, *Mier Expedition Diary*, p. 45.

20. *Telegraph and Texas Register*, August 2, 1843.

21. Stapp, *Prisoners*, p. 33; McCutchan, *Mier Expedition Diary*, p. 46.

22. Green, *Journal*, pp. 91–92.

23. McCutchan, *Mier Expedition Diary*, pp. 46–47; Green, *Journal*, pp. 92–93; Stapp, *Prisoners*, pp. 33–34. For more on Mexican army firearms, see [Angelina] Nieto, [John Nicholas] Brown, and [J.] Hefter, *El soldado mexicano, 1837–1847*, pp. 53–54.

24. Green, *Journal*, pp. 93–94.

25. Duval, *Big Foot Wallace*, p. 180; Green, *Journal*, p. 94; Stapp, *Prisoners*, p. 34.

26. *Telegraph and Texas Register*, August 2, 1843; Ampudia to Tornel, December 29, 1842, *El Siglo XIX*, March 1, 1843.

27. Green, *Journal*, p. 99.

28. *Telegraph and Texas Register*, August 2, 1843.

29. Ibid.

30. Ibid. Numerous reports confirm Fisher's belief that the general panic and confusion which seized the Texans during the cease-fire impaired their ability to continue the battle. See New Orleans *Daily Picayune*, February 8, 1843; Winkler, ed., "Bryan-Hayes Correspondence," *SHQ* 25:106; *Telegraph and Texas Register*, February 15, 1843; and Israel Canfield, "Israel Canfield on the Mier Expedition," ed. James Day, *TMH* 3:170.

31. Green, *Journal*, p. 93.

32. James A. Glasscock, "Diary of James A. Glasscock, Mier Man," ed. James Day, *Texana* 1:89–90; Canfield, "Israel Canfield," *TMH* 3:170.

33. *Telegraph and Texas Register*, August 2, 1843. Joseph McCutchan agreed with Fisher that any efforts to fight their way out of Mier would have ended in disaster. Of the sixty men in favor of this "mad attempt," he wrote, no more than ten "would have got one mile from town." McCutchan, *Mier Expedition Diary*, p. 57.

34. Clarksville *Northern Standard*, January 14, 1843.

35. *Telegraph and Texas Register*, August 2, 1843.

36. Green, *Journal*, p. 104.

37. Duval, *Big Foot Wallace*, p. 170.

38. A third, Nelson Lee, also claimed to have escaped from Mier after the battle, although no other source mentions him as a participant. Lee's name appears on the muster rolls of Captain Philip H. Coe's company on the Somervell Expedition, but I have been unable to find any evidence to corroborate or refute his contention that he joined Fisher's army and marched into Mexico. Nonetheless, in his book *Three Years among the Camanches*, Lee provides a vivid and detailed account of his escape, claiming to have hidden underneath a chaparral fence overgrown with weeds when Fisher's men marched into the square to stack

their arms. When night fell he succeeded in making his escape, and after several adventures, returned to San Antonio. Lee, *Three Years among the Camanches,* pp. 62–68.

39. Erath, "Memoirs," *SHQ* 27:48.

40. Green, *Journal,* p. 115.

41. Houston *Morning Star,* January 10, 1843.

42. *Telegraph and Texas Register,* January 18, 1843.

43. Green, *Journal,* pp. 107, 443.

44. Antonio Canales to D. José María Tornel, December 26, 1842, *El Siglo XIX,* January 7, 1843.

45. Ampudia to Tornel, December 26, 1842, ibid.

46. According to A. J. Sowell, many *presidiale* troops were killed during the three assaults on the Texas position. A. J. Sowell, *History of Fort Bend County,* p. 188.

47. Green, *Journal,* p. 111.

48. Houston *Morning Star,* March 7, 1843.

49. *Telegraph and Texas Register,* August 2, 1843.

50. Green, *Journal,* pp. 106–107.

51. Ibid., p. 107.

52. Ampudia seems to have adopted a view similar to that of General Adrian Woll, who remarked to Judge Anderson Hutchinson after the capture of San Antonio that "now, since the recognition of Texas by other nations, the war would be conducted according to the usages of civilized warfare." E. W. Winkler, ed., "The Bexar and Dawson Prisoners," *TSHAQ* 13:296.

53. Fay[ette] Robinson, *Mexico and Her Military Chieftains,* p. 259.

54. Pedro Ampudia to Señoritas de la villa de Mier, December 31, 1842, *Diario del Gobierno,* February 24, 1843.

55. William S. Fisher and Thomas Jefferson Green to Pedro Ampudia, January 11, 1843, *Telegraph and Texas Register,* May 3, 1843.

56. Fanny Chambers Gooch-Iglehart, *Boy Captive of the Mier Expedition,* Ch. 12 passim.

57. Duval, *Big Foot Wallace,* p. 185.

58. McCutchan, *Mier Expedition Diary,* p. 53.

59. *Telegraph and Texas Register,* August 2, 1844.

6. "OUR NATIONAL CALAMITY"

1. *El Siglo XIX,* January 6, 1843. Unless otherwise indicated, translations from Spanish are mine.

2. Van Zandt to Gen[era]l, March 5, 1843, Van Zandt Papers.

3. J. N. Almonte to Ministro de Relaciones Exteriores y Gobernación [José María de Bocanaegra], January 25, 1843, No. 10, Archivo de la Secretaría de Relaciones Exteriores, 1842–1847, Barker Transcripts, Archivo General de México 571:124; same to same, February 7, 1843, No. 13, ibid., p. 125.

4. Houston to George Hill, January 24, 1843, *Houston Writings* 3:305.

5. *Telegraph and Texas Register,* January 18, 1843.

6. Ibid., February 1, 1843.

7. Bollaert, *Bollaert's Texas,* p. 160.

8. Houston *Morning Star,* March 25, 1843.

9. E. S. C. Robertson to Van Zandt, April 8, 1843, Van Zandt Papers.

10. New Orleans *Commercial Bulletin,* January 21, 1843.

11. Van Zandt to Anson Jones, March 15, 1843, Jones, *Memoranda and Official Correspondence,* p. 211.

12. Bollaert, *Bollaert's Texas,* p. 167.

13. Samuel Swartwout to James Morgan, April 2, 1843, Bass and Brunson, eds., *Fragile Empires,* pp. 199–200.

14. Ashbel Smith to Anson Jones, March 31, 1843, *DCRT* (Part III) 3:1427–1430.

15. Smith to Jones, June 16, 1843, *DCRT* (Part III) 3:1449–1450.

16. Jules Edouard de Cramayel to François Guizot, February 4, 1843, No. 10, Nancy Nichols Barker, ed., *The French Legation in Texas* 2:406.

17. Richard Pakenham to Lord Aberdeen, February 24, 1843, No. 8, FO 50/161, Public Record Office (Great Britain); hereafter cited as PRO.

18. Pakenham to Aberdeen, January 24, 1843, No. 3, ibid.

19. Yoakum, *History of Texas* 2:395; Eve to Houston, April 11, 1843, Andrew Jackson Houston Collection.

20. Van Zandt to Jones, April 21, 1843, *DCRT* (Part II) 2:168–169.

21. Van Zandt to Daniel Webster, March 23, 1843, ibid., p. 155.

22. Van Zandt to Jones, April 21, 1843, ibid., pp. 168–169.

23. Waddy Thompson to Webster, May 16, 1843, No. 20, National Archives: Despatches from United States Ministers to Mexico, vol. 11.

24. Webster to Thompson, January 31, 1843, Shewmaker et al., eds., *The Papers of Daniel Webster: Diplomatic Papers* 1:474.

25. Thompson to Webster, March 14, 1843, William R. Manning, ed., *Diplomatic Correspondence of the United States: Inter-American Affairs, 1831–1860* 8:542; hereafter cited as *DCUS-IAA.* See also Webster to Thompson, February 7, 1843, Shewmaker et al., eds., *The Papers of Daniel Webster: Diplomatic Papers* 1:474.

26. Van Zandt to Jones, March 13, 1843, *DCRT* (Part II) 2:133.

27. Van Zandt to Gen[era]l, March 5, 1843, Van Zandt Papers.

28. Van Zandt to Jones, March 13, 1843, *DCRT* (Part II) 2:133–134.

29. William Henry Daingerfield to Jones, March 10, 1843, ibid., p. 130.

30. Van Zandt to Gen[era]l, March 5, 1843, Van Zandt Papers.

31. Houston to Eve, February 17, 1843, *DCRT* (Part II) 2:128.

32. Jones to Van Zandt, February 10, 1843, ibid., p. 123.

33. Washington D. Miller to President Tyler, January 30, 1843, Washington Daniel Miller Papers.

34. Houston to Charles Elliot, January 24, 1843, *Houston Writings* 3:299–302.

35. Ibid., p. 299.

36. Ibid., p. 300.

37. Ibid.
38. George L. Rives, *The United States and Mexico, 1821–1848* 1:517–521.
39. Houston to the Texas Congress, December 29, 1842, *Houston Writings* 3:255.
40. Thompson to Webster, March 14, 1843, *DCUS-IAA* 8:542.
41. Ibid.
42. Thompson to Webster, April 11, 1843, ibid., pp. 543–544.
43. Elliot to Aberdeen, February 5, 1843, *BDC*, p. 162.
44. Elliot to Henry Unwin Addington, November 15, 1842, ibid., p. 126.
45. Daingerfield to Jones, February 4, 1843, Jones, *Memoranda and Official Correspondence*, p. 209.
46. Cramayel to Guizot, February 5, 1843, No. 11, Barker, ed., *The French Legation in Texas* 2:406.
47. Ibid., p. 407.
48. Van Zandt to Jones, March 13, 1843, *DCRT* (Part II) 2:136.
49. Elliot to Aberdeen, February 5, 1843, *BDC*, p. 162.
50. Stapp, *Prisoners*, p. 44; Green, *Journal*, p. 118.
51. Canfield, "Israel Canfield," *TMH* 3:171; Green, *Journal*, pp. 118–119.
52. Green, *Journal*, p. 120; Stapp, *Prisoners*, p. 45.
53. John Warren Hunter, *Adventures of a Mier Prisoner: Being the Thrilling Experiences of John Rufus Alexander, Who Was with the Ill-Fated Expedition Which Invaded Mexico* [p. 5]. Alexander's account was also serialized in the *LaGrange Journal*, March 12 to April 23, 1936.
54. Duval, *Big Foot Wallace*, pp. 187–188, 192.
55. Stapp, *Prisoners*, pp. 49–50.
56. Green, *Journal*, p. 123.
57. Ibid., pp. 124–125.
58. Walker, *Samuel Walker's Account*, p. 39; Green, *Journal*, p. 126.
59. Stapp, *Prisoners*, p. 51.
60. Ibid.; McCutchan, *Mier Expedition Diary*, p. 69; Canfield, "Israel Canfield," *TMH* 3:172–173.
61. Green, *Journal*, p. 126; Green to Felix Huston and Colo[nel] Bailey Peyton, January 12, 1843 (Archives Division, Texas State Library).
62. Duval, *Big Foot Wallace*, p. 191; *Telegraph and Texas Register*, January 25, 1843.
63. Walker, *Samuel Walker's Account*, p. 40; Green, *Journal*, p. 129.
64. The city's name was spelled Monterey in 1843. I have used the present spelling, Monterrey, throughout this book.
65. Yoakum, *History of Texas* 2:377–378. The Battle of Lipantitlan is examined in Nance, *Attack and Counterattack*, pp. 229–254.
66. Gooch-Iglehart, *Boy Captive of the Mier Expedition*, p. 207.
67. Stapp, *Prisoners*, pp. 53–54; Walker, *Samuel Walker's Account*, pp. 39–40; Duval, *Big Foot Wallace*, p. 192.
68. Duval, *Big Foot Wallace*, pp. 196–197; Stapp, *Prisoners*, pp. 56–57. Some of the prisoners blamed Charles Keller Reese for the aborted escape attempt. Israel Canfield believed that Reese had refused to take the position as-

signed to him, while Samuel Walker maintained that Reese had actually informed Colonel Manuel R. Barragán of the Texans' plans. Canfield, "Israel Canfield," *TMH* 3:173; Walker, *Samuel Walker's Account*, p. 42.

69. Green, *Reply [of] Gen. Thomas J. Green*, p. 43.
70. Green, *Journal*, pp. 132–134.
71. Winkler, ed., "The Bexar and Dawson Prisoners," *TSHAQ* 13:299–300n.
72. Stapp, *Prisoners*, pp. 65–66.
73. Canfield, "Israel Canfield," *TMH* 3:173; Walker, *Samuel Walker's Account*, p. 42.
74. Gregg, *Diary and Letters* 2:238.
75. Green, *Journal*, pp. 146–147; Stapp, *Prisoners*, p. 67.
76. Green, *Journal*, pp. 146–147.

7. THE BLACK BEAN EPISODE

1. Hunter, *Adventures of a Mier Prisoner* [p. 6]; Walker, *Samuel Walker's Account*, p. 44.
2. Wade, *Notes and Fragments* 1:52. In July 1843 Thomas Jefferson Green would escape with Reese from Perote prison (see Green, *Journal*, Ch. 9). In Reese's defense, Green would later write: "Captain Reese and his party have been severely censured by many of his comrades for not joining them in their attempt to reach home, and some have ascribed the worst motives for his not so doing. Captain Reese is too tried a soldier and devoted a patriot to allow a suspicion of either want of bravery or patriotism." Green, *Journal*, pp. 177–178.
3. Canfield, "Israel Canfield," *TMH* 3:176; Hunter, *Adventures of a Mier Prisoner* [p. 6].
4. Canfield, "Israel Canfield," *TMH* 3:174.
5. Green, *Journal*, p. 147.
6. Deposition of Colonel Severo Ruiz, February 22, 1843, "Calendar of Documents regarding Mier in National Archives of Mexico," Houston Wade Papers.
7. "Sketches of Mier, Hacienda del Salado, and Castle of Perote," Mier Expedition, Military Rolls (Texas State Library).
8. Duval, *Big Foot Wallace*, p. 203.
9. Hunter, *Adventures of a Mier Prisoner* [pp. 6–7].
10. George Washington Trahern, "Reminiscences" (Texas State Library), p. 8.
11. Sowell, *The Life of "Big Foot" Wallace*, p. 53.
12. Walker, *Samuel Walker's Account*, p. 44.
13. Green, *Journal*, pp. 148–149; *Diario del Gobierno*, February 24, 1843.
14. H. A. Adams, "Expedition against the Southwest," p. 65.
15. Clarksville *Northern Standard*, June 8, 1843.
16. Percy Doyle to Lord Aberdeen, April 24, 1843, FO 50/161, PRO.
17. Richard Pakenham to Aberdeen, March 22, 1843, No. 16, FO 50/161, PRO.

18. Wade, *Notes and Fragments* 1:70; Hunter, *Adventures of a Mier Prisoner* [p. 7].

19. Stapp, *Prisoners,* p. 72. According to Israel Canfield, fifteen Texans remained behind with Captain Reese. Canfield, "Israel Canfield," *TMH* 3:176.

20. Duval, *Big Foot Wallace,* p. 205; Walker, *Samuel Walker's Account,* p. 47.

21. Some believed the traveler to be an American, who had sent the Mexican the prisoners had found the night before to guide them through the mountains. Stapp, *Prisoners,* p. 75; Tho[ma]s Bell, *Narrative of the Capture and Subsequent Sufferings of the Mier Prisoners in Mexico,* pp. 29–30.

22. Stapp, *Prisoners,* p. 75. For details on Mexican efforts to recapture the prisoners, see *Diario del Gobierno,* March 24 and March 31, 1843, and *El Siglo XIX,* March 20, 1843.

23. *El Siglo XIX,* March 20, 1843.

24. Trahern, "Reminiscences," pp. 8–9.

25. Stapp, *Prisoners,* pp. 81–82.

26. Hunter, *Adventures of a Mier Prisoner* [p. 8]; Stapp, *Prisoners,* p. 82.

27. Walker, *Samuel Walker's Account,* pp. 50–51.

28. Duval, *Big Foot Wallace,* p. 210.

29. Stapp, *Prisoners,* pp. 82–83.

30. Duval, *Big Foot Wallace,* p. 216.

31. Lord, "George Lord," *Frontier Times* 15:546–547.

32. Stapp, *Prisoners,* pp. 83–84; Duval, *Big Foot Wallace,* p. 214.

33. Hunter, *Adventures of a Mier Prisoner* [p. 9].

34. Ibid.

35. Wade, *Notes and Fragments* 1:81.

36. Lord, "George Lord," *Frontier Times* 15:547.

37. Francisco Mejía to Ministro de Guerra y Marina [Tornel], March 1, 1843, *El Siglo XIX,* March 20, 1843.

38. Canfield, "Israel Canfield," *TMH* 3:178; Mejía to [Tornel], March 1, 1843, *El Siglo XIX,* March 20, 1843.

39. Duval, *Big Foot Wallace,* pp. 216–217. According to Israel Canfield, who was also a member of Cameron's party, the Mexican soldiers had no water at this encampment and were unable to furnish their captives with any until they reached the water hole at Boca de los Tres Ríos the next day. Canfield, "Israel Canfield," *TMH* 3:178.

40. Canfield, "Israel Canfield," *TMH* 3:179.

41. Walker, *Samuel Walker's Account,* pp. 52–53.

42. Duval, *Big Foot Wallace,* p. 220. The symptoms described by the Texans are entirely consistent with medical studies of the effects of dehydration. See, for example, A. V. Wolf, *Thirst: Physiology of the Urge to Drink and Problems of Water Lack,* pp. 219–222.

43. Canfield, "Israel Canfield," *TMH* 3:179.

44. Wade, *Notes and Fragments* 1:81–82.

45. Hunter, *Adventures of a Mier Prisoner* [p. 9].

46. Ibid. [p. 14].

47. New Orleans *Commercial Bulletin*, April 19, 1843; *Telegraph and Texas Register*, April 26, 1843.

48. Those known to have returned to Texas were John Alexander, George Oldham, Thomas W. Cox, and J. D. Blackburn. New Orleans *Commercial Bulletin*, April 19, 1843. Those believed to have perished in the mountains were George Anderson, F. Bray, William Morehead, William Cody, Sanford Rice, and A. J. Lewis. Perry Randolph and William Mitchell died shortly after their recapture. McCutchan, *Mier Expedition Diary*, pp. 192−201; Green, *Journal*, p. 444; Canfield, "Israel Canfield," *TMH* 3:179.

49. Stapp, *Prisoners*, p. 87.

50. *El Siglo XIX*, March 20, 1843; *Político Semanario*, March 9, 1843.

51. Gregg, *Diary and Letters* 2:231.

52. Francisco Mejía's resignation address was published in *El Voto de Coahuila*, March 25, 1843. Mejía's decision does not appear to have interfered with his political and military career. After leaving his post as governor of Coahuila, he served under General Woll as commander of the Army of the North's reserve brigade. In the Mexican War, he was appointed general-in-chief of Mexico's northern forces. *El Siglo XIX*, July 14, 1843; Albert Carreño, *Jefes del ejército mexicano en 1847*.

53. Houston *Morning Star*, June 27, 1843. For more on Waddy Thompson, see Louis Cleveland Pitchford, "The Diplomatic Representatives from the United States to Mexico, 1826−48" (Ph.D. dissertation, University of Colorado, 1965), Chs. 4−5.

54. Bocanegra to Webster, May 12, 1842, *DCUS-IAA* 8:488; Webster to Thompson, July 8, 1842, Shewmaker et al., eds., *The Papers of Daniel Webster: Diplomatic Papers* 1:452−453.

55. Waddy Thompson, *Recollections of Mexico*, pp. 73−74.

56. Thompson to Webster, April 11, 1843, *DCUS-IAA* 8:543−544.

57. Pakenham to Aberdeen, March 22, 1843, No. 16, FO 50/161, PRO.

58. Jose M. Rincón to Ministro de Guerra y Marina [Tornel], April 1, 1843, *El Cosmopolita*, April 19, 1843.

59. In 1800 a filibustering expedition into Texas led by Philip Nolan was defeated by Spanish troops. The government condemned one of the nine captured survivors to death and sentenced the others to ten-year prison terms. The punishments were decided by the roll of a dice. The man rolling the lowest number was hanged.

60. *El Siglo XIX*, April 11, 1843.

61. Emerich de Vattel, *The Law of Nations*, ed. Joseph Chitty, pp. 348, 353.

62. Thompson, *Recollections of Mexico*, pp. 73−74.

63. Thompson to Webster, April 11, 1843, *DCUS-IAA* 8:543−544.

64. Green, *Journal*, Chs. 13−14 passim.

65. Green, *Journal*, pp. 216−217.

66. Stapp, *Prisoners*, pp. 89−90; Walker, *Samuel Walker's Account*, p. 56.

67. Stapp, *Prisoners*, p. 90; Manuel Montero to Commandant General of the Department, February 23, 1843, Houston Wade Papers.

68. Walker, *Samuel Walker's Account*, p. 57.

69. Duval, *Big Foot Wallace*, p. 228.
70. Stapp, *Prisoners*, p. 99.
71. Juan Ortiz to Gobernador y Comandante General del Departmento de San Luis Potosí, March 27, 1843, *El Cosmopolita*, April 19, 1843. Some of the prisoners believed these were the same soldiers who had been put to flight by the Texans on February 11. Israel Canfield, on the other hand, believed that the infantry under Huerta's command were "*fresh* troops." Canfield, "Israel Canfield," *TMH* 3:181.
72. Colonel Domingo Huerta was *mayor de la plaza* of Saltillo.
73. Stapp, *Prisoners*, p. 91.
74. Duval, *Big Foot Wallace*, p. 229.
75. Ibid., p. 230. According to historian Houston Wade, it was James Wilson, who was not an officer himself, who advised the Texan leaders to "dip deep." Wade, *Notes and Fragments* 2:140.
76. Duval, *Big Foot Wallace*, p. 233.
77. Clarksville *Northern Standard*, February 10, 1844.
78. Stapp, *Prisoners*, p. 92.
79. Duval, *Big Foot Wallace*, p. 232.
80. Ibid., p. 233.
81. Trahern, "Reminiscences," p. 11. Like many Texans, Whaling does not appear to have been bothered by inconsistencies in the spelling of his surname. Although listed in Public Debt Papers, Texas State Archives, as Henry Whaling, he is identified as Henry Whelan in Refugio County probate records. See Huson, *Refugio* 1:481, 483.
82. Trahern, "Reminiscences," p. 11.
83. Wade, *Notes and Fragments* 1:144–145. The original Dunham letter is on display in the Alamo Museum.
84. Bell, *Narrative*, p. 38.
85. Stapp, *Prisoners*, p. 93.
86. Lord, "George Lord," *Frontier Times* 15:549.
87. Vito Alessio Robles, *Coahuila y Texas*, pp. 280–281; Stapp, *Prisoners*, p. 96; Gregg, *Diary and Letters* 2:231–232.

8. "THERE IS NO HOPE OF RELEASE"

1. Stapp, *Prisoners*, p. 97.
2. Ibid., pp. 98–102.
3. Ibid., p. 98.
4. Bell, *Narrative*, pp. 42–44.
5. Canfield, "Israel Canfield," *TMH* 3:184.
6. Clarksville *Northern Standard*, February 10, 1844.
7. Yoakum, *History of Texas* 2:377–378.
8. Percy Doyle to Lord Aberdeen, May 25, 1843, No. 17, FO 50/162, PRO.
9. Ibid.
10. Bell, *Narrative*, p. 44.

11. Gooch-Iglehart, *Boy Captive of the Mier Expedition*, pp. 227–242 passim. Although the authorized biography of John Hill, this is a highly fictionalized account, containing many inaccuracies. In describing the meeting between Hill and Santa Anna, the author also placed General José María Tornel and Valentín Gómez Farias at the scene; the latter, however, was at this time a bitter enemy of Santa Anna, living in exile in New Orleans. Perhaps Hill in later years had a limited recall of events; in any case, Gooch-Iglehart seems to have relied heavily upon her own imagination and some rather uneven research.

12. Lon Tinkle, *Thirteen Days to Glory*, pp. 234–235.

13. Thompson, *Recollections of Mexico*, p. 77.

14. Albert Gilliam, *Travels in Mexico during the Years 1843 and 1844*, pp. 87–89.

15. Dennis Berge, "The Mexican Response to United States' Expansionism, 1841–48" (Ph.D. dissertation, University of California at Berkeley, 1965), p. 85.

16. Waddy Thompson to Abel Upshur, October 29, 1843, *DCUS-IAA* 8:565.

17. Doyle to Aberdeen, April 24, 1843, No. 13, FO 50/161, PRO.

18. Ibid.

19. Duval, *Big Foot Wallace*, p. 241.

20. Ibid. Wallace gave more than one explanation of how he came by his nickname. When interviewed by A. J. Sowell, Wallace stated that he had acquired the eponym as early as 1839, when his footprints were mistaken for those of an Indian named Big Foot, who had been seen prowling around the homes of Austin. Sowell, *The Life of "Big Foot" Wallace*, pp. 20–21.

21. Stapp, *Prisoners*, p. 113.

22. Bell, *Narrative*, pp. 48–50.

23. Stapp, *Prisoners*, p. 117.

24. Ibid., p. 120; McCutchan, *Mier Expedition Diary*, p. 96.

25. Walker, *Samuel Walker's Account*, pp. 69–70.

26. Stapp, *Prisoners*, pp. 120–121.

27. The modern spelling, Veracruz, is used throughout rather than the earlier Vera Cruz.

28. Stapp, *Prisoners*, p. 164.

29. R. A. Barclay to My frends [*sic*], June 18, 1843, Spellman, ed. "Letters of the 'Dawson Men,'" *SHQ* 38:254–255.

30. *The Monument*, September 3, 1851, reprinted in the *LaGrange Journal*, July 20, 1933; see also Green, *Journal*, pp. 240–241.

31. Major General William J. Worth, who led the advance columns of Winfield Scott's army in the Mexican War, estimated that Perote had quarters for two thousand men and their officers. George Winston Smith and Charles Judah, eds., *Chronicles of the Gringos*, p. 223.

32. J. Jacob Oswandel, *Notes of the Mexican War*, p. 180.

33. McCutchan, *Mier Expedition Diary*, p. 131.

34. For a detailed description of the fortress, see Miguel A. Sánchez Lamego, *El Castillo de San Carlos de Perote*. See also J. J. McGrath and Walace Hawkins, "Perote Fort—Where Texans Were Imprisoned," *SHQ* 48:340–345, and Oswandel, *Notes of the Mexican War*, pp. 180–182.

35. For a list of the officer staff at Perote at this time, see *El Siglo XIX*, January 5, 1843; Green, *Journal,* pp. 267–268.

36. In order to provide a thorough description of prison life at Perote, I have drawn upon the letters, diaries, and other writings of many Texas prisoners incarcerated there during the years 1843–1844. Although the main body of Mier prisoners would not arrive until some months later, their impressions of Perote were much the same as those of the Texans imprisoned in the spring of 1843, and I have therefore included some of their observations, as well as those of the Bexar prisoners, in this chapter.

37. Eduard Harkort, *In Mexican Prisons: The Journal of Eduard Harkort,* ed. Louis E. Brister, pp. 27–29.

38. Rena Maverick Green, ed., *Samuel Maverick, Texan, 1803–1870,* p. 240; see also James L. Truehart, *The Perote Prisoners,* ed. Frederick C. Chabot, p. 274.

39. Green, *Journal,* p. 264.

40. Stapp, *Prisoners,* pp. 158–159.

41. Green, *Journal,* pp. 253–255.

42. Ibid., pp. 264–265; McCutchan, *Mier Expedition Diary,* pp. 124–125.

43. Green, *Journal,* pp. 264–265.

44. Ibid., pp. 264–266. See also Kenneth Franklin Neighbours, *Robert Simpson Neighbors and the Texas Frontier, 1836–1859,* p. 20.

45. McCutchan, *Mier Expedition Diary,* pp. 109–110.

46. Bell, *Narrative,* p. 72.

47. William F. Wilson to Brother, April 22, 1844, "Two Letters from a Mier Prisoner," *TSHAQ* 2:233.

48. C. K. Gleason to R. H. Gleason, May 4, 1843, Friend, ed., "Sidelights and Supplements," *SHQ* 69:92.

49. Green, *Journal,* pp. 244, 267–268.

50. Yoakum, *History of Texas,* 2:398–399.

51. Green, *Journal,* pp. 245–246.

52. Ibid., p. 246; Oswandel, *Notes of the Mexican War,* p. 186.

53. Willis Coplan, "Interesting Incidents in the Life of Brother Willis Coplan, While a Prisoner in Mexico during the Texas and Mexican War, Given in His Own Words, Taken from Memory," p. 8 (Texas State Library).

54. McCutchan, *Mier Expedition Diary,* p. 123.

55. R. A. Barclay to Henry Gonsalvo Woods, May 8, 1843, Spellman, ed., "Letters of the 'Dawson Men,'" *SHQ* 38:253.

56. Green, *Journal,* pp. 268–289; Neighbours, *Robert Simpson Neighbors,* p. 21.

57. Green, *Journal,* pp. 270–272.

58. Ibid., p. 277.

59. Ibid., pp. 320–322.

60. Samuel Maverick to Mary Maverick, March 15, 1843, Green, ed., *Samuel Maverick, Texan,* pp. 236–237.

61. Norman Woods to Jane Woods, October 17, 1843, Spellman, ed., "Letters of the 'Dawson Men,'" *SHQ* 38:266.

62. Norman Woods to Jane Woods, July 20, 1843, ibid., pp. 260–261.

63. Norman Woods to Henry Gonsalvo Woods, July 21, 1843, ibid., p. 265.

64. Maverick to Bocanegra, January 21, 1843, Green, ed., *Samuel Maverick, Texan,* pp. 212–222.

65. Barclay to My frends [*sic*], April 10, 1843, Spellman, ed., "Letters of the 'Dawson Men,'" *SHQ* 38:251.

66. Barclay to Henry Gonsalvo Woods, May 8, 1843, ibid., p. 253.

67. Peter Maxwell to Samuel Walker, October 18, 1843, Thomas Jefferson Green Papers.

68. *Telegraph and Texas Register,* July 16, 1843.

69. Fenton Gibson to Waddy Thompson, September 12, 1843, Friend, ed., "Sidelights and Supplements," *SHQ* 68:490.

70. *Brazos Planter,* June 4, 1843.

71. Barclay to H. G. Woods, May 8, 1843, Spellman, ed., "Letters of the 'Dawson Men,'" *SHQ* 38:252.

72. Maxwell to Walker, October 18, 1843, T. J. Green Papers.

73. *Telegraph and Texas Register,* March 9, 1843.

74. Canfield, "Israel Canfield," *TMH* 3:197–198.

75. Thompson, *Recollections of Mexico,* pp. 75–76.

76. Andrew Jackson to Waddy Thompson, July 12, 1843, John S. Bassett, ed., *Correspondence of Andrew Jackson* 6:224.

77. Francis Blair to Jackson, February 27, 1843, ibid., p. 21.

78. Jackson to Thompson, July 12, 1843, Waddy Thompson Letters. See also Bassett, ed., *Correspondence of Andrew Jackson* 6:224.

79. Jackson to Santa Anna, March 1, 1844, Bassett, ed., *Correspondence of Andrew Jackson* 6:268–289. Several letters petitioning Andrew Jackson to intercede on behalf of Mier prisoners can be found in Friend, ed., "Sidelights and Supplements," *SHQ* 68:489–496; 69:88–95, 224–230, 377–385, 516–524 passim.

80. Four Mier men won their freedom as a result of the personal—but unofficial—intercession of Richard Pakenham, Percy Doyle, and Charles Bankhead. Green, *Journal,* p. 445. Shortly before the release of all the prisoners on September 16, 1844, Bankhead secured the release of fourteen other men born in the British Isles. Bankhead to Aberdeen, September 29, 1844, No. 76, FO 50/176, PRO.

81. Thompson to Webster, March 18, 1843, Shewmaker et al., eds., *The Papers of Daniel Webster: Diplomatic Papers* 1:481.

82. Canfield, "Israel Canfield," *TMH* 3:197–198.

83. In a letter to Sidney Breese dated April 25, 1844, John Quincy Adams declined to intercede on behalf of Mier prisoner Peter Maxwell. New Orleans *Daily Picayune,* August 22, 1844. Andrew Jackson was also reluctant to issue direct personal appeals to Santa Anna after the release of Bexar prisoner William Bradley, although he made an exception in the case of Mier man Patrick Lusk. Jackson to Thompson, July 12, 1843, Bassett, ed., *Correspondence of Andrew Jackson* 6:224; Friend, ed., "Sidelights and Supplements," *SHQ* 69:227–228.

84. Rives, *The United States and Mexico* 1 : 548–549.

85. Thomas Jefferson Green to Santa Anna, March 28, 1843, T. J. Green Papers.

86. I have been unable to find any evidence to support Green's claim that he helped pay for Santa Anna's travel expenses to Washington, D.C. In his book, *The Life and Select Literary Remains of Sam Houston*, p. 123, William Carey Crane states that the transportation costs of Santa Anna's trip were paid for by Bernard Bee.

87. Green to Santa Anna, March 28, 1843, T. J. Green Papers. There may have been some truth to Green's claim that he had given Santa Anna a coat in 1836. Many years later, Green recalled that he had given an expensive cloak to Sam Houston, who had in turn given it to Santa Anna, who was still a prisoner in Texas, in exchange for a gold snuffbox. Green, who had received nothing from these transactions, believed that Houston had never intended to wear the coat, but wished to give Santa Anna an expensive gift in order to obtain the more valuable snuffbox, which Green estimated to be worth one thousand dollars. Green, *Reply [of] Gen. Thomas J. Green*, pp. 63–64.

9. "A MYSTERIOUS SILENCE"

1. Stapp, *Prisoners*, pp. 121–122.

2. Houston to William Christy, May 7, 1843, *Houston Writings* 4 : 201.

3. H. Bailey Carroll, "Steward A. Miller and the Snively Expedition of 1843," *SHQ* 54 : 261–286.

4. *New Orleans Bee*, quoted in *Niles' National Register*, May 20, 1843.

5. Charles Elliot to Lord Aberdeen, June 8, 1843, *BDC*, p. 207.

6. Ibid.

7. Houston to Elliot, May 7, 1843, *Houston Writings* 4 : 197–198.

8. Houston to Elliot, May 13, 1843, *BDC*, pp. 211–212; Anson Jones to Isaac Van Zandt, *DCRT* (Part II) 2 : 235.

9. Elliot to Aberdeen, June 8, 1843, *BDC*, p. 207.

10. Elliot to Percy Doyle, June 21, 1843, ibid., p. 226.

11. "Injustice to Our Imprisoned Countrymen," Houston *Morning Star*, June 3, 1843.

12. Houston to Christy, May 7, 1843, *Houston Writings* 4 : 201.

13. Cramayel to Guizot, May 22, 1843, No. 23, Barker, ed., *The French Legation in Texas* 2 : 436.

14. Elliot to Aberdeen, May 9, 1843, No. 9, *BDC*, p. 182.

15. Elliot to Aberdeen, May 29, 1843, No. 10, ibid., p. 199.

16. *New Orleans Bee*, May 4, 1843, quoted in *Niles' National Register*, May 13, 1843.

17. Houston *Morning Star*, May 13, 1843.

18. Bollaert, *Bollaert's Texas*, p. 169.

19. Houston *Morning Star*, May 13, 1843.

20. Ibid., May 4, 1843; *Houston Writings* 4 : 185–186n.

21. Houston *Morning Star,* May 4, 1843.

22. Ibid., May 10, 1843.

23. R. A. Barclay to Henry Gonsalvo Woods, May 8, 1843, Spellman, ed., "Letters of the 'Dawson Men,'" *SHQ* 38:250.

24. Few people seem to have accepted the extraordinary theory posited by one west Texas newspaper, which maintained that the demonstration of Texas arms at the battle of Mier had so intimidated the Mexicans that the centralist government was now forced to come to terms: "Well Santa Anna knew from that hour that the scene of war was changed, and that unless negotiation could stay its progress, that the Republic of Texas had no longer limits to its boundary." Quoted in Houston *Morning Star,* May 23, 1843.

25. Bocanegra to Thompson, August 23, 1843, *DCUS-IAA* 8:555–557.

26. E. D. Adams, *British Interests and Activities,* pp. 128–137 passim.

27. Thompson, *Recollections of Mexico,* pp. 95–96.

28. Houston to Joseph Eve, April 22, 1843, *Houston Writings* 4:181–184.

29. Washington D. Miller to James Robinson, August 23, 1848, Miller Papers.

30. In the letter to Robinson cited above, Miller states that Robinson's April 10, 1843, correspondence with Santa Anna "was written out on the day following your [Robinson's] arrival at Washington by General Houston, and was copied and signed by you." See also *Houston Writings* 3:353n.

31. Robinson to Santa Anna, April 10, 1843, *Houston Writings* 3:351–353.

32. Quoted in *Telegraph and Texas Register,* July 19, 1843.

33. Houston *Morning Star,* May 1, 1843.

34. New Orleans *Daily Picayune,* May 20, 1843.

35. Ashbel Smith to Anson Jones, July 31, 1843, *DCRT* (Part III) 2:1118–1119.

36. Smith to Miller, November 21, 1843, Miller Papers.

37. Miller to Van Zandt, November 1, 1843, and E. L. Barnard to Van Zandt, October 9, 1843, Van Zandt Papers.

38. Cramayel to Guizot, October 4, 1843, No. 35, Barker, ed., *French Legation in Texas* 2:474.

39. Houston *Morning Star,* June 29, 1843.

40. J. H. Kuykendall to James Grant, August 20, 1843, Jonathan Hampton Kuykendall Papers, vol. 2, book 6, p. 16.

41. O. M. Roberts to Miller, September 12, 1843, Miller Papers.

42. New Orleans *Daily Picayune,* September 7, 1843.

43. New Orleans *Commercial Bulletin,* June 5, 1843.

44. *Telegraph and Texas Register,* August 2, 1843.

45. Kuykendall to Grant, August 20, 1843, Kuykendall Papers, vol. 2, book 6.

46. Houston to George Hockley, May 13, 1843, *Houston Writings* 4:206.

47. Houston to Ashbel Smith, July 21, 1843, *Houston Writings* 3:418.

48. Houston to E. L. R. Wheelock, July 1, 1843, *Houston Writings* 3:413.

49. Yoakum, *History of Texas* 2:411.

50. Ibid.

51. Canfield, "Israel Canfield," *TMH* 3:189.

52. Stapp, *Prisoners,* pp. 134–137.

53. Ibid., p. 137.

54. Coplan, "Interesting Incidents in the Life of Brother Willis Coplan," p. 6.

55. Ibid., p. 7. Also spelled Willis Copeland.

56. Walker, *Samuel Walker's Account,* pp. 76–78; Clarksville *Northern Standard,* November 18, 1843.

57. Walker, *Samuel Walker's Account,* p. 79.

58. Coplan, "Interesting Incidents in the Life of Brother Willis Coplan," p. 7.

59. Canfield, "Israel Canfield," *TMH* 3:188.

60. Thomas Jefferson Green to John Tyler, January 11, 1843, Shewmaker et al., eds., *The Papers of Daniel Webster: Diplomatic Papers* 1:463–464. See also John C. Calhoun to Daniel Webster, February 23, 1843, Clyde N. Wilson, ed. *The Papers of John C. Calhoun,* 16:687.

61. Charles Reese to Santa Anna, April 16, 1843, T. J. Green Papers.

62. McCutchan, *Mier Expedition Diary,* p. 103.

63. Green, *Journal,* p. 304.

64. Ibid., pp. 306–308.

65. Ibid., p. 313.

66. Truehart, *The Perote Prisoners,* p. 218.

67. Green, *Journal,* pp. 326–364 passim.

10. "A FRAGILE PEACE"

1. Glasscock, "Diary," *Texana* 1:110; Truehart, *The Perote Prisoners,* p. 238.

2. Glasscock, "Diary," *Texana* 1:110.

3. Fisher to Green, August 26, 1843, T. J. Green Papers.

4. Bell, *Narrative,* p. 60. According to San Antonio prisoner James Truehart, Brigadier General José María Jarero arrived at the fortress on September 18, 1843. Initially, this appears to have been a temporary assignment, owing to General Durán's illness. After two months, however, Jarero received his commission as commandant of the fortress, officially serving in that capacity from November 21, 1843, until December 20, 1844. Truehart, *The Perote Prisoners,* p. 234; Sánchez Lamego, *El Castillo de San Carlos de Perote,* p. 97.

5. Bell, *Narrative,* p. 63; Stapp, *Prisoners,* p. 155.

6. Glasscock, "Diary," *Texana* 1:101.

7. Truehart, *The Perote Prisoners,* p. 243; Canfield, "Israel Canfield," *TMH* 3:191.

8. Stapp, *Prisoners,* pp. 156–158.

9. Ibid., p. 164.

10. Truehart, *The Perote Prisoners,* pp. 255–279 passim. When the U.S. Army captured Perote in the Mexican War, it proved similarly unable to cope with the ravages of disease which plagued the fort. Five hundred soldiers were confined to the hospital, but one recruit faulted the men "for not taking proper care of themselves; they eat too much fruit and green vegetables." Oswandel, *Notes of the Mexican War,* p. 215.

11. Duval, *Big Foot Wallace*, pp. 254–255; see also Canfield, "Israel Canfield," *TMH* 3:196.

12. Duval, *Big Foot Wallace*, p. 245.

13. Stapp, *Prisoners*, p. 159.

14. Canfield, "Israel Canfield," *TMH* 3:195.

15. P. M. Maxwell to [?], January 23, 1844, Waddy Thompson Letters.

16. Bell, *Narrative*, p. 58.

17. Canfield, "Israel Canfield," *TMH* 3:196.

18. Ibid., p. 195.

19. One American newspaper predicted that the depredations against Mexican citizens committed by these gangs, if allowed to continue, would cause Texas "to sink lower and lower in character, and in the estimation of the world." It added, "Better it would be if these young men were at the plough, or in the mechanic's shop at work. But the Government of Texas cannot stop them; and all that these marauders have to do is to indite the stealing of horses 'capturing' or to designate merchants whom they rob as 'Mexican smugglers' or churches that they may plunder 'the hiding places of thieves' to secure booty enough, and to be hailed as heroes by a large portion of the population." *Daily National Intelligencer*, June 10, 1843.

20. *Telegraph and Texas Register*, December 24, 1842.

21. John J. Linn, *Reminiscences of Fifty Years in Texas*, pp. 322–324; Houston *Morning Star*, May 30, 1843; *El Siglo XIX*, August 2, 1843; Jones to Elliot, August 28, 1843, Jones, *Memoranda and Official Correspondence*, p. 248.

22. "Proclamation of Martial Law between the Nueces, the Frio, and the Rio Grande," *Houston Writings* 3:366–367.

23. Bollaert, *Bollaert's Texas*, p. 276n.

24. Doyle to Aberdeen, September 29, 1843, No. 74, FO 50/164, PRO. Lord Aberdeen was by no means pleased with Doyle's rash response in the flag episode, and lost no time in accepting the explanation tendered by the Mexican government, which insisted that no insult to Great Britain had been intended. Aberdeen to Doyle, November 29, 1843, No. 34, FO 50/160, PRO.

25. Jones to Elliot, July 30, 1843, *DCRT* (Part III) 2:1115.

26. Elliot to Doyle, February 8, 1843, *BDC*, p. 244.

27. Doyle to Aberdeen, May 25, 1843, No. 24, FO 50/162, PRO.

28. *Telegraph and Texas Register*, October 11, 1842.

29. "Proclamation Demanding the Release of Mexican Prisoners in Texas," *Houston Writings* 3:427–428. See also Jones to Elliot, September 4, 1843, *DCRT* (Part III) 2:1126.

30. Margaret Swett Henson, *Samuel May Williams*, pp. 118–119.

31. "A Speech Delivered at the Presbyterian Church (Huntsville) on November 8, 1842," *Houston Writings* 3:443–444.

32. *New Orleans Bee*, quoted in *Niles' National Register*, June 10, 1843, pp. 229–231. See also New Orleans *Commercial Bulletin*, April 26, 1843.

33. William Murphy to Hugh S. Legaré, June 5, 1843, No. 1, National Archives: Despatches from United States Ministers to Texas, vol. 20.

34. *National Vindicator,* July 1, 1843; July 3, 1843 (Enclosures); Murphy to Legaré, July 16, 1843, No. 3, National Archives: Despatches from United States Ministers to Texas, vol. 2.

35. Doyle to Aberdeen, June 24, 1843, FO 50/162, PRO.

36. Murphy to Upshur, September 23, 1843, No. 4, National Archives: Despatches from United States Ministers to Texas, vol. 2.

37. Frederick Merk, *Slavery and the Annexation of Texas,* pp. 11–32.

38. Thomas Jefferson Green to Calhoun, June 24, 1843, T. J. Green Papers.

39. Houston to Jones, July 30, 1843, Jones, *Memoranda and Official Correspondence,* p. 233; Henson, *Samuel May Williams,* pp. 122–123.

40. Jones to Elliot, September 11, 1843, Jones, *Memoranda and Official Correspondence,* pp. 250–253.

41. Houston to Jones, July 30, 1843, ibid., p. 233.

42. Henson, *Samuel May Williams,* p. 124.

43. Ibid., pp. 124–125.

44. Washington D. Miller to Tyler, September 16, 1843, Miller Papers.

45. Van Zandt to Jones, September 18, 1843, DCRT (Part II) 2:207–210.

46. Houston to Van Zandt, January 29, 1844, *Houston Writings* 3:538–541.

47. Houston to Hockley and Williams, February 3, 1844, DCRT (Part II) 2:786–789. See also Henson, *Samuel May Williams,* p. 126.

48. Henson, *Samuel May Williams,* p. 126; Hockley to Jones, February 28, 1844, Jones, *Memoranda and Official Correspondence,* pp. 324–325.

49. *Daily National Intelligencer,* March 16, 1844; Merk, *Slavery and the Annexation of Texas,* p. ix.

50. Houston to Santa Anna, July 29, 1844, *Houston Writings* 4:346–348.

51. Elliot to Aberdeen, October 31, 1843, BDC, p. 271.

52. Elliot to Jones, January 8, 1844, Jones, *Memoranda and Official Correspondence,* p. 301.

53. Elliot to Aberdeen, February 17, 1844, No. 6, BDC, pp. 299–300.

54. Elliot to Aberdeen, April 7, 1844, ibid., p. 308.

55. Houston to Jones, April 20, 1844, *Houston Writings* 4:303–304.

56. William Kennedy to Aberdeen, June 18, 1844, BDC, p. 339; Henson, *Samuel May Williams,* pp. 129–130.

57. Joseph Smith to Jones, December 9, 1843, Jones, *Memoranda and Official Correspondence,* pp. 282–283.

58. H. P. N. Gammell, comp., *The Laws of Texas, 1822–1897* 2:17, 67–68, 116–117.

59. Galveston *Evening News,* May 11, 1844.

60. Walker to Green, October 28, 1843, T. J. Green Papers.

61. J. H. Kuykendall, "Sketches of Early Texians," p. 10 (Barker Texas History Center).

62. "A Speech Delivered at the Presbyterian Church (Huntsville) on November 8, 1843," *Houston Writings* 3:447–448.

63. Bollaert, *Bollaert's Texas,* p. 308.

64. "Names of Texian Prisoners Who Died in Perote Castle," April 8, 1844 (Texas State Library). Of the twenty-two men on this list, all but two died be-

tween the months of September 1843 and January 1844, presumably of typhus. Shields Booker and Richard Jackson, both Bexar prisoners, died before the outbreak of the epidemic. See also Glasscock, "Diary," *Texana* 1:111–119 passim.

65. Norman Woods to brothers and sisters, etc., October 17, 1843, Spellman, ed., "Letters of the 'Dawson Men,'" *SHQ* 38:267.

66. William E. Millen to the Honorable Charge Affairs of the Republic of Texas [Isaac Van Zandt], February 1, 1844, Van Zandt Papers.

67. Canfield, "Israel Canfield," *TMH* 3:196.

68. Glasscock, "Diary," *Texana* 1:234.

69. New Orleans *Daily Picayune,* July 10, 1844. McCutchan, *Mier Expedition Diary,* p. 123.

70. Henry Journeay, who worked as a cabinetmaker before joining the expedition, made at least one of these violins, which is on display in the Pease Gallery, Texas State Library.

71. Glasscock, "Diary," *Texana* 1:232.

72. Stapp, *Prisoners,* p. 165.

73. Glasscock, "Diary," *Texana* 1:89.

74. Truehart, *The Perote Prisoners,* p. 267. In November, Mexican authorities arrested four Americans near Santa Anna's estate. Although charged with plotting to assassinate the President, they appear to have been treasure-hunters in search of a cache of gold left by the Spanish during the War for Independence. Doyle to Aberdeen, November 29, 1843, No. 94, FO 50/165, PRO.

11. THE ANNEXATION CRISIS

1. Waddy Thompson to Abel Upshur, October 2, 1843, No. 21, National Archives: Despatches from United States Ministers to Mexico, vol. 11.

2. Pitchford, "The Diplomatic Representatives from the United States to Mexico," p. 206.

3. William E. Millen to the Honorable Charge Affairs of the Republic of Texas [Isaac Van Zandt], February 1, 1844, Van Zandt Papers.

4. Pitchford, "The Diplomatic Representatives from the United States to Mexico," p. 237.

5. Thompson to Andrew Jackson, May 20, 1843, *Niles' National Register,* January 27, 1844.

6. Thompson, *Recollections of Mexico,* p. 231.

7. Thompson to Upshur, March 25, 1844, *DCUS-IAA* 8:581.

8. Thompson, *Recollections of Mexico,* pp. 77–78. Once again, a discrepancy exists between Thompson's account in his autobiography and his despatches to the State Department. In a letter to the secretary of state shortly after his meeting with Santa Anna, Thompson refers only to the San Antonio prisoners, but makes no mention of his request for the release of the Mier inmates. Thompson to Secretary of State, March 25, 1844, National Archives: Despatches from United States Ministers to Mexico, vol. 11.

9. Thompson, *Recollections of Mexico,* p. 78.

10. Thompson to Upshur, March 25, 1844, *DCUS-IAA* 8:581.

11. Noah Smithwick, *The Evolution of a State: Or, Recollections of Old Texas Days,* pp. 276–277.

12. Thompson, *Recollections of Mexico,* p. 231.

13. Ibid., p. vi.

14. Bell, *Narrative,* pp. 71–72; Stapp, *Prisoners,* pp. 169–171.

15. New Orleans *Daily Picayune,* April 2, 1844.

16. Thomas Jefferson Green to My Dear Friends, February 20, 1844, T. J. Green Papers.

17. Reuben Potter to James Miller, No. 1636, July 16, 1844, and Potter to Miller, No. 1642, August 7, 1844, *Texas Treasury Papers,* ed. Seymour V. Connor, 3:1022–1025, 1027–1031.

18. Ibid., pp. 1027–1031.

19. Glasscock, "Diary," *Texana* 1:228; McCutchan, *Mier Expedition Diary,* pp. 121–122.

20. W. P. Zuber, "The Number of 'Decimated Mier Prisoners,'" *TSHAQ* 5:167.

21. Berge, "The Mexican Response to United States' Expansionism," p. 109.

22. Bocanegra to Benjamin Green, May 30, 1844, *DCUS-IAA* 8:587.

23. Benjamin Green to Bocanegra, May 31, 1844, ibid., p. 593.

24. Justin H. Smith, *The Annexation of Texas,* p. 289.

25. David M. Pletcher, *The Diplomacy of Annexation,* p. 185.

26. E. D. Adams, *British Interests and Activities,* p. 167.

27. Ibid., p. 176.

28. New Orleans *Daily Picayune,* August 2, 1844.

29. Glasscock, "Diary," *Texana* 1:234, 229.

30. New Orleans *Daily Picayune,* July 7, 1844.

31. William Bradburn to Thomas Jefferson Green, December 30, 1844, T. J. Green Papers.

32. *Telegraph and Texas Register,* September 4, 1844; September 24, 1844.

33. *LaGrange Intelligencer,* July 4, 1844.

34. McCutchan, *Mier Expedition Diary,* p. 116.

35. Ibid., pp. 125–126.

36. Green, ed., *Samuel Maverick, Texan,* p. 246.

37. *Telegraph and Texas Register,* September 25, 1844.

38. William Ryon to Abner Harris, June 6, 1844, Louis Wiltz Kemp Collection.

39. McCutchan, *Mier Expedition Diary,* p. 126.

40. William E. Millen to the Honorable Charge Affairs of the Republic of Texas [Isaac Van Zandt], February 1, 1844, Van Zandt Papers.

41. New Orleans *Daily Picayune,* August 22, 1844; Stapp, *Prisoners,* pp. 214–216. Glasscock, "Diary," *Texana* 1:230.

42. McCutchan, *Mier Expedition Diary,* p. 127.

43. Ibid., pp. 142–143. A companion of Thurmond's, G. W. Bush, also escaped, and was not recaptured.

44. Ibid., p. 134.

45. Pitchford, "Diplomatic Representatives from the United States to Mexico," p. 280.

46. Wilson Shannon to John C. Calhoun, September 21, 1844, No. 2, National Archives: Despatches from United States Ministers to Mexico, vol. 12. See also Trahern, "Reminiscences," pp. 13–14.

47. Duval, *Big Foot Wallace,* p. 246.

48. Andrew Jackson to Santa Anna, March 1, 1844, Bassett, ed., *Correspondence of Andrew Jackson* 6:268–289. Bankhead to Aberdeen, September 29, 1844, No. 76, FO 50/176, PRO.

49. Wilson Shannon to John C. Calhoun, August 28, 1844 [No. 1], National Archives: Despatches from United States Ministers to Mexico, vol. 12. Fortunately for Shannon, most of his belongings had been sent to the capital by separate coach. As a result, the bandits made off with only an expensive cloak, about eighty dollars, a watch, and a pencil case. New Orleans *Daily Picayune,* October 1, 1844. According to Brantz Mayer, the Mexican government had recently stepped up its efforts to eliminate banditry along the Veracruz–Mexico City highway, making numerous arrests. The convicted *ladrones* were garotted in pairs in towns along the road. Brantz Mayer, *Mexico: Aztec, Spanish and Republican* 2:149–150.

50. W. H. Callcott, *Santa Anna,* pp. 200–203.

51. E. D. Adams, *British Interests and Activities,* Ch. 8 passim; Smith, *The Annexation of Texas,* p. 389.

52. Berge, "The Mexican Response to United States' Expansionism," p. 122; John R. Tymitz, "British Influence in Mexico, 1840–48" (Ph.D. dissertation, Oklahoma State University, 1973), p. 88.

53. Benjamin Green to Calhoun, August 1844, Benjamin Green Papers.

54. Green to Calhoun, September 12, 1844, B. Green Papers.

55. McCutchan, *Mier Expedition Diary,* p. 148.

56. Glasscock, "Diary," *Texana* 1:237.

57. Ibid.

58. Shannon to Calhoun, September 21, 1844, No. 2, National Archives: Despatches from United States Ministers to Mexico, vol. 12.

59. Ibid.

60. Ibid.

61. New Orleans *Daily Picayune,* October 16, 1844.

62. Waddy Thompson to the Editors of the *National Intelligencer,* July 3, 1844, Thomas W. Streeter, *Texas as Province and Republic, 1795–1845,* no. 1540, reel 30.

63. New Orleans *Daily Picayune,* August 24, 1844.

64. In all, Santa Anna liberated 120 Texas prisoners by the edict of September 16, 1844. In addition to the 104 men at Perote, 2 Mier participants were released in Matamoros, 1 in Puebla, 3 in Mexico City, and 10 in Veracruz. Shannon to Calhoun, September 21, 1844, No. 2, National Archives: Despatches from United States Ministers to Mexico, vol. 12.

65. Bell, *Narrative*, p. 76; McCutchan, *Mier Expedition Diary*, p. 154.
66. McCutchan, *Mier Expedition Diary*, p. 152.
67. Bell, *Narrative*, p. 75.
68. *LaGrange Intelligencer*, September 10, 1851.
69. McCutchan, *Mier Expedition Diary*, p. 153.
70. Ibid., p. 154.

12. EPILOGUE

1. McCutchan, *Mier Expedition Diary*, pp. 185–186.
2. Coplan, "Interesting Incidents in the Life of Brother Willis Coplan," p. 10.
3. McCutchan, *Mier Expedition Diary*, p. 164.
4. Houston to Santa Anna, December 10, 1844, *Houston Writings* 4:405–406. José Antonio Navarro would soon be released from San Juan de Ulloa and placed on parole in Veracruz. A few weeks later he escaped on a ship bound for New Orleans.
5. Shannon to Calhoun, October 14, 1844, *DCUS-IAA* 8:644–649.
6. Manuel C. Rejón to Shannon, October 31, 1844, ibid., pp. 654–663; Shannon to Rejón, November 4, 1844, ibid., pp. 663–664.
7. Rejón to Shannon, November 6, 1844, ibid., pp. 664–665; Shannon to Rejón, November 8, 1844, ibid., pp. 666–675.
8. Shannon to Calhoun, November 12, 1844, No. 4, National Archives: Despatches from United States Ministers to Mexico, vol. 12.
9. Clarksville *Northern Standard*, January 14, 1846.
10. *American Whig Review* 2 (1845): 543.
11. "A Speech Made at the Methodist Church," Houston, December 17, 1845, *Houston Writings* 4:435.
12. Houston to Hamilton Stuart, December 21, 1845, *Houston Writings* 4:441.
13. Reinhardt, "The Public Career of Thomas Jefferson Green in Texas," pp. 126, 129.
14. "Speech on Texan Affairs," August 1, 1854, *Houston Writings* 6:74–93.
15. Ibid.
16. Green, *Reply [of] Gen. Thomas J. Green*, p. 9.
17. T. E. Dansbee to brother and sister, October 14, 1846, T. E. Dansbee Collection.
18. John Warren Hunter, "Life of Creed Taylor, or Eighty-three Years on the Frontiers of Texas" (Part 2), pp. 17–18.
19. Frank S. Edwards, *A Campaign in New Mexico with Colonel Doniphan*, p. 156.
20. Robert W. Johannsen, *To the Halls of the Montezumas*, p. 134.
21. Samuel Walker to J. T. Walker, August 4, 1849, Walker Papers.
22. Smith and Judah, eds., *Chronicles of the Gringos*, pp. 269–271.
23. Walter P. Lane, *The Adventures and Recollections of a San Jacinto Veteran*, pp. 67–69.

24. *Democratic Telegraph and Texas Register,* July 13, 1848; September 28, 1848.

25. *The Monument,* July 30, 1851.

26. "An act for the relief of certain persons, formerly Prisoners of War in Mexico," February 9, 1850, Gammel, comp., *The Laws of Texas, 1822–1897* 3:594–595. This piece of legislation entitled the Mier men to receive $22.50 per month from the time they were mustered into service until their release, plus $65 to each man for the "loss of his horse, arms, and accoutrements."

Bibliography

PRIMARY SOURCES

Unpublished Materials

Adams, Harvey Alexander. "Diary of Harvey Alexander Adams, in Two Parts: Rhode Island to Texas and Expedition against the Southwest in 1842 and 1843." Typescript. Barker Texas History Center, University of Texas (Austin). [Manuscript diary is also in the Barker collection. All page citations are to the typescript.]

Archivo General de México. Archivo de la Secretaría de Relaciones Exteriores, Barker Transcripts. Barker Texas History Center, University of Texas (Austin).

Army Papers, 1835–1846. Adjutant General's Record Group, Archives Division, Texas State Library (Austin).

Bear, M. M. Letter to Father, May 13, 1843. Archives Division, Texas State Library (Austin).

Bryan, James. Papers. Barker Texas History Center, University of Texas (Austin).

Canfield, Israel. Diary [of the Mier Expedition]. Archives Division, Texas State Library (Austin).

Chalk, Whitfield. Reminiscences. Rosenberg Library (Galveston).

Coplan, Willis. "Interesting Incidents in the Life of Brother Willis Coplan, While a Prisoner in Mexico during the Texas and Mexican War, Given in His Own Words, Taken from Memory." Archives Division, Texas State Library (Austin).

Dansbee, T. E. Collection. Tennessee State Library and Archives (Nashville).

De la Garza, José Antonio. Letter to Dr. José Luis Gonzaga García, December 15, 1842. Manuscript Collection, Archives Division, Texas State Library (Austin).

Duerr, Christian Friederich. Diary. Barker Texas History Center, University of Texas (Austin).

Eaves, N. R. Collection. South Caroliniana Library, University of South Carolina (Columbia).

Eberstadt Collection. Barker Texas History Center, University of Texas (Austin).

Ford, John S. Memoirs. Barker Texas History Center, University of Texas (Austin).

Green, Benjamin. Papers. Duff Green Collection, University of North Carolina (Chapel Hill).

Green, Thomas Jefferson. Letter to Felix Huston and Colo[nel] Bailey Peyton, January 25, 1843. Manuscript Collection, Archives Division, Texas State Library (Austin).

———. Papers. University of North Carolina (Chapel Hill).

Hearne, Madge Williams. Collection. Barker Texas History Center, University of Texas (Austin).

Hearne, Sam Houston. Collection. Barker Texas History Center, University of Texas (Austin).

Houston, Andrew Jackson. Collection. Archives Division, Texas State Library (Austin).

Hunter, John Warren. "Life of Creed Taylor, or Eighty-three Years on the Frontiers of Texas" (ms.). Manuscript Collection, Archives Division, Texas State Library (Austin).

Kemp, Louis Wiltz. Collection. Barker Texas History Center, University of Texas (Austin).

Kuykendall, Jonathan Hampton. Papers. Barker Texas History Center, University of Texas (Austin).

———. "Sketches of Early Texians." Barker Texas History Center, University of Texas (Austin).

Lenz, Louis. Collection. Barker Texas History Center, University of Texas (Austin).

Military Rolls, 1835–1861. Adjutant General's Records Group, Archives Division, Texas State Library (Austin).

Miller, Washington Daniel. Papers, 1833–1860. Archives Division, Texas State Library (Austin).

Morgan, James. Papers. Rosenberg Library (Galveston).

"Names of Texian Prisoners who died in Perote Castle," April 8, 1844. Manuscript Collection. Archives Division, Texas State Library (Austin).

National Archives (Washington, D.C.). Despatches from United States Consuls in Veracruz, 1822–1906, vols. 4–5.

———. Despatches from United States Ministers to Mexico, 1826–1906, vols. 10–12.

———. Despatches from United States Ministers to Texas, 1836–1845, vol. 2.

———. Despatches Received by the Department of State from U.S. Consuls in Matamoros, 1826–1906, vol. 4.

———. Diplomatic Instructions of the Department of State, 1801–1906, Mexico, vol. 15.

Public Debt Papers. Archives Division, Texas State Library (Austin).

Public Record Office (Great Britain). Foreign Office, General Correspondence: Mexico, vols. 159–176.

Rusk, Thomas Jefferson. Papers. Barker Texas History Center, University of Texas (Austin).

Smith, Ashbel. Papers. Barker Texas History Center, University of Texas (Austin).

Smith, Sam S. Collection. Barker Texas History Center, University of Texas (Austin).

Taylor, Creed. *See* Hunter, John W.
Thompson, Waddy. Letters. Barker Texas History Center, University of Texas (Austin).
Thomson Family Papers. Woodson Research Center, Rice University (Houston).
Trahern, George Washington. "Reminiscences." Manuscript Collection. Archives Division, Texas State Library (Austin).
Van Zandt, Isaac. Papers. Barker Texas History Center, University of Texas (Austin).
Walker, Samuel Hamilton. Papers. Archives Division, Texas State Library (Austin).
Wallace, William A. A. Letter to Nora Franklin, September 24, 1888. Archives Division, Texas State Library (Austin).
———. Papers. Barker Texas History Center, University of Texas (Austin).
Williams, Samuel May. Papers. Rosenberg Library (Galveston).
Woods, Norman. Letters. Barker Texas History Center, University of Texas (Austin).

Printed Government Documents

Texas Congress. *Journals of the House of Representatives of the Seventh Congress of the Republic of Texas.* Washington, Texas: Thomas Johnson, 1843.
———. *Journals of the House of Representatives of the Eighth Congress of the Republic of Texas.* Houston: Cruger & Moore, 1844.
———. *Journals of the Sixth Congress of the Republic of Texas.* Edited by Harriet Smither. 3 vols. Austin: Von Boeckmann–Jones, 1940.
Texas Treasury Papers: Letters Received in the Treasury Department of the Republic of Texas, 1836–46. Edited by Seymour V. Connor. 3 vols. Austin: Texas State Library, 1955.

Books and Pamphlets

Adams, Ephraim D., ed. *British Diplomatic Correspondence Concerning the Republic of Texas, 1836–1846.* Austin: Texas State Historical Association, 1917.
Barker, Nancy Nichols, ed. *The French Legation in Texas.* 2 vols. Austin: Texas State Historical Association, 1971–1973.
Bass, Feris A., and B. R. Brunson, eds. *Fragile Empires: The Texas Correspondence of Samuel Swartwout and James Morgan, 1836–1856.* Austin: Shoal Creek, 1978.
Bassett, John S., ed. *Correspondence of Andrew Jackson.* 6 vols. Washington, D.C.: Carnegie Institute, 1926–1933.
Bell, Tho[ma]s W. *A Narrative of the Capture and Subsequent Sufferings of the Mier Prisoners in Mexico, Captured in the Cause of Texas, Dec. 26th, 1842 and liberated Sept. 16th, 1844.* Edited by James A. Day. Waco: Texian Press, 1964.
Binkley, William C., ed. *Official Correspondence of the Texas Revolution, 1835–1836.* 2 vols. New York: D. Appleton & Co., 1936.

Bollaert, William. *William Bollaert's Texas*. Edited by Eugene W. Hollon and Ruth Lapham Butler. Norman: University of Oklahoma Press, 1956.

Calderon de la Barca, Fanny. *Life in Mexico: The Letters of Fanny Calderon de la Barca*. Edited by Howard T. Fisher and Marion Hall Fisher. New York: Doubleday & Co., 1966.

Calhoun, John C. *See* Wilson, Clyde N., ed.

Dresel, Gustav. *Gustav Dresel's Houston Journal: Adventures in North America and Texas, 1837–1841*. Translated and edited by Max Freund. Austin: University of Texas Press, 1954.

Edwards, Frank S. *A Campaign in New Mexico with Colonel Doniphan*. Philadelphia: Carey and Hart, 1847.

Ford, John Salmon. *Rip Ford's Texas*. Edited by Stephen B. Oates. Austin: University of Texas Press, 1963. (Reprinted with revised notes, 1987.)

Gammel, H. P. N., comp. *The Laws of Texas, 1822–1897*. 10 vols. Austin: Gammel Book Co., 1898.

García, Carlos Bosch. *Material para la historia diplomática de México: México y los Estados Unidos, 1820–1848*. Mexico City: Escuela Nacional de Ciencias Políticas y Sociales, 1957.

Garrison, George P., ed. *Diplomatic Correspondence of the Republic of Texas*. Annual Report of the American Historical Association, 1907–1908. 3 vols. Washington, D.C.: U.S. Government Printing Office, 1908–1911.

Gilliam, Albert. *Travels in Mexico during the Years 1843 and 1844*. Aberdeen: George Clark and Son, 1847.

Green, Rena Maverick, ed. *Samuel Maverick, Texan, 1803–1870: A Collection of Letters, Journals, and Memoirs*. San Antonio, 1952.

Green, Thomas Jefferson. *Journal of the Texian Expedition against Mier*. New York: Harper & Bros., 1845.

———. *Reply [of] Gen. Thomas J. Green, to the Speech of General Sam Houston, in the Senate of the United States, August 1, 1854*. Washington, D.C., February 15, 1855. (Pamphlet. A copy is in Texas State Library, Archives Division.)

Gregg, Josiah. *Diary and Letters of Josiah Gregg*. Edited by Maurice Garland Fulton. 2 vols. Norman: University of Oklahoma Press, 1941–1944.

Harkort, Eduard. *In Mexican Prisons: The Journal of Eduard Harkort, 1832–1834*. Edited by Louis E. Brister. College Station: Texas A&M University Press, 1986.

Houston, Sam. *The Writings of Sam Houston*. Edited by Amelia Williams and Eugene C. Barker. 8 vols. Austin: Jenkins Publishing Co., 1970.

Houstoun, Matilda C. *Texas and the Gulf of Mexico; or, Yachting in the New World*. 2 vols. London: John Murray, 1844.

Hunter, John Warren. *Adventures of a Mier Prisoner: Being the Thrilling Experiences of John Rufus Alexander, Who Was with the Ill-Fated Expedition Which Invaded Mexico*. Bandera: Frontier Times, n.d.

Jenkins, John Holland. *Recollections of Early Texas: The Memoirs of John Holland Jenkins*. Edited by John Holmes Jenkins III. Austin: University of Texas Press, 1958.

Jones, Anson. *Memoranda and Official Correspondence Relating to the Republic of Texas.* New York: Appleton & Co., 1859.

Kendall, George Wilkins. *Narrative of the Texan Santa Fe Expedition, Comprising a Description of a Tour through Texas and across the Great Southwestern Prairies, the Camanche Caygüa Hunting-Grounds, with an Account of the Sufferings from Want of Food, Losses from Hostile Indians, and Final Capture of the Texans and Their March, as Prisoners, to the City of Mexico.* 2 vols. New York: Harper & Bros., 1850.

Lane, Walter P. *The Adventures and Recollections of a San Jacinto Veteran: Containing Sketches of the Texian, Mexican and Late Wars, with Several Indian Fights Thrown In.* Marshall: Tri-Weekly Herald, 1887.

Latham, Francis. *Travels in the Republic of Texas, 1842.* Austin: Encino Press, 1971.

Lee, Nelson. *Three Years among the Camanches* [sic]: *The Narrative of Nelson Lee, the Texas Ranger, Containing a Detailed Account of His Captivity among the Indians, His Singular Escape through the Instrumentality of His Watch, and Fully Illustrating Indian Life as It Is on the War Path and in the Camp.* Albany: Baker Taylor, 1859.

Linn, John J. *Reminiscences of Fifty Years in Texas.* New York: D & J Sadler, 1883.

Lockhart, John Washington. *Sixty Years on the Brazos: The Life and Letters of Dr. John Washington Lockhart.* Edited by Jonnie Lockhart Wallis and Laurence Hill. Waco: Texian Press, 1967.

Lubbock, Francis Richard. *Six Decades in Texas; or, Memoirs of Francis Richard Lubbock, Governor of Texas in War-Time, 1861–63.* Edited by C. W. Raines. Austin, 1900.

McCutchan, Joseph D. *Mier Expedition Diary: A Texan Prisoner's Account.* Edited by Joseph Milton Nance. Austin: University of Texas Press, 1978.

Manning, William R., ed. *Diplomatic Correspondence of the United States: Inter-American Affairs, 1831–1860,* vol. 8. Washington, D.C.: Carnegie Endowment for International Peace, 1932–1939.

Mayer, Brantz. *Mexico: Aztec, Spanish and Republican.* 2 vols. Hartford: S. Drake and Company, 1852.

Nance, Joseph Milton, ed. See McCutchan, Joseph D.

Neighbours, Kenneth Franklin. *Robert Simpson Neighbors and the Texas Frontier, 1836–1859.* Waco: Texian Press, 1975.

Nichols, James Wilson. *Now You Hear My Horn: The Journal of James Wilson Nichols, 1820–1887.* Edited by Catherine W. McDowell. Austin: University of Texas Press, 1967.

Oswandel, J. Jacob. *Notes of the Mexican War, 1846–47–48.* Rev. ed. Philadelphia, 1885.

Polk, James K. *The Correspondence of James K. Polk,* vol. 6. Edited by Wayne Cutler. Nashville: Vanderbilt University Press, 1983.

Rayburn, John C., and Virginia Kemp Rayburn, eds. *Century of Conflict, 1821–1913: Incidents in the Lives of William Neale and William A. Neale, Early Settlers in South Texas.* Waco: Texian Press, 1964.

Reid, Samuel C. *Scouting Expeditions of McCulloch's Texas Rangers.* Philadelphia, 1847.

Santa Anna, Antonio de López de. *The Eagle: The Autobiography of Santa Anna.* Edited by Ann Fears Crawford. Austin: Pemberton Press, 1967.

Shewmaker, Kenneth, et al., eds. *The Papers of Daniel Webster: Diplomatic Papers, Vol. 1, 1841–43.* Hanover, N.H.: University Press of New England, 1983.

Sibley, Marilyn McAdams. *See* Walker, Samuel.

Smith, George Winston, and Charles Judah, eds. *Chronicles of the Gringos: The U.S. Army in the Mexican War, 1846–1848; Accounts of Eyewitnesses and Combatants.* Albuquerque: University of New Mexico Press, 1968.

Smithwick, Noah. *The Evolution of a State; Or, Recollections of Old Texas Days.* Austin: Gammel Book Co., 1900. (New ed., Austin: University of Texas Press, 1983.)

Spurlin, Charles D., comp. *Texas Veterans in the Mexican War: Muster Rolls of Texas Military Units.* Victoria, Tex.: Victoria College, 1984.

Stapp, William Preston. *The Prisoners of Perote.* Austin: University of Texas Press, 1977. (First published in 1845.)

Streeter, Thomas W. *Bibliography of Texas, 1795–1845.* Rev. ed. Woodbridge, Conn.: Research Publications, 1983.

———. *Texas as Province and Republic, 1795–1845, as Based on the Bibliography by Thomas W. Streeter.* Microfilm. 33 reels. Woodbridge, Conn.: Research Publications, 1983.

Thompson, Waddy. *Recollections of Mexico.* New York: Wiley and Putnam, 1846.

Truehart, James L. *The Perote Prisoners: Being the Diary of James L. Truehart.* Edited by Frederick C. Chabot. San Antonio: Naylor Co., 1932.

Tyler, Lyon Gardiner, ed. *The Letters and Times of the Tylers.* New York: Da Capo Press, 1970.

Vattel, Emerich de. *The Law of Nations; or, Principles of the Law of Nature, Applied to the Conduct and Affairs of Nations and Sovereigns, from the French Monsieur de Vattel.* Edited by Joseph Chitty. Philadelphia: T. & J. W. Johnson & Co., 1857.

A Voice from the West!!! Broadside, published by Austin *City Gazette* [1842]. Barker Texas History Center, University of Texas (Austin).

Walker, Samuel. *Samuel Walker's Account of the Mier Expedition.* Edited by Marilyn McAdams Sibley. Austin: Texas State Historical Association, 1978.

Webster, Daniel. *See* Shewmaker, Kenneth, et al., eds.

Wilson, Clyde N., ed. *The Papers of John C. Calhoun,* vol. 16. Columbia: University of South Carolina Press, 1985.

Wilson, Robert A. *Mexico and Its Religion.* New York: Harper & Bros., 1855.

Zuber, William Physick. *My Eighty Years in Texas.* Edited by Janis Boyle Mayfield. Austin: University of Texas Press, 1971.

Articles

Bell, Thomas W. "Thomas W. Bell Letters." Edited by Llerena B. Friend. *Southwestern Historical Quarterly* 63(April 1960):589–599.

Canfield, Israel. "Israel Canfield on the Mier Expedition." Edited by James Day. *Texas Military History* 3(Fall 1963):165–199.

Day, James, ed. *See* Canfield, Israel; Glasscock, James A.

Erath, George B. "Memoirs of George B. Erath." Edited by Lucy Erath. *Southwestern Historical Quarterly* 25(1922–1923):207–233, 255–279; 27(1923–1924):27–51.

Eve, Joseph. "A Letter Book of Joseph Eve." Edited by Joseph Milton Nance. *Southwestern Historical Quarterly* 43(January–April 1940):369–374, 486–510; 44(July 1940):96–107.

Friend, Llerena B., ed. "Sidelights and Supplements on the Perote Prisoners." *Southwestern Historical Quarterly* 68(January–April 1965):366–374, 489–496; 69(July–October 1965):88–95, 224–230; 69(January–April 1966):377–385, 516–524.

―――. *See* Bell, Thomas W.

Glasscock, James A. "Diary of James A. Glasscock, Mier Man." Edited by James Day. *Texana* 1(Spring 1963):85–119; 1(Summer 1963):225–238.

Harris, Lewis Birdsall. "Journal of Lewis Birdsall Harris, 1836–1842." Edited by Adele B. Looscan. *Southwestern Historical Quarterly* 25(July 1921):63–71; 25(October 1921):131–146; 25(January 1922):185–197.

Hendricks, Sterling Brown. "The Somervell Expedition to the Rio Grande, 1842." *Southwestern Historical Quarterly* 23(October 1919):112–140.

Lord, George. "George Lord: Mier Prisoner." Edited by C. T. Traylor. *Frontier Times* 15(1938–1939):533–552.

Nance, Joseph M., ed. *See* Eve, Joseph; Woll, Adrian

Spellman, L. U., ed. "Letters of the 'Dawson Men' from Perote Prison, Mexico, 1842–1843." *Southwestern Historical Quarterly* 38(April 1935):246–269.

Sterne, Adolphus. "Diary of Adolphus Sterne." Edited by Harriet Smither. *Southwestern Historical Quarterly* 35(October 1931):151–168.

Wilson, William F. "Two Letters from a Mier Prisoner." *Texas State Historical Association Quarterly* 2(January 1899):233–236.

Winkler, E. W., ed. "The Bexar and Dawson Prisoners." *Texas State Historical Association Quarterly* 13(1909–1910):292–324.

―――. "The Bryan-Hayes Correspondence." *Southwestern Historical Quarterly* 25(October 1921):98–120; 25(January 1922):198–221; 25(April 1922):274–299.

Woll, Adrian. "Brigadier General Adrian Woll's Report of His Expedition into Texas in 1842." Translated and edited by Joseph Milton Nance. *Southwestern Historical Quarterly* 58(April 1955):523–552.

Zuber, W. P. "The Number of 'Decimated Mier Prisoners.'" *Texas State Historical Association Quarterly* 5(July 1901–April 1902):165–168.

Newspapers

City Gazette (Austin), 1841–1842.
Commercial Bulletin (New Orleans), 1843–1844.
El Cosmopolita (Mexico City), 1843.
Daily Bulletin (Austin), 1841–1842.
Daily National Intelligencer (Washington, D.C.), 1843–1844.
Daily Picayune (New Orleans), 1842–1844.
Daily Plebian (New York), 1843.
Democratic Telegraph and Texas Register (Houston), 1848.
Diario del Gobierno (Mexico City), 1842–1844.
Evening News (Galveston), 1843–1844.
The Galveston Civilian (Galveston), 1843.
LaGrange Intelligencer (LaGrange), 1843–1844.
LaGrange Journal (LaGrange), 1933–1936.
The Monument (LaGrange), 1850–1851.
Morning News (New York), 1843–1844.
Morning Star (Houston), 1839–1845.
National Vindicator (Washington-on-the-Brazos), 1843.
New York Herald (New York), 1843–1844.
Niles' National Register (Washington, D.C.), 1842–1845.
Northern Standard (Clarksville), 1843–1846.
The Planter (Columbia, S.C.), 1843.
Político Semanario (Monterrey, N.L., Mexico), 1842–1843.
El Siglo Diez y Nueve (Mexico City), 1843.
Telegraph and Texas Register (Houston), 1835–1846.
Texas Sentinel (Austin), 1841.
Texas Times (Galveston), 1842.
Texian and Brazos Farmer (Washington-on-the-Brazos), 1843.
United States Magazine and Democratic Review (Philadelphia), 1849.
El Voto de Coahuila (Saltillo, Coah., Mexico), 1842–1843.
The Weekly Texian (Austin), 1841–1842.

SECONDARY SOURCES

Unpublished Materials

Barker, Bernice. "The Texian Expedition to the Rio Grande in 1842." Master's thesis, University of Texas, 1929.

Berge, Dennis. "The Mexican Response to United States' Expansionism, 1841–48." Ph.D. dissertation, University of California at Berkeley, 1965.

Brack, Gene Martin. "Imperious Neighbor: The Mexican View of the United States, 1841–46." Ph.D. dissertation, University of Texas at Austin, 1967.

Brennan, Mary Estes. "American and British Travellers in Mexico, 1822–1846." Ph.D. dissertation, University of Texas at Austin, 1973.

Catterton, C. D. "The Political Campaigns of 1841 and 1844 in the Republic of Texas." Master's thesis, University of Texas, 1935.

Cook, Berenice S. "Texas as Seen in the New York Press, from 1835 to 1845." Master's thesis, Columbia University, 1935.

Huson, Hobart. "Iron Men: A History of the Republic of the Rio Grande and the Federalist Wars in Northern Mexico." Archives Division, Texas State Library (Austin).

McClendon, Earl. "Daniel Webster and Mexican Relations." Master's thesis, University of Texas, 1924.

Pierce, Gerald Swetnam, "The Army of the Texas Republic, 1836–45." Ph.D. dissertation, University of Mississippi, 1963.

Pitchford, Louis Cleveland. "The Diplomatic Representatives from the United States to Mexico, 1826–48." Ph.D. dissertation, University of Colorado, 1965.

Reinhardt, Ina Kate. "The Public Career of Thomas Jefferson Green in Texas." Master's thesis, University of Texas, 1939.

Tymitz, John R. "British Influence in Mexico, 1840–48." Ph.D. dissertation, Oklahoma State University, 1973.

Wade, Houston. Papers. Archives Division, Texas State Library (Austin).

Books

Adams, Ephraim D. *British Interests and Activities in Texas, 1838–1846.* Baltimore: Johns Hopkins Press, 1910.

Adolph, E. F., et al. *Physiology of Man in the Desert.* New York: Hafner Publishing Co., 1969.

Alessio Robles, Vito. *Coahuila y Texas: Desde la consumación de la independencia hasta el tratado de paz de Guadalupe Hidalgo.* Mexico City: Talleres Gráficos de la Nación, 1946.

———. *Coahuila y Texas en la epoca colonial.* Mexico City: Editorial Cultura, 1938.

Anderson, John Q. *Tales of Frontier Texas.* Dallas: Southern Methodist University Press, 1966.

Bancroft, Hubert Howe. *History of Northern Mexican States and Texas.* 2 vols. San Francisco: A. L. Bancroft & Co., 1883.

Billington, Ray Allen. *America's Frontier Heritage.* New York: Holt, Rinehart & Winston, 1966.

Binkley, William C. *The Expansionist Movement in Texas, 1836–1850.* Berkeley: University of California Press, 1925. Reprint, New York: Da Capo Press, 1970.

Blake, Clagett. *Charles Elliot, R.N., 1801–1875; A Servant of Britain Overseas.* London: Cleaver Hume Press, 1960.

Brown, John Henry. *History of Texas from 1685 to 1892.* 2 vols. St. Louis: L. E. Daniell, 1892. Reprint, Austin: Jenkins Publishing Co., 1970.

———. *Indian Wars and Pioneers of Texas.* Austin: L. E. Daniell, n.d.

Callcott, W. H. *Santa Anna: The Story of an Enigma Who Once Was Mexico.* Norman: University of Oklahoma Press, 1936.

Carreño, Alberto M., ed. *Jefes del ejército mexicano en 1847: Biografías de generales de división y brigada y de coroneles del ejército mexicano por fines del año de 1847.* Mexico City: Imprenta de la Secretaría de Fomento, 1914.

Chase, Mary Katherine. *Négociations de la République du Texas en Europe, 1837–1845.* Paris: Librairie Ancienne Honoré Champion, 1932.

Clark, Mary Whatley. *David G. Burnet: First President of Texas.* Austin: Pemberton Press, 1969.

Crane, William Carey. *Life and Select Literary Remains of Sam Houston.* Dallas: William G. Scarff & Co., 1884.

Day, James M. *Black Beans and Goose Quills.* Waco: Texian Press, 1970.

Duval, John C. *The Adventures of Big Foot Wallace.* Edited by Mabel Major and Rebecca Smith Lee. Lincoln: University of Nebraska Press, 1936.

Fehrenbach, T. R. *Fire and Blood: A History of Mexico.* New York: Macmillan Press, 1973.

———. *Lone Star: A History of Texas and the Texans.* New York: Macmillan Press, 1980.

Friend, Llerena. *Sam Houston: The Great Designer.* Austin: University of Texas Press, 1954.

Gambrell, Herbert Pickens. Anson Jones: *The Last President of Texas.* 2d ed. Austin: University of Texas Press, 1964.

———. *Mirabeau Buonaparte Lamar, Troubadour and Crusader.* Dallas: Southwest Press, 1934.

Gooch-Iglehart, Fanny Chambers. *Boy Captive of the Mier Expedition.* San Antonio: Passing Show, 1910.

Gouge, William M. *The Fiscal History of Texas, Embracing an Account of Its Revenues, Debts, and Currency, From the Commencement of the Revolution in 1834 to 1851–52, With Remarks on American Debts.* Philadelphia: Lippincott, Grambo, & Co., 1852.

Green, Wharton. *Recollections and Reflections.* Raleigh: Edwards and Broughton Printing Company, 1906.

Greer, James Kimmins. *Colonel Jack Hays: Texas Frontier Leader and California Builder.* Rev. ed. College Station: Texas A&M University Press, 1987.

Gregory, Jack, and Rennard Strickland. *Sam Houston with the Cherokees, 1829–1833.* Austin: University of Texas Press, 1967.

The Handbook of Texas. Vols. 1–2, edited by Walter Prescott Webb et al. Austin: Texas State Historical Association, 1952. Vol. 3, edited by Eldon Stephen Branda. Austin: Texas State Historical Association, 1976.

Hanighen, Frank. *Santa Anna: The Napoleon of the West.* New York: Coward, 1934.

Henson, Margaret Swett. *Samuel May Williams: Early Texas Entrepreneur.* College Station: Texas A&M University Press, 1976.

Hogan, William Ransom. *The Texas Republic: A Social and Economic History.* Norman: University of Oklahoma Press, 1946.

Horgan, Paul. *Great River: The Rio Grande in North American History.* 2 vols. New York: Rinehart & Co., 1954.

Horsman, Reginald. *Race and Manifest Destiny: The Origins of American Racial Anglo-Saxonism.* Cambridge: Harvard University Press, 1981.

Huson, Hobart. *Refugio: A Comprehensive History of Refugio County from Aboriginal Times to 1953.* 2 vols. Houston: Guardsman Publishing Co., 1953–1955.

James, Marquis. *The Raven.* New York: Bobbs Merrill, 1929. Reprint, Austin: University of Texas Press, 1988.

Johannsen, Robert W. *To the Halls of the Montezumas: The Mexican War in the American Imagination.* New York: Oxford University Press, 1985.

Kirwan, Albert D. *John J. Crittenden: The Struggle for the Union.* Lexington: University of Kentucky Press, 1962.

Lander, Ernest McPherson, Jr. *Reluctant Imperialists: Calhoun, the South Carolinians, and the Mexican War.* Baton Rouge: LSU Press, 1980.

Lester, C. Edwards. *Life and Achievements of Sam Houston, Hero and Statesman.* New York: Hurst & Co., 1883.

Loomis, Noel M. *The Texan–Santa Fe Pioneers.* Norman: University of Oklahoma Press, 1958.

McComb, David G. *Houston: The Bayou City.* Austin: University of Texas Press, 1969.

———. *Galveston: A History.* Austin: University of Texas Press, 1986.

Merk, Frederick. *Manifest Destiny and Mission in American History.* New York: Alfred A. Knopf, 1963.

———. *The Monroe Doctrine and American Expansionism, 1843–49.* New York: Alfred A. Knopf, 1966.

———. *Slavery and the Annexation of Texas.* New York: Alfred A. Knopf, 1972.

Montaigne, Sanford H. *Blood over Texas.* New Rochelle, N.Y.: Arlington House, 1976.

Nackman, Mark E. *A Nation within a Nation: The Rise of Texas Nationalism.* New York: Kennikat Press, 1975.

Nance, Joseph Milton. *After San Jacinto: The Texas-Mexican Frontier, 1836–1841.* Austin: University of Texas Press, 1963.

———. *Attack and Counterattack: The Texas-Mexican Frontier, 1842.* Austin: University of Texas Press, 1964.

Nieto, [Angelina], [John Nicholas] Brown, and [J.] Hefter. *El soldado mexicano, 1837–1847: Organización, vestuario, equipo/The Mexican Soldier, 1837–1847: Organization, Dress, Equipment.* Mexico City: Documentos Históricos Militares, 1958.

Pierson, George Wilson. *Tocqueville and Beaumont in America.* New York: Oxford University Press, 1938.

Pletcher, David M. *The Diplomacy of Annexation: Texas, Oregon, and the Mexican War.* Columbia: University of Missouri Press, 1973.

Ramos, Samuel. *Profile of Man and Culture in Mexico.* Translated by Peter G. Earle. Austin: University of Texas Press, 1962.

Reeves, Jesse. *American Diplomacy under Tyler and Polk.* Baltimore: Johns Hopkins Press, 1907.

Riva Palacios, Vicente, ed. *México a través de los siglos,* vol. 4. Barcelona, n.d.

Rives, George L. *The United States and Mexico, 1821–1848.* 2 vols. New York: Scribner's, 1913.

Robinson, Fay[ette]. *Mexico and Her Military Chieftains: From the Revolution of Hidalgo to the Present Time.* Hartford: Andrus & Son, 1851. Reprint, Glorieta, N.M.: Rio Grande Press, 1970.

Roemer, Ferdinand. *Texas: With Particular Reference to German Immigration and the Physical Appearance of the Country.* Translated by Oswald Mueller. San Antonio: Standard Printing Company, 1935.

Sánchez Lamego, Miguel A. *El Castillo de San Carlos de Perote.* Veracruz: Colección Suma Veracruzana, n.d.

———. *The Second Mexican-Texan War, 1841–1843.* Waco: Texian Press, 1972.

Schmitz, Joseph William. *Texan Statecraft, 1836–1845.* San Antonio: Naylor Co., 1941.

Seale, William. *Sam Houston's Wife: A Biography of Margaret Lea Houston.* Norman: University of Oklahoma Press, 1970.

Siegel, Stanley. *A Political History of the Texas Republic, 1836–1845.* Austin: University of Texas Press, 1956.

Sierra, Justo. *The Political Evolution of the Mexican People.* Translated by Charles Ramsdell. Austin: University of Texas Press, 1969.

Smith, Justin H. *The Annexation of Texas.* New York: AMS Press, 1971.

———. *The War with Mexico.* New York: Macmillan, 1919.

Sowell, A. J. *History of Fort Bend County: Containing Biographical Sketches of Many Noted Characters.* Houston: W. H. Coyle & Co., 1904.

———. *The Life of "Big Foot" Wallace.* Bandera, Tex.: Frontier Times, 1927.

Thompson, Henry T. *Waddy Thompson, Jr.* Columbia, S.C.: R. L. Bryan Co., 1929.

Thrall, Homer S. *A Pictorial History of the Republic of Texas: From the Earliest Visits of European Adventurers to A.D. 1879.* St. Louis: N. D. Thompson & Co., 1879.

Tinkle, Lon. *Thirteen Days to Glory: The Siege of the Alamo.* New York: McGraw-Hill, 1958. Reprint, College Station: Texas A&M University Press, 1985.

Wade, Houston. *The Dawson Men of Fayette County.* Houston, 1934.

———. *Notes and Fragments of the Mier Expedition.* 2 vols. LaGrange: LaGrange Journal, 1936.

Webb, Walter Prescott. *The Texas Rangers: A Century of Frontier Defense.* 2d ed. Austin: University of Texas Press, 1965.

Weinberg, Albert K. *Manifest Destiny: A Study of Nationalist Expansion in American History.* Gloucester: Peter Smith, 1958.

Wells, Tom Henderson. *Commodore Moore and the Texas Navy.* Austin: University of Texas Press, 1960.

Wheeler, Kenneth W. *To Wear a City's Crown: The Beginnings of Urban Growth in Texas, 1836–1865.* Cambridge: Harvard University Press, 1968.

Wolf, A. V. *Thirst: Physiology of the Urge to Drink and Problems of Water Lack.* Springfield, Ill.: Charles Thomas, Publisher, 1958.

Yoakum, Henderson. *History of Texas: From Its First Settlement in 1685 to Its Annexation to the United States in 1846.* 2 vols. New York: J. S. Redfield, 1855.

Articles

Barker, Eugene C. "The Annexation of Texas." *Southwestern Historical Quarterly* 50(July 1946):49–74.

Barton, Henry W. "The Problem of Command in the Army of the Republic of Texas." *Southwestern Historical Quarterly* 62(January 1959):299–311.

Binkley, William Campbell. "The Last Stage of Texan Military Operations against Mexico, 1843." *Southwestern Historical Quarterly* 22(January 1919):260–271.

Carroll, H. Bailey. "Steward A. Miller and the Snively Expedition of 1843." *Southwestern Historical Quarterly* 54(January 1951):261–286.

Gailey, Harry A., Jr. "Sam Houston and the Texas War Fever, March–August, 1842." *Southwestern Historical Quarterly* 62(July 1958):29–44.

García, Carlos Bosch. "Dos diplomáticas y un problema." *Historia Mexicana* 2 (July–September 1952):46–63.

McGrath, J. J., and Walace Hawkins. "Perote Fort—Where Texans Were Imprisoned." *Southwestern Historical Quarterly* 48(January 1945):340–345.

Nackman, Mark. "Anglo-American Migrants to the West: Men of Broken Fortunes? The Case of Texas, 1821–46." *Western Historical Quarterly* 5(October 1974):441–455.

———. "The Making of the Texan Citizen-Soldier, 1835–1860." *Southwestern Historical Quarterly* 77(January 1975):231–253.

Oates, Stephen B. "The Texas Rangers in the Mexican War." *Texas Military History* 3(Summer 1963):65–84.

Wilcox, Seb. "Laredo during the Texas Republic." *Southwestern Historical Quarterly* 42(October 1938):83–107.

Winfrey, Dorman H. "The Texan Archives War of 1842." *Southwestern Historical Quarterly* 64(October 1960):172–184.

Winston, J. E. "The Attitude of the Newspapers of the United States towards Texan Independence." *Proceedings of the Mississippi Valley Historical Association* 8(1914–1915):160–175.

Wooster, Ralph A. "Texas Military Operations against Mexico, 1842–43." *Southwestern Historical Quarterly* 67(April 1964):465–484.

Maps

Abbot, T. S. *Carta general del estado de Coahuila de Zaragoza formada por disposición del gobierno del mismo estado.* 1905.

Arbingast, Stanley A., Calvin P. Blair, James R. Buchanan, et al. *Atlas of Mexico.* Austin: Bureau of Business Research, University of Texas at Austin, 1975.

Canalizo, Valentín. "Plano topográfico que comprehende por el N. hasta Vejar, por el E. hasta San Patricio, por S.E. hasta Camargo, por el S.O. hasta Saltillo, por el O. hasta Monclova." 1838. (Barker Texas History Center.)

Mapa de los Estados Unidos de México. New York: J. Disturnell, 1847.

von Humboldt, Alexander. *Atlas géographique et physique des royaumes de la Nouvelle-Espagne, fondé sur des observations astronomiques, des mesures trigonométriques et des nivellemen[t]s barométriques.* Paris: G. Durfour, 1812.

Index